SCHOOL-FOCUSED INSERVICE: DESCRIPTIONS AND DISCUSSIONS

Kenneth R. Howey
Richard Bents
and
Dean Corrigan
Editors
1981

Association of Teacher Educators
Reston, Virginia

Spring 1980

The work presented in this project was performed pursuant to Grant No. G007801498 from the U.S. Office of Education, Bureau for the Handicapped, Division of Personnel Preparation. However, the opinions expressed herein do not necessarily reflect the position or policy of the Office of Education, and no official endorsement by the Office of Education should be inferred.

Appreciation for editorial assistance by
Renee Brimfield, University of Maryland
Janet Rosenberg, University of Minnesota

Library of Congress No. 81-66929

April 1981

Published by
ASSOCIATION OF TEACHER EDUCATORS
1900 Association Drive, Suite ATE
Reston, Virginia 22091
703/620-3110

TABLE OF CONTENTS

Foreword..
List of Contributors ....
List of Figures ....

PART I. PERSPECTIVE

    Chapter 1. Overview   1
                Richard Bents
          2. The Concept of School-focused Inservice   5
                Kenneth R. Howey

PART II. SCENARIOS

    Chapter 3. A School-focused Teacher Educator: A Scenario of a Public School Teacher with Staff Development Responsibilities   25
                Jennifer Smith
          4. A University-employed Teacher Educator: A Week in the Life of a Field-based Teacher Educator   37
                Gwen P. Yarger

PART III. INTERVIEWS

    Chapter 5. An Interview with Sue Brown: A Public School Teacher Assigned to Assist Other Teachers   55
          6. An Interview with Fred Baker: A College Teacher Educator with a School-focused Role   65
          7. An Interview with Frank Lyman: A Public School Teacher Educator with Joint Responsibilities with a University   77

PART IV. DESCRIPTIONS AND DISCUSSION OF THE ISSUES

    Chapter 8. Variant Approaches to School-focused Inservice   97
                Richard Bents
          9. A Discussion of Issues Relating to School-focused Teacher Education   109
                Fred Baker
                Tom Kromer
                Mike Wolf

PART V. SPECIFIC APPROACHES TO SCHOOL-FOCUSED INSERVICE

Chapter 10. The Advisory Approach as a Form of Professional Growth   123
Robert P. Mai

11. Staff Development via Colleague Training   143
Willis D. Copeland

12. Organizational Development and Public Law 94-142 in Jefferson Elementary School   159
Charles W. Case

13. Inservice for Team Teaching to Promote Professional Growth through Team Teaching   171
Gerald D. McDermot
Kenneth R. Howey

14. School-focused Inservice Education: An All School Approach   179
Clifford D. Sibley

15. Interactive Research and Development as a Form of Professional Growth   187
William J. Tikunoff
Beatrice A. Ward
Gary A. Griffin

16. Professional Development Through Inservice That Works   215
Henrietta Barnes
Joyce Putnam

PART VI. P.L. 94-142 AND SCHOOL FOCUSED INSERVICE EDUCATION

17. Achieving the Goals of P.L. 94-142 Through School Focused Inservice Education: Implications for Leadership   231
Dean C. Corrigan

CONTRIBUTORS

Fred Baker
    Central Michigan University
Henrietta Barnes
    Michigan State University
Richard Bents
    University of Maryland
Susan Brown
    Lincoln, Nebraska Public Schools
Charles Case
    University of Iowa
Willis Copeland
    University of California, Santa Barbara
Dean Corrigan
    Texas A & M
Gary A. Griffin
    Research and Development Center
    For Teacher Education, University of Texas
Kenneth R. Howey
    University of Minnesota
Thomas Kromer
    Central Michigan University
Frank Lyman
    Teacher Education Center, Howard County, Maryland
Robert Mai
    Missouri State Department of Education
Gerald D. McDermot
    Fon du Lac, Wisconsin Public Schools
Joyce Putnam
    Michigan State University
Clifford Sibley
    Lincoln, Nebraska Public Schools
Jennifer Smith
    Minneapolis, Minnesota Public Schools

William Tikunoff
  Far West Laboratory
Betty Ward
  Far West Laboratory
Michael Wolf
  Central Michigan University
Gwen Yarger
  Syracuse University

Chapter 1:

Overview

Richard Bents

The primary purpose of this book is to explore and describe the notion of school-focused inservice. The book contains six interrelated sections. Part I provides the context for this document and a perspective of school-focused inservice. Part II explores the day to day realities of a school-focused educator in the form of scenarios. The interviews in Part III focus on the type of planning, decision-making, assessment, and collaboration skills that are appropriate for school-focused educators. Part IV, then, describes programs designed to prepare individuals to work in a school setting as leaders of inservice that take into account the uniqueness of a particular educational system. Part V offers seven specific approaches to school-focused inservice ranging from organizational development to colleague training to interactive research. Finally, Part VI, the Summary, discusses the implications that school-focused inservice may have for educational leaders and the compliance to the Public Law 94-142.

More specifically, Part I provides an overview, rationale, and conceptual framework for the notion of school-focused inservice. In Chapter 2 school-focused inservice is explicated. Kenneth Howey indicates that the term "school-focused" specifies what the focus (not the base) is. "School-focused inservice more literally *focuses* on the specific interests and needs of teachers and others in their work setting" (p. 12).

Part II describes the myriad activities of two school-focused teacher educators. In Chapter 3, Jennifer Smith, a public school teacher with staff development responsibilities, discusses her role in the development, planning, and evaluation of inservice activities. She indicates how working with the administration, conducting tours of the school, writing proposals, and on occasion assuming teaching responsibilities can all play a part in staff development. She concludes by stating, "To do this job effectively, I need to be able to counsel, to organize, to teach, to listen, to lead, to influence, and to guide" (p. 36).

Gwen Yarger, in Chapter 4, provides a scenario of a university-employed teacher-educator in a school-focused role. Gwen discusses the difficult role of meeting multiple demands. In her own words, the scenario presents "evidence which indicates that field-based teacher educators: 1) can meet extensive demands placed upon their time and energies, 2) can meet academic expectations in higher education, 3) are able to contribute to a better understanding of teacher training, and 4) are able to provide a vehicle for bridging theory into practice" (p. 54).

Part III is a series of interviews with school-focused teacher educators. Chapter 5 is an interview with a public school teacher specifically assigned to assist other teachers in the area of main-streaming. This "Helping Teacher" role provides a renewal capacity to both the teachers in the district and the Helping Teacher. The interview focuses on the planning, coordination, and administration of the role. In addition, the skills necessary to meet the demands of the role and the acquisition of those skills are discussed.

Chapter 6 consists of an interview with Fred Baker, an employee of higher education with a school-focused role which addresses both pre- and inservice teacher education. Fred elaborates on the type of commitments necessary to appreciably impact both the pre-service and the inservice dimension of teacher education.

Frank Lyman, in Chapter 7, gives the reader a review of school-focused inservice from the perspective of a public school teacher with joint responsibilities with a university. Frank emphasizes the interpersonal skills that are crucial to the success of a school-focused educator. "One goal [of staff development] is improvement of professional self-concept. The teacher must see her/himself as one who is effective with kids" (p. 89). This issue of self-concept, according to Lyman, can best be addressed by utilizing support and encouragement coupled with specific, concrete suggestions for the improvement of instruction. Frank gives many examples of this interpersonal notion.

Part IV is an overview of approaches to prepare school-focused educators. Chapter 8 reviews three programs; 1) the Vermont Consulting Teacher Program, 2) the University of Southern California/Lynwood Unified School Trainer of Trainers Program, and 3) the Lincoln Public Schools Helping Teacher Cadre. The programs are reviewed to indicate the diversity of training approaches. They represent respectively a statewide network of consulting teachers, a collaborative effort between a university and a public school, and an independent public school effort. In addition, these efforts reflect efforts to address the pedagogical, organizational, and personal development dimensions in the training of school-focused teacher educators.

Chapter 9 is a discussion of the issues involved in providing school-focused inservice as well as a discussion of the skills necessary for the school-focused educator. The discussants agree that "the role is definitely unique." Issues such as the support of the college or university for school-focused programs, role definition, interpersonal skills, professional affiliations, and certification for school-focused teacher educators are all touched upon.

Part V offers seven specific approaches to school-focused inservice. The first two chapters of this section address approaches which most directly impact the personal dimension of inservice. In Chapter 10, Robert Mai outlines the "advisory approach" as a form of professional growth. Mai makes a strong case for the inclusion of the role of advisor as a strategy for the school-focused educator. The "combination of enthusiasm for teaching and an unobtrusive style in working with other professionals" are necessary qualities of advisors. Mai goes on to describe what advisors do as listeners and observers, curriculum developers, and models for their peers. The chapter concludes by providing an outline of a problem solving orientation critical to the advisory approach.

Willis Copeland, in Chapter 11, continues the personal interaction approach through a colleague training strategy. Copeland notes, "There is a potentially powerful pool of resources for helping individual teachers solve instructional problems—other teachers" (p. 145). By drawing on clinical supervision skills, Copeland outlines a colleague training approach that "would focus on the perceived needs of individual teachers, would recognize and encourage the power of teachers to improve their instruction, and would employ a systematic strategy for developing and testing strategies for improvement. This strategy would, above all, cast the teacher in the central role of staff development as a source of energy, direction, and motivation" (p. 156).

Chapters 12, 13 and 14 provide insight into the organizational development dimension of school-focused inservice. In Chapter 12 Charles Case focuses attention on change in a specific elementary school. Using the basic tenets of organizational development, a school-focused educator can produce systematic change. Case provides a scenario of how this occurs.

Gerald McDermot and Kenneth Howey stress the "human element" in organization development and present a Team Teaching approach to inservice in Chapter 13. They discuss convergent staff training and divergent exploration as major dimensions of teaming. "Convergent staff development tends to focus on those processes and elements that are necessary in making a team teaching model functional. Divergent exploration includes more self-directed inservice activities aimed at individuals and teams in order to analyze and promote aspects of their individual realm of responsibility" (p. 172). Critical elements in developing functional team teaching are then discussed and implementation strategies are explored.

Clifford Sibley, in Chapter 14, underscores the importance of the role of the principal in an "all school approach" to inservice. He concludes by stating: "Inservice programs will likely be more successful if the principal assumes a central but not dominant role in the process" (p. 185).

The next two chapters represent more collaborative approaches to school-focused inservice. In Chapter 15 William Tikunoff, Beatrice Ward, and Gary Griffin present an interactive research and development approach to professional growth. This chapter examines the collaboration necessary in effective coupling of *teacher* and *researcher* and the maintaining of integrity of the classroom. The chapter provides a summary of outcomes of the *Interactive Reasearch and Development on Teaching Study* done at the Far West Laboratory for Educational Research and Development in 1979.

In Chapter 16, Henrietta Barnes and Joyce Putnam discuss the collegial model for inservice education which was developed by the staff at Michigan State University. This chapter "describes the necessary criteria for the establishment of a collegial model and a released time system for accomplishing professional growth" (p. 216).

In the summary of this document, Dean Corrigan explores the potential impact this school-focused notion might have for colleges, universities, and schools as they move to meet the mandates of Public Law 94-142 and the continuing education of teachers.

Chapter 2:

The Concept of School-focused Inservice

Kenneth R. Howey

Background

Our goal in this collection of writings is a modest one. It is to share briefly some of the ways that inservice or staff development for school personnel can be focused more effectively on specific needs and interests. We are deeply indebted to the several persons who work in a teacher education capacity at school sites for the many insights which they have shared with us in this manuscript.

This effort has been possible thanks largely to the foresight and wisdom of Dr. Thomas Behrens in the Office of Special Education. If I may be allowed a personal statement, I wish to take this opportunity along with Dean and Dick, my co-editors, to acknowledge our sincere gratitude for his assistance and support. The federal legislation P.L. 94–142 (The Education of All Handicapped Children Act) requires that all students assessed as handicapped in some manner be provided education in the *least restrictive environment.* This law also calls for an individual education plan (IEP) to be jointly developed for each handicapped learner. Classroom teachers, special education personnel, other supervisory and support personnel, school administrators, and parents are required by this legislation to work together in deciding and providing appropriate educational activities for these students. This far-reaching legislation has served as a catalyst for altered and hopefully improved approaches to planning and providing instruction for *all* youngsters.

Obviously new approaches present new problems and obstacles as well. While often the problems are similar in nature from one school to the next, the particular condition in any given school and classroom also demands inservice and assistance responsive to those unique situations. More effective *school-focused* inservice is not a new need. P.L. 94-142 has only further underscored that coordinated and coherent forms of inservice which address specific needs at a school site are often lacking.

Dr. Behrens and his colleagues were willing to support our efforts to visit, interview, observe, and dialogue with teacher educators who worked in a collaborative manner in a variety of inservice activities at specific school sites. While several of these inservice approaches did not focus, as such, on the needs of the handicapped learner, it was assumed that bridges could be built by the reader between these practices and ways in which the critical needs of the handicapped might better be met. Thus, while this book hopefully will be of some help to all interested in improving inservice teacher education, our special desire is that it contribute to those engaged in attempting to better respond to the needs of the handicapped.

By way of background, it should also be noted that this book is a compendium edition to an earlier publication which Dean Corrigan and I edited with a similar goal in mind. *Special Education in Transition— Concepts to Guide the Education of Experienced Teachers* was published by the Council for Exceptional Children in 1980. In this first book of readings we attempted to identify some of the understandings and skills which a school-focused teacher educator would need in order to assume leadership in providing more continuing and coherent forms of inservice education. In an attempt to provide some framework for the selection and preparation of school-focused teacher educators or staff developers, we identified three basic domains of study these school-focused teacher educators should engage in:
  1. inquiry into what is known about how adults (teachers) learn and develop
  2. inquiry into how organizations (schools and classrooms) affect how teachers learn and develop
  3. inquiry into what is known about the organization, management, and delivery of (inservice) teacher education.

While the emphasis was on school-focused inservice in the first collection of writings, our strategy for better understanding this form of inservice varied considerably from that pursued in this book. The first phase of our inquiry into the concept of school-focused inservice was conducted by bringing together scholars in the above domains. Thus, we called upon the thinking and research of those who had attempted to study how adults (including teachers) develop and learn, how organziations, especially schools and classrooms, affect teaching and teacher education, and, of course, what we know about the education of teachers in general. Treatises developed by selected scholars were filtered through the reactions and criticisms of teachers, teacher educators, and special educators. These papers were further revised in light of visits to sites which prepared different types of school-focused teacher educators and then published as a collection of writings. The earlier material complements those writings included in this current book.

In the following chapters we try to share not only specific examples of how teacher educators work at school sites but to illustrate distinctively different forms of inservice as well. Educators in a variety of roles engage in school-focused forms of inservice and employ a diversity of teacher education approaches. We attempt, here, to demonstrate some of this diversity.

In this chapter, I wish to 1) briefly review the justification for school-focused forms of inservice, 2) identify some general attributes of this concept, 3) speak briefly to some specific varieties of inservice which appear especially suitable for use at the school site.

Why School-focused Inservice?

Advocacy of more school-focused forms of inservice (and I might add more participatory forms of inservice) is not uncommon. The case for this form of inservice has been developed to some extent empirically and several political and economic arguments have also been put forth. From this perspective, collective experience and common sense argue persuasively for this approach as well.

There is little doubt in this country that many teachers desire more inservice which is focused on their specific needs. The plea is not only for *more* but *better* inservice of this type. The most recent survey of inservice with which this writer was involved (Yarger, Howey, & Joyce, 1980) clearly underscores the problem. Less than 20 percent of the respondents across the country reported they were able on any kind of regular basis to participate in inservice or staff development activities which varied from the after school course or workshop. Further, only 1 in 7 teachers reported any kind of follow-up in his or her classroom to these inservice offerings. Thus, for the vast majority of teachers in this country, we have a picture of inservice as an activity which follows a full day's work, in a setting apart from their own instruction, with no attempt made at any time to pursue the subject matter, whatever it may be, into the teacher's classroom. Lawrence (1977) analyzed the formal evaluations and assessments of almost 100 different inservice projects and concluded:

> Teacher attitudes are more likely to be influenced in school-based than in college-based inservice programs . . .
>
> Inservice programs in schools and on college campuses are equally capable of affecting teacher behavior but the school settings appear to be capable of influencing more complex behavior changes in teachers . . .
>
> School-based programs in which teachers participate as helpers to each other and planners of inservice activities tend to have greater success in accomplishing their objectives than do programs which are conducted by colleges or other outside personnel without the assistance of teachers. (1977, pp. 2, 3)

McLean and Brison (1976) reviewed various research and development activities at the Ontario Institute for Studies in Education which were intended to effect school change and offered the following advice to educational researchers and developers.

> *Collaborative relationships.* So far, we haven't seen a good example anywhere of school change that did not (a) evolve slowly as a result of basic research findings, (b) come about because of a dramatic change in society, e.g. Sputnik, or (c) result from people in schools working out a "new" way, with or without the help of outsiders. In part II, we gave several examples of change processes with which we are familiar. From these and other samples we have formed our opinion that to save itself the R & D community will have to lose itself, i.e. that it will have to share control with practitioners at all stages, from selection of the problem through working out the solution to implementing the result. Note that this implies that the practitioners will also share some control, including close collaboration in the classrooms as the implementation stage is worked out. (1976, p. 43)

The Rand Corporation's (1976) widely cited nationwide survey of 293 "change agent" projects identified a limited number of factors and conditions common to those relatively few projects successful at achieving desired change. McLaughlin and Marsh (1978) analyzed these data in terms of their implications for staff development. They concluded that the process by which change or innovation occurs is mutually adaptive (that is, modifications occur in the proposed innovation as well as in the users of that innovation) and heuristic in nature. Teachers begin "where they are at" in their specific context and to some degree invariably "reinvent the wheel." They also concluded that in the most successful change efforts staff development activities were closely related to the teacher's day-to-day responsibilities and consideration was given to the total school as an organization.

These empirically-supported findings undergird the political and economic arguments which, for a considerable time, have been made by teachers and teacher organizations and more recently supported by governmental funding agencies. The teachers' case rests on the most sensible premise (and, I might add, proven principle of learning) that one should be centrally involved in deciding his or her own continuing education. This appears especially true of adults. Involvement and ownership is central to authentic forms of learning. While this argument is not identical to calling for school-focused inservice, it certainly is parallel. Teacher ownership is considerably enhanced when inservice or staff development focuses upon the concerns he or she has identified in his or her own classroom.

Teacher center sponsored forms of inservice tend to place teachers more centrally in all aspects of inservice. The federally funded teacher centers in this country are required to have a governance body comprised of a majority of classroom teachers. Certainly the call for more participatory and school-focused forms of inservice is not limited to this country. In Canada, Northern and Western Europe, Australia, New Zealand, and Japan, governmental policies have directed inservice monies to efforts which are more responsive to specific school sites. Several British educators and government-sponsored advisory groups, for example, have for some time called for more school-focused forms of inservice. A milestone report of the British Schools Council (1975) illustrates this:

> ... we want to highlight what we see as being the key concepts in our report. Among the most important of these is the idea of the school as a centre of curriculum development. We believe the improvement of the secondary-school curriculum must rest upon an acknowledgement of the central role of the teacher. All worthwhile proposals for curriculum change are put to the test in classrooms and only come to fruition if the practicing teacher has the resources, support, training and self-confidence to implement them. Teachers are in a unique position to know and understand the needs of pupils and from them should come the principal pressure for increasingly effective programmes of teaching and learning. Because we see the development of the curriculum and the self-development of the teacher as being inseparable, we call for vigorous programmes of in-service education and school-based curriculum development, both of which are essential if the teachers are to perform their role to the full. (p. 80)

In Australia, and especially the state of Victoria, policies related to inservice call not only for teachers but for parents to be more involved in deciding priorities. Inservice is viewed as directly related to school improvement, and the decision-making, problem-solving process itself is seen as a form of inservice. Ingvarson (1978) refers to a recent Schools Commission paper which underscores such involvement in decision making:

> The Commission has consistently taken the view that the improvement of schools lies not just in the quality of the actual decisions taken about how to improve them, but in the processes through which those decisions are reached. Three of its special programs . . . actively promote a process which encourages people to analyze the situation in which they are placed, to identify directions of needed change and improvement, and to propose actions addressed to them. This is the process which is central to improved school effectiveness through extended school-based decision-making. It is designed to encourage initiative, self-reliance, and commitment among people who will implement changed directions of action. (1978, p. 13)

The argument for school-focused forms of inservice appears at this point to have largely been made on other than economic grounds. There is little cost-effectiveness data for teacher education (or education for that matter), in general, let alone for school-focused forms of inservice. Some have argued that school-focused inservice is likely to be less costly given the time and travel needed for teachers to engage in other forms of inservice external to the school site. However, others who view school-focused forms of inservice as hopefully more comprehensive and continuing in nature suggest it will be more costly.

It doesn't, from this perspective, make a lot of sense to argue in the abstract and general one way or the other. What *is* needed are cost-effectiveness evaluations of both specific forms of school-focused and more general forms of inservice. Specific school-focused forms of inservice are outlined in this book. They include forms of team teaching, organizational development, clinical supervision and psychological consultation framed in concepts of adult psychological development. For too long we have treated inservice as a relatively undifferentiated concept (I believe often implicitly assuming a course or workshop format). Better assessments of both effectiveness and cost will be made *when we more precisely define the type of outcomes and processes we are referring to when we use the term "inservice."*

Nonetheless, one might make the general argument that much of current inservice which tends largely *not* to focus on the *specific* problems of schools and interests of those who work in these schools is *not* cost-effective. For example, in our 17,000 school districts, there are almost 100,000 principals and vice-principals who have some responsibility for inservice. There are more persons than that in local and intermediate education districts in line or staff positions who also have some responsibilities for inservice. Plus, there are numerous consultants in other government agencies, educational and educationally-related organizations, and the private sector who provide inservice in myriad ways. An estimate of a quarter of a million people directly connected with inservice is likely conservative. Yet our survey (Yarger, Howey, & Joyce, 1980) suggests that teachers largely reject many of these "helpers" at least in the way they typically attempt to provide inservice. It would appear that many current human resources (both in roles as *providers* and *receivers* of inservice) are not making the best use of their time and talents. Many efforts at inservice could be construed as dysfunctional and likely even debilitating in effect. The costs then in terms of time, emotions, and dollars can likely not even be estimated well at this time. However, there is no doubt there is room for considerable improvement in many instances.

This present set of conditions surrounding inservice can be summarized as follows:

1) Inservice generally appears in need of improvement.
2) While not all inservice or continuing education can or should take place at the school site, many growth activities can reasonably be integrated into the on-going activities associated with schools and focus more directly on the problems of the school and the teachers in it.
3) One reason inservice is generally such a fragmented process at many schools is that *no single person* in the schooling enterprise has the basic responsibility for a coordinated approach to inservice or staff development. Principals, for example, generally have other priorities and a variety of support personnel tends to address only certain aspects of inservice. Professors are usually too removed from a school site.
4) A second reason inservice is generally such a fragmented process is that the concept invariably lacks conceptual and operational coherency. Rarely, for example, is staff development interrelated with forms of organizational development and even more rarely is the question considered of how the personal or psychological development of the teacher might interact with the professional role.
5) There are still ample personnel resources in the rather vast super-

structure of the schooling enterprise, in colleges and universities, and among teachers themselves (roughly one in seven teachers desires some opportunity to provide continuing education to their peers) to identify persons who could be selected and prepared to serve in more school-focused capacities and assume responsibilities for more coordinated and coherent forms of inservice.
6) There is also a knowledge base to draw upon for training school-focused teacher educators. Adult development, clinical supervision, research on teaching, and organizational development are just some of the areas of study which might be pursued by such teacher educators.
7) An appropriate function for many institutions of higher education and local school districts (either alone or, hopefully, in many cases in a cooperative manner) would be to initiate or further augment programs for preparing school-focused teacher educators.

What is School-focused Inservice?

What does the term *school-focused* suggest? Certainly, not all inservice should be *based* at the school site. On the contrary, more opportunities are needed for teachers and other school personnel to periodically get out of their immediate environment. Developmental psychologists such as Sprinthall (1980) suggest that adult psychological development is fostered when one engages in cycles of action (when possible in a new context and new role) followed by periods of guided reflection or introspection. Opportunities in the often frenetic world of teaching (think of teaching five different sections of 30 students day after day, for example) allow little opportunity either for extended reflection and relaxed dialogue or well-conceived experimentation in different contexts. It is likely that one of the major contributing factors to what is commonly referred to as teacher "burn-out" is the perceived, if not real, inability to periodically engage in renewing experiences of a kind different than those activities they engage in on a repeated basis in the confines of their classroom and school.

School-focused inservice more literally *focuses* on the specific interests and needs of teachers and others in their work setting. This activity can and should be periodically engaged in away from the work setting. This form of inservice also focuses upon concerns and interests which are cross-cutting in nature, which have *school-wide* as well as individual implications. This is a critical point. Several of the factors which appear to contribute significantly to student success in schools appear to lie beyond the confines of an individual classroom as such. Rutter (1979) for example, in his longitudinal study of successful and less successful schools in London, looked not only at differences in student achievement but at differences in student attitudes in the form of attendance, number of behavior problems, and incidents of vandalism. His team of researchers found that successful schools could be differentiated from less successful ones in terms of such factors as the general ethos of the school, the working relationships between teachers and the consistency and quality of goals held for students *among teachers*, both in terms of academic achievement and social behavior. It is increasingly obvious that a number of desired pupil outcomes are enhanced when certain behaviors are exemplified by the faculty as a whole and when key curriculum decisions are well-articulated at the school across grade levels.

A school-focused inservice agenda should have as a priority the improvement of those conditions and processes which most directly affect the quality of education of *students* within a given school. How and when and where different students might productively and humanely be engaged with different persons, different subject matter, and different contextual settings and resources are the salient decisions which teachers make. These decisions should not be bounded by the confines of a single classroom. School-focused inservice should address how those decisions can best be made not only by individual teachers within the context of an individual classroom but *between* teachers in the context of the larger school/community. Much of what contributes to the qualitative "climate" of a school is determined by the type of interactions among teachers.

Bolam (1978), in an attempt to explicate the concept of school-focused inservice with the Department of Education and Science (D.E.S.) in England, provided multiple examples of school-focused inservice. These included:

- A home economics teacher spends a day in another school to find out about a new child-care course.
- Two deputy heads in very different primary schools exchange jobs for one week to broaden their experience.
- A large comprehensive school timetable frees staff for one week each year to work on materials preparation with the resource center coordinator.
- Two colleagues in the same school systematically observe each other teaching over a term and discuss their observations after each session.
- A group of comprehensive school staff developing a new integrated-

studies curriculum invites a teachers' center warden to coordinate a term-long school-based course involving outside speakers.
- A college of education offers a week-long course for primary schools for four weeks in succession. Each of four members of the staff attend in turn, thus having a similar experience. College staff follow-up by visiting the schools.
- Two LEA advisers offer a school-based course of eight weekly sessions on primary math. They spend from 3:00 to 3:45 working with teachers in their classrooms and from 4:00 to 5:30 in follow-up workshop discussion sessions.
- A university award-bearing course for a group of staff from the same school includes a substantial school-based component.
- A school runs a conference on "Going Comprehensive" which begins on Friday morning, in school time, and ends on Saturday afternoon. Outside speakers include a chief adviser, a comprehensive head, and a university lecturer. As a result, several working parties run throughout the following year. (1978, pp. 7, 8)

Without doubt, several other examples could readily be provided by the reader. Hopefully, however, this concept will be planned at specific school sites as more than a rather random set of activities. In this book we emphasize that inservice of both an all-school and individual nature be planned within a framework which attempts to assess two types of powerful interacting variables: the first, social and organizational, and the second, personal and individual. Those who plan staff development or inservice activities should consider both the social norms and conventions and the specific organizational features of a given school. They should also consider to the extent feasible, how the personal and psychological development of teachers interacts with their professional growth and performance. Miles (1978), for example, has identified the following common properties of schools as organizations:

- goal diffuseness
- technical capability is often sub-optimal
- co-ordination problems
- boundary management problems
- owned by their environment, survival guaranteed and (are) non-competitive for resources
- form a constrained, decentralized system.

Likewise, one could identify common and relatively unique characteristics of teachers as learners in attempting to better understand personal or psychological development. Martin Haberman (1979), in a report co-

authored by this writer and Dean Corrigan, identified factors which tended to make teacher education different from other forms of adult education. Factors he identified included:
> 1. *Required study.* The factor of state mandated coursework or some sort of professional updating is a significant one. Compulsion as an initial impetus for undertaking further study has an abiding impact; one does not readily forget that one is being required to participate.
> 2. *Proficiency.* Unlike a class in general education or in some personal skill, teachers are expected to master the content of their professional studies and to demonstrate their learnings in subsequent performance. The realization that one will have to perform something at a high level cannot help but become a factor which affects his/her learning experience.
> 3. *Professional.* Learning things which, while they may or may not be enriching to the teachers, are *intended* to implement learning in others is a distinctive feature of inservice education.
> 4. *Situation-specific.* Teachers work in school settings. Their learnings are valid to the degree that they are operationallly successful in such settings. Teachers cannot be offered ideas in a vacuum or without reference to the context in which the new ideas are to be implemented.
> 5. *Accountability.* Teachers will in several ways be evaluated on what they have learned, or more precisely, on what their students have learned.

School-focused inservice then specifies what the focus (not the base) is. It is conceived of in a framework which calls for attention to the interaction of social/organizational variables with personal/psychological ones. This writer has also identified a number of other desired characteristics of school-focused inservice. These attributes evolved from a review of several school-focused activities in this country and Western Europe and from discussions with several participants in these activities. The school-focused characteristics below were summarized for the National Institute of Education in 1980:
> 1. It is viewed as but one aspect, however crucial, of a larger scheme of continuing development.
> 2. Assumptions about how adults (teachers) best *learn* and continue to *develop* along several dimensions are made explicit.
> 3. Interactions between the teacher as person, the teacher as learner, and the teacher as teacher in the school site are given

consideration in designing school-focused inservice.
4. Interactions between organizational changes, curricular changes, and inservice are noted and incorporated into planning; implications for resocialization and role-change are given special attention.
5. Teachers are centrally involved in all aspects of the process.
6. Needs and interests of students and parents are of special importance in this form of inservice.
7. Attention is given not only to individual teachers but to key functioning groups and entire faculties.
8. Regardless of the number of teachers or size of group, individual differences are accommodated.
9. School-focused inservice goes beyond the sharing of ideas to include demonstration, experimentation, supervised trials, and feedback; often these take place at the school site.
10. Building administrations can assume a number of responsibilities in this endeavor but the most critical one is a reciprocal responsibility to provide both material and psychological support for teachers who venture into new growth experiences.
11. There is continuity; school-focused inservice is seen as a process, often a developmental or incremental one, and not an event.
12. There are ample opportunities for *reflection* about as well as *action* and experimentaion. Time is taken for consideration of alternatives.
13. School-focused inservice frequently is concerned with teacher changes which are implied in resolving cross-cutting school problems and in achieving school-wide goals.
14. A common form of school-focused inservice is experimentation and problem-solving which is integrated into the daily instructional tasks of the teacher; it is differentiated from teaching only by its intent and the type of examination and sharing which takes place later.
15. School-focused inservice has a primary *focus*, quality education for students in a specific school through quality education of the teacher.

Obviously, it is extremely rare when such attributes do or will exist in a single inservice project or school setting. However, one of the essential processes in the development of a concept—and we are examining a developing or perhaps better, evolving, concept here—is the identification of attributes of that concept. The above characteristics are offered as an initial, tentative set of positive attributes with the purpose of more clearly defining an important form of professional growth. Hopefully, more conceptual clarity will lead to more coherent plans and actions.

Strategies Consonant with the Concept of School-focused Inservice

An attempt has been made to synthesize the rationales put forth for more school-focused forms of inservice and then to more clearly define the concept. This chapter concludes with a brief review of some instructional strategies which appear especially appropriate for school-focused teacher educators to employ. Each of these approaches is addressed by separate authors in more detail later in the book.

There are a number of general factors which contribute to teacher growth. Distinctions between various aspects of teacher daily planning or problem-solving and inservice can be artificial, especially when the former promote teacher growth. Growth is the basic first-order goal of inservice activities and obviously considerable teacher growth occurs over time in the process of refining one's skills while engaging in one's craft. Equally as obvious is that given more optimal work conditions, more teacher growth could occur. Several factors and conditions which appear to promote teacher growth in the work context are readily identifiable. These include:

1. Clear understanding of what is successful with different pupils.
2. Accurate perceptions of what one is actually doing as a teacher and what other events are occurring in the classroom and school context.
3. Ready opportunities to call upon the experience and wisdom of others in planning and problem-solving.
4. Frequent validation of one's personal and professional worth.
5. The skills and support needed to engage in forms of systematic inquiry in the classroom.
6. Opportunities for sharing and demonstrating one's insights with others.
7. Time for introspection and reflection.

The way in which teachers are organized for instruction speaks to some extent to whether the above desired conditions are likely to exist. It would appear that for many teachers both performance in their job and continued growth related to that job are constrained. These teachers can be characterized as working basically alone and with extended, often unrealistic, expectations placed upon them (especially elementary teachers asked to teach in up to 10 different subject areas). These expectations tend not only to be additive in nature but often mixed and unclear.

Accurate and salient feedback about their specific activities as teachers is minimal. Planned forms of psychological counseling and support for teachers in their work place are even rarer. Typically the teacher seeks assurance (and assistance) wherever and whenever he/she can. In a time of teacher displacement, a sense of competition rather than collaboration is further heightened. Teachers are seen as "consumers" rather than as "producers" of research and new knowledge. A concomitant hierarchical sense of status results. This is but one of the undesirable spin-offs of current role-expectations for teachers and the way in which they are organized for instruction in many schools.

Certainly there are teachers who perform admirably in rather self-contained settings. There are also many highly *self*-renewing teachers in such contexts. (How and why certain teachers perform better and continue to grow in school settings highly similar to those in which other teachers perform less adequately and appear to stagnate in their growth should be an expanded priority for research.) Some alternative organizational schemes already exist. Likely even better ones could be created which would allow more teachers to function in more realistic and productive ways.

Team teaching (or, more accurately, team planning) can, if well conceived, contribute to more ideal conditions for teacher growth and performance. There are many varieties of team or cooperative teaching. Historically, efforts in this direction have met with mixed success at best, however. The reasons as to why the potential power of this concept has often not been realized are readily identifiable. Cooperative teaching arrangements are undergirded by a well-delineated *division of labor* concept. Persons engaged in teaming, while usually in agreement on major goals, should be differentiated in terms of competence and complement one another. In this way, the whole is truly greater than the sum of its parts and opportunities for students are expanded and enriched. Yet, the considerable homogeneity of teachers in terms of background, preparation, and role-expectation continues to constrain against genuine forms of teacher specialization and division of labor, especially in our elementary schools. Teaming has failed in most instances because in reality teachers have only marginally complemented or been of assistance to one another.

There were historically and are today, other obstacles to effective teaming. Special skills are needed in working effectively in a small group, let alone in making *joint*—as opposed to individual—curriculum decisions. Little preparation was typically provided for this type of joint decision-making and communication, and almost none in terms of how teaming could be used as a form of staff development. Leadership is essential to this concept but again has not been adequately considered. Even such basic considerations as needed time and space for collaborative planning and teaching were frequently slighted. It is little wonder from this perspective, then, that the concept of teaming, especially in terms of its implications for further teacher growth, has not realized anywhere near its full potential. Thus, this writer, along with Gerry McDermot (who was one of the pioneers in implementing effective teaming designs) address this concept more fully later in the book. Strategies for both developing more collaborative structures and for maximizing teacher growth through teaming are reviewed based upon our experiences with this concept.

While clusters of teachers working closely together are a critical aspect of the school organization to focus upon in terms of both instruction for pupils and the further development of teachers, all-school as well as individual teacher considerations are also important. Schools as organizations must be studied and understood at several levels of functioning. This is why we advocate the study of the school as an organization with the aim of *collective* as well as individual development as a core component of school-focused inservice. Charles Case is familiar first hand with systemic approaches to *organizational development* in both K-12 and post-secondary institutions. In his contribution to this book he looks specifically at the organizational implications of P.L. 94-142 for a total elementary school community. He employs proven principles from systems theory to examine an individual school as it interacts with the larger school district or "macro system." In organizational development terms, specific "inputs" into the school, key internal processes within the school, relevant "outputs," and means of feedback are outlined in the scenario he develops for us. The implications of this approach for teacher growth individually and especially as a collective unit are readily apparent.

Attempts to involve teachers in both the formulation of relevant researchable problems and hypotheses and then in the subsequent conduct of that research in a scientifically rigorous manner are rare. There are a few notable exceptions, however. For several years now Bill Tikunoff and Betty Ward have been engaged in the development of an *interactive model of research and development.* They have studied this approach to research and development to determine what essential requirements and characteristics would predict the successful use of such a strategy. Their Interactive Research and Development on Teaching (IR&DT) model calls for teachers, researchers and teacher educators/developers to work together as a team and to engage in research on questions which emanate from the classroom teacher's concerns.

They have identified three basic assumptions about the nature of research in an "interactive" design and five criteria which the design should meet. They hold the following assumptions:

> Assumption 1: Research on the teaching-learning process must take place where the teaching and learning is occurring: on site at public schools.
> Assumption 2: The personnel conducting the research must be sensitive to and sympathetic with the situational pressures on the classroom teacher.
> Assumption 3: Research on the teaching-learning process must be seen as consistent with the group norms of the setting in which it is occurring. (Tikunoff, Ward, 1977, p. 10)

The criteria they generated for defining an interactive approach include:

> (1) The results of educational research should be available for widespread classroom application within a reasonably short time.
> (2) The delivery system for disseminating research results should move directly from research to the classroom with minimal reliance upon intermediate training products.
> (3) The R&D process should be an interactive one, and should include daily, ongoing communication between teachers, researchers, trainers of teachers, and others involved in the process.
> (4) Research on teaching and the corollary training of teachers should be concerned with the multiple dimensions of the teaching act, emphasizing the context within which teaching occurs.
> (5) Research on teaching should emphasize the most effective forms of teaching. (Tikunoff, Ward, 1977, p. 6)

This writer had the privilege of working with Tikunoff and Ward in one of the schools in which they had conducted collaborative research and the opportunity to interview an entire school faculty in terms of their perceptions of how this joint inquiry had contributed to their own professional growth (Howey, 1980). The teachers and administrators at this particular school were uniformly positive about the benefits of this collaborative research for teacher growth and shared numerous ways in which they perceived themselves to have grown professionally. There is little doubt, in this writer's mind at least, of the potential of well-conceived collaborative forms of inquiry for teacher growth.

For over a decade now in this country and for longer than that in

England, a unique type of teacher educator referred to as an *advisor* has been at work in several schools and school districts. These advisors have approached teachers not as supervisors but rather as a human resource to be used as teachers see fit. Christine San Jose (1979) has defined the nature of their work as follows:

> It's fairly easy to walk in and tell someone what to do. It's not too difficult to listen to a problem and say what you would do. To listen to people and then help them think through what is the next best step for them, that is an extraordinarily demanding way to work.

Gretchen Thomas (1979) reviewed teachers' perceptions of the advisor:

> Educators who believe learning takes place best among colleagues exploring a subject together, who believe that the desire to learn must come from the learner, and who believe that learning must be individualized so that it suits the specific people involved and their particular situation.
>
> Someone who helps teachers examine what they want to have happen with their students and why, and then demystifies the process of going about it . . .
>
> Someone who practices the art of drawing out the best in a teacher and in a school. Not master teachers who "have the answers" but colleagues committed to working and learning along-side teachers . . .

We have asked Bob Mai, because of his extended experience with this approach, to address matters of selection, preparation and practice for the advisor role, and the problems and successes encountered with it. The advisory approach is most consonant with school-focused inservice and also with the strategies employed by many who work in teacher centers. Thus, interviews with and scenarios of such outstanding school-focused teacher educators and teacher center pioneers as Gwen Yarger, Frank Lyman, and Fred Baker are also included in our collection of writings. We also dialogue at length with exemplary classroom teachers such as Jennifer Smith and Sue Brown, who have assumed major staff development responsibilities in specific school sites.

Clinical supervision is not a new concept and the basic elements of this approach need not be reviewed here. There are, however, as with most approaches to any instructional (teacher education) approach, multiple variations on the theme. This writer, for example, has worked with *students* in elementary classrooms in training them to systematically record dimensions of classroom activity. Employing easy-to-use recording devices, these pupils might look at patterns of verbal or nonverbal discourse, the functioning behavior of students in groups, reinforcement behaviors of teachers, decision-making patterns, or the use of time for specific purposes. Decisions are jointly made between teachers and pupils as to what might be interesting and helpful to examine in the classroom. Information collected is examined not only in terms of teacher role and responsibility but the students' responsibility individually and as a group for the achievement of classroom goals. This approach is one aspect of and one variation on the clinical supervision model. In this collection, we have asked Willis Copeland, both because of his knowledge of clinical supervison and his extensive work with teachers, to outline a collegial approach among teachers which employs the basic principles of clinical supervison.

Finally, whatever instructional strategies one decides to employ as a form of inservice, necessary time and resources are invariably important factors to achieving success. The roles and relationships assumed by key persons other than teachers within the schools, as well as institutions and persons external to the school, can be critical. Thus, we include in this book what we believe to be a viable leadership role in terms of inservice for a most key person—the building principal. We also share one way in which an external agency—an institution of higher education preparing teachers—can link a pre-service and inservice program to the benefit of both beginning and more experienced teachers. Clifford Sibley outlines the central role a principal can assume in a systematic school-wide approach to inservice and speaks to the resources and support he or she can provide. Henrietta Barnes and Joyce Putnam share with us a unique pre/inservice model which emphasizes reciprocity. They amply illustrate how the use of preservice students and college faculty can contribute to effective school-focused inservice. Their approach can be characterized as a structured *action/reflection model*.

In summary, this chapter has attempted to provide a rationale not only for more but for *better* school-focused inservice education. In an attempt to promote better forms of this type of inservice, essential characteristics of effective school-focused inservice were identified. The author has also identified several specific approaches to this form of inservice (which are amplified more fully later in the text). These approaches include 1) team teaching, 2) organizational development, 3) collaborative research, 4) advisory models, 5) collegial forms of clinical supervision, 6) school-wide goal setting (emphasizing the role of the principal) and 7) a structured action/reflection model (emphasizing the role of higher education) as consonant with the notion of school-focused inservice.

References

Berman, P., et al. Federal programs supporting educational change. A monograph; *Executive Summary*. Santa Monica, Calif.: The Rand Corporation, 1976.

Bolam, R., et al. Making INSET work. A discussion paper. Chesham, England: Department of Education and Science and the Welsh Office, Her Majesty's Stationary Office, STP Ltd., 1978.

British Schools Council. The whole curriculum 13-16: Working Paper 53. London, England, 1975.

Howey, K. R., Corrigan, D., & Haberman, M. Adult learning and development: Implications for inservice teacher education. Paris: Organization for Economic Cooperation and Development/Center for Educational Research and Innovation. CERI/TE 79.04; 9th May, 1979.

Howey, K.R. A review of NIE/OECD. Sponsored conferences and literature on school-focused inservice education: Implications for research and development. Monograph, Draft copy. 1980.

Ingvarson, L., et al. *School-focused and school based in-service education in Australia*. (Draft copy.) Canberra, 1978.

Lawrence, G., et al. *Patterns of effective inservice education*. Syracuse, NY: Inservice National Council of States on Inservice Education, Syracuse University, 1977.

McLaughlin, M. W., & Marsh, D. Staff development and school change. *Teacher's College Record*, 1(80), September 1978.

McLean, L. D., & Brison, D. W. *Making a difference at school—The R & D challenge*. The Ontario Institute for Studies in Education. (Draft copy.) Ferbruary 1976.

Miles, M. et al. *O.D. in schools: The state of the art*. A paper presented at the American Educational Research Association Annual Meeting, Toronto, March 27-31, 1978.

Rutter, M. *Fifteen thousand hours*. Cambridge, Mass.: Harvard University Press, 1979.

San Jose, C. Staffing a teachers' center. In K. Devaney (Ed.), *Building a teachers' center*. San Francisco: Teachers' Centers Exchange, Far West Laboratory for Educational Research and Development, 1979.

Tikunoff, W. T. et al. *Toward an operational definition of the interactive model of research and development in teaching. Some assumptions and characteristics*. San Francisco: Far West Laboratory for Research and Development, 1977.

Thomas, G. *The advisor: Emissary from teachers' center to classroom*. San Francisco: Teachers' Centers Exchange, Occasional Paper No. 6, Far West Laboratory for Educational Research and Development, October 1979.

Yarger, S., Howey, K., & Joyce, B. *Inservice teacher education*. Palo Alto: Booksend Laboratories, 1980.

Chapter 3:

A School-focused Teacher Educator: A Scenario of a Public School Teacher with Staff Development Responsibilities

Jennifer Smith

Overview

My job as inservice coordinator for Hans Christian Andersen Elementary School is described here as it pertains to the staff of an elementary school which is committed to open education. Andersen A is one of three alternative schools located in a large building complex. Each school (Andersen A, B, and C) offers a different educational program from which parents and students can choose. The complex is located in an inner-city neighborhood. More than 45% of its population is minority, with over 35% being American Indian. Approximately 36% of the total school population (1600 students) qualifies for Title I supplementary services.

Each alternative program has a population of about 500 students. The building is subdivided and each program is located in separate wings of the complex. Gymnasiums, music and art rooms as well as a media center are all shared facilities. Each staff of the three schools consists of a principal, licensed teachers, and instructional and clerical aides.

The open education program with which I work has twenty-five licensed teachers and fifteen aides on the staff. Seventeen of the teachers are full-time classroom teachers that work in teams of four or five members. The six part-time teachers work as Title I tutors. In addition, this open education program has two SLBP teachers that service children with special learning and behavior problems. All of the aides work with children in classrooms under the direct supervision of the teachers or as clerical assistants.

My role as the inservice coordinator in this open school is to encourage and facilitate the continuing professional education of the teaching staffs. I work collaboratively with the teachers to establish learning goals that are appropriate for the individual teachers and the staff as a whole. Learning activities may be planned for an individual, a team, or perhaps the entire staff. Most of the planned learning experiences occur at the school site. However, some of the needs of teachers require an experience apart from the school setting.

Although the primary focus of my job is inservice education, it is by no means my only responsibility. Curriculum planning, the purchasing of learning materials and the supervision of Title I services are also a part of the role of the school-based inservice coordinator. It is important to note that these "extra" responsibilities gradually became a part of my role not because there was no one else to do them, although that does happen, but because these activities are an integral part of the total inservice program.

The model for curriculum planning used by the school staff would be an example of such an integration of responsibilities. Each staff member serves on one of the four major curriculum committees (social studies, science, reading/language arts, and math). The committees, with representatives from each team, meet on a regular basis to define goals, identify the scope and sequence of the program, plan special activities for the students, report on meetings attended outside of the school, and evaluate the program. I attend these meetings to provide direction to the task and to respond to the staff needs that often become apparent during these sessions. At times a committee feels that the total staff should participate in a specific type of learning experience appropriately related to their curriculum area. In that instance, I then investigate the inservice possibilities and report the necessary arrangements back to the committee. In the interim, the committee members, being representatives of their respective teams, report back to their team members and explain the position and ideas of their committee. Then, at a subsequent staff meeting the committee members present their ideas, I share my perspectives as inservice coordinator, and a consensus decision regarding the type and time for the inservice is made by the staff. If the decision is made to pursue the committee's ideas, then I, with the help of the committee, assume the responsibility for planning and carrying out the inservice. This type of participative curriculum planning by the staff increases not only the teachers' awareness of their students' needs but also makes them aware of their own strengths and weaknesses. With the cooperation and commitment of the entire staff, I, in the role of inservice coordinator, can facilitate the improvement of the curriculum through the larger inservice program.

The effectiveness of my role, however, is also dependent upon the support of the building principal. It is imperative that the principal and I communicate regularly on a number of issues. The principal in this open school recognizes the need for the inservice coordinator to be actively involved in decisions related to curriculum, staffing, and budget. Although the principal is ultimately responsible for these decisions, he seeks out the opinions and ideas of the coordinator and other staff members. The principal and I, then, work as a team, each doing our part for the staff, students and parents in this alternative school setting.

It is important to note, however, that I do not participate in any way in staff evaluations. Evaluating teacher effectiveness is totally the responsibility of the building principal. Both the principal and I recognize the importance of the teachers being able to consult with me without fear of jeopardizing themselves or their jobs. Teacher growth does not occur without honestly accepting the need for change. The atmosphere of trust that fosters that growth must always be maintained.

The effectiveness of the inservice coordinator is often contingent upon the relationships maintained not only with the open school staff members but also with resource people within the complex and the school district. I recognize the need to spend time developing good lines of communication with other coordinators and curriculum resource people. Many of my hours of meeting time are spent discussing the mutual needs of teachers in open settings and other alternative programs. Many times district inservice goals are a direct result of these meetings.

A large school district often has many resource people that can help support the inservice efforts of a school staff. It is my role as inservice coordinator to identify these resource people and to enlist their support when needed.

At this point my role in this open school is evolving—constantly changing. Each day is different. Although the primary focus of my position is to facilitate the continuing teacher education process, many different tasks are involved. Some are related to the long-term goals of the staff; others are more crisis-centered. The following description of my major responsibilities and activities during a regular working week may help the reader to better understand the role of the inservice coordinator in this open setting.

MONDAY

    8:00 Inservice planning meeting
    9:00 Evaluation of new learning materials
  11:00 Parents Tour
  12:00 Lunch
    1:00 Meeting
    4:45 ———

Inservice Planning Meeting

Monday morning begins with an 8:00 planning meeting. Two teachers, one aide, the chemical dependency counselor, and I are meeting to plan a series of inservice sessions for the entire staff on the topic of chemical dependency and its impact on elementary children. In response to a request from the staff, I have assumed the responsibility for conducting the planning meeting and coordinating the inservice activities. Representatives from the staff have been asked to meet with the counselor so that the relevant issues regarding chemical dependency can be explored from a variety of perspectives.

The meeting begins with a brief review of the charge of the group. I remind the committee that we are here to plan one or more inservice sessions on chemical dependency problems in the elementary school. After a brief exchange of questions, answers, and lengthy discussion between the committee members and the counselor, the committee concludes that three one-hour sessions will be adequate to cover the initial concerns of the staff. It is decided that these sessions will occur during the staff planning time before school on three successive Tuesday mornings. A general outline for each day's activities is recommended by the committee. Final planning is then delegated to the counselor and myself who will both serve as resource persons for the inservice sessions. The meeting ends after an hour of intense discussion and planning.

Learning Materials Evaluation

The next two hours of my time is spent evaluating new learning materials. Several teachers have requested materials that appear to be quite costly. It is the responsibility of the inservice coordinator to consider these requests and to evaluate the materials. Then, after consulting with each curriculum committee, I will decide which materials should be purchased for the entire school and which materials would most appropriately be purchased in limited quantities to be used as resource materials.

I am asked by the principal to come to his office. Upon arriving, I am introduced to two parents who have indicated an interest in enrolling their child in the open school. The principal, indicating that she has another commitment, asks me to tour the parents through the building, explain the program to them, and answer any questions that they might have.

Parents Tour

Occasionally, the coordinator assumes this role of "tour guide" at the request of the staff or principal. There seems to be a definite need for someone who understands the philosophy of the open school, is aware of the goals of the program, and can explain them to interested parents or visitors who may be unfamiliar with alternative education models. The inservice coordinator is often in a position of serving as an advocate for the open program and its teachers. The flexibility of my work schedule greatly enhances my availability. Therefore, the role of guide is merely an extension of my position.

Lunch

After spending an hour with the parents, I then join several staff members for lunch in the teachers' cafeteria. Although this period of time is not part of the teacher's working day, it is an important time for me to meet on an informal basis with the teachers. I regularly make myself available to interact with staff members on both personal and professional issues during this time. After a hectic morning with children, teachers are often willing to seek out advice and assistance on problems that they are having within their classrooms. They often need and want support and help from their peers. It is at this point that other staff members, outside resource people or other learning experiences can be mentioned as resources available to the classroom teacher. It is the responsibility of the inservice coordinator in this situation to provide the appropriate resources and ensure that these resources assist the teacher. Follow-up activities serve to strengthen and evaluate the overall effectiveness of the resources that were used. These lunchtime informal discussions are some of the most productive meetings that occur during the school day because they provide a non-threatening and supportive problem-solving atmosphere for the entire staff.

Meeting

Immediately following lunch, I leave the building for a meeting with twenty other Title I coordinators in the school district. The agenda for the meeting includes: (a) a presentation by a resource person on the differences between criterion and norm-referenced tests and their uses in the

Title I evaluation process, (b) an update on the latest supplementary reading and math materials developed by the district for Title I students, and (c) a discussion on the plans for Title I summer school.

The purpose of the meeting is to disseminate current information to the various school staffs involved in servicing Title I students. In this situation, the inservice coordinator reports back to the staff the information that is particularly relevant to them. Depending on the situation it may be necessary for the coordinator to plan a meeting or an inservice session to effectively disseminate the information and/or materials.

TUESDAY

  8:15 Inservice Planning
  9:00 Proposal Writing
12:00 Lunch
12:45 Administrative Meeting
  4:00 Math Inservice
  7:00 ———

Inservice Planning

An 8:15 meeting with one of the open school teams and two resource teachers starts my day. The two language arts specialists from the district office are here at my request to help plan a writing inservice. Several teachers from one intermediate-age team have become increasingly frustrated with the writing ability of their students. After attempting to remedy this problem on their own, the teachers approached me with their frustrations. We agreed that someone with specific expertise in the area of writing would be helpful in giving direction to the teachers involved. This meeting then is the first of several that will be needed to plan such an inservice for teachers.

I begin the meeting with brief introductions and a review of the situation that made the meeting necessary. The team members are anxious to explain their problem and identify their goals. The discussion starts immediately. After a lengthy exchange of ideas, all of those in attendance agree that several inservice sessions would be most desirable. However, the group concurs that several hours of uninterrupted time is most appropriate to accomplish this task. It is agreed that a proposal to the district staff development committee will be written by the inservice coordinator. The proposal will ask for the necessary money to pay for after-school inservice time. If the proposal is not funded, I will then reconvene this group to investigate other possibilities. The meeting ends with everyone understanding that I, as the inservice coordinator, will assume the responsibility for the next steps in the planning process.

The planning process cannot continue until the funding is secured. With that in mind, I decide to put everything else aside until the proposal is completed. The rest of the morning then is spent writing the proposal and securing the necessary support for the project from the principal and the district staff development specialist. No further planning can now be done until the funding committee makes its decision.

Administrative Meeting

After lunch, the coordinator and the principal attend a meeting on computerized record-keeping. The school administrators (all three principals from each school in the complex) are investigating the possibility of computerizing all of the records including those kept by teachers. In attendance are the three principals, two computer experts, and myself. I have specifically been asked to attend this meeting because of my familiarity with the records kept by teachers and my knowledge of computers. In addition, it is likely that I will be asked to plan the training sessions that will be needed to acquaint teachers with the computer if the plan for computerized record-keeping becomes a reality.

The meeting begins with the listing of several questions that the building administrators would like answered by the computer specialists before the meeting is concluded. These questions initiate a rather technical and lengthy discussion. It is clear as the meeting continues that many of the questions cannot be easily or immediately answered. More information is necessary. Each person in attendance agrees to follow-up on some aspect of the discussion and report back to the next meeting of this group. It is my responsibility to draw up an accurate list of all of 1) the necessary inservice records and 2) the records on resource materials, pupil progress, curriculum materials and the like that teachers keep on their own. Also included in the report should be the reasons for keeping each type of record. Each teacher and team of teachers will have to be consulted so that no pertinent information is excluded. The group agrees to meet again the following week.

Math Inservice

My day, as busy as it has been already, seems as though it is just getting started. I still have the responsibility to facilitate a math inservice session for the primary team. This meeting which begins at 4:00 and concludes at 7:00 p.m. is the fourth in a series of six inservice sessions on the use of Piagetian concepts and tasks in a primary math program. This particular session is focusing on the materials now available to support such a program. Another teacher and I will present the materials and demonstrate some of their possible uses.

This exciting inservice project is the result of one team member's insistence that the teachers should be doing more for the children in their team. After becoming familiar with Piaget's theories through a graduate course at a local university, I became increasingly critical of the lack of *planned* "hands on" experiences for children within the school. As I began to try new techniques and materials with some of the children, the rest of the team members began to notice a change in the students' attitudes toward math. The teachers were intrigued and wanted to know more. The discussions, the planning and the proposal writing started. Within a few weeks, the inservice session began and a major change in the primary math program was underway.

WEDNESDAY

8:00 Welcome Student Teachers
8:45 Classroom Teaching
1:00 Field Trip
4:00 ———

Welcome Student Teachers

My role at the open school is not only committed to inservice education, but it also supports preservice teacher education. Pre-service teachers doing practicums and student teaching are integrated into the activities of the school for experiences in a variety of learning situations. I work cooperatively with the classroom teachers and the university supervisor to provide a valuable learning experience for these preservice teachers.

This is the first day for the student teachers and all of the teachers have gathered to meet and welcome them. I have provided coffee and doughnuts for the informal time before the meetings so that the atmosphere is warm and relaxed.

The meeting is called to order by the principal who welcomes the students and encourages them to visit with her when they have questions or concerns. After making a few announcements, she turns the meeting over to me. At my request, each supervising teacher introduces his/her student teacher to the staff. After the introductions, the teachers not responsible for student teachers return to finish their planning for the day. The students and the supervising teachers remain with me for a brief review of the requirements and expectations of the student teaching program. Following the question and answer period, everyone adjourns to greet the arriving students.

I will again formally meet with the student teachers later in the week to establish a seminar schedule and to address in more detail some of their questions and concerns.

Classroom Teaching

On occasion, the role of the inservice coordinator calls for me to assume the responsibilities of a classroom teacher. I do this so that the teacher may participate in a learning experience that is only available during the school day. Today, I am releasing a primary teacher so that she can demonstrate a language arts lesson to another team of teachers. This teaching responsibility also provides an opportunity for me to try some new techniques that I will later share with other teachers. Perhaps more importantly I am able to interact with the students that provide much of the challenge to the teachers.

Although my classroom teaching does not happen frequently, I do encourage teachers to learn from each other by exchanging teaching responsibilities. To facilitate this learning, I feel that I must provide specific time and arrange schedules for this to happen. It then becomes evident that individual teachers are not the only ones benefitting from this exchange. The total school environment is enhanced. Teaming and space problems, management difficulties and a lack of curriculum materials all become more obvious when experienced from the perspective of a colleague. After teaching, even for such a short time, I am more appreciative of the overwhelming responsibilities of the teacher. I feel that I also gain a certain credibility with the staff that may not necessarily exist when I have been out of the classroom for an extended period of time.

Field Trip

Today, unlike some days that seem to be filled with endless meetings, I am able to spend time with students and interact with teachers in a somewhat different context. This afternoon I am accompanying a group of intermediate-age students and their teacher on a field trip. The purpose of the trip is to gather data for a social studies unit which is being developed by the teacher with the help of the students. I was invited by the teacher in order to help give direction to the project and to ascertain the feasibility of using this site as a learning center for other students and teachers. The site is accessible via the public bus system and is only a short distance from the school. Although the resources are seemingly unlimited, after observing the site, we note that to use them effectively the students would need a great deal of direction from an adult. As the planning of the unit continues, the teacher and I agree that the site should be used but only with considerable pre-planning and teacher supervision. After returning to the school, the teacher, students, and I discuss their experiences and the unit. Plans are then made to pursue other resources for information and ideas. I am anxious to be a continuing part of a group that is so excited about learning.

This day has been a truly eventful day for me. I have learned much about the program, the staff, and the students of our open school.

THURSDAY

8:00 Inservice Day

Thursday is a district-wide inservice day for all teachers. The students are dismissed from school for the day so that the teachers can participate in activities not otherwise available to them. This particular day is the fourth inservice day out of a total of seven days provided each year by the school district.

Today the staff is joining 200 other open school teachers for what has been termed a "Renewal Day." Speakers, small group sessions, and informal discussion times have been planned. The purpose of this day is to provide new information about and renewed interest in the open school movement. Job stress and outside pressures have been taking their toll on the open school teachers. Everyone has agreed that what is needed is a new focus on open schools.

I have been actively involved in the preplanning for virtually all aspects of the "Renewal Day." As a member of the steering and program committees, as well as facilitator of one of the discussion groups, much time and effort has already been expended. However, this type of involvement allows me to interject the needs and ideas of my staff into the planning process. I realize that much of what will occur today will have a direct immediate impact on the teachers in my building. I really have a vested interest to ensure that all things go well.

As the day progresses my role changes dramatically. At one point I am a resource person to a group of teachers seeking information. At another point I am a facilitator of a discussion group. Later I become a participant, joining other staff members in group information sessions and informal discussions.

Following the staff development day, I will systematically help the teachers evaluate their experiences, set any personal or group goals that seem appropriate, and initiate the planning of other learning experiences that are needed to meet these goals.

FRIDAY

   8:00 Coordinators Meeting
11:00 Student Teachers Meeting
12:00 Lunch
   1:00 Administrative Meeting
   4:00 ——

Coordinators Meeting

Each building in the complex has a staff person that has specific coordinating responsibilities. Each person in the role of coordinator does not have the same job focus. The coordinator in the open school (me), as has been pointed out, is a facilitator of continuing or inservice teacher education. The coordinators in the other two schools function as team leaders. Their primary responsibilities are to see that the teams are functioning efficiently and that all of the teachers' tasks are being completed. It is important to note that each coordinator's job has a different focus because the staffs, principals and coordinators of each school are committed to different goals. Each school then has defined the coordinator's position so that the coordinator may best serve the unique needs of his/her school.

On this Friday morning, the coordinators are meeting regarding a problem that affects all three schools. Standardized test scores in math are unacceptably low and the teachers in each school are concerned. Since all three buildings have students from the same geographic area of the city, the problems of poor attendance, lack of motivation and poor basic skills are shared by all three programs. A committee that has met previously has recommended that a math maintenance project be developed. The coordinators have been delegated the responsibility of carrying out that charge.

After discussing the issues in detail, the coordinators decide that two representatives from each program and two math resource teachers from the district should be recruited to serve on a writing task force. It also is agreed that I should organize and chair this group. However, each coordinator will secure their own representatives from his/her program. As the meeting ends, each coordinator agrees to identify his/her representatives by Monday.

Student Teachers Meeting

As this appears to be a day of meetings, I then join the student teachers and their university supervisor. They are meeting to debrief the students' teaching experiences during their first week in the school. We would also like to establish a seminar schedule for the remainder of the quarter. Both the supervisor and I recognize the need for the student teachers to share their successes and frustrations with others. Without any special preparation, the student teachers are often asked to function effectively in situations with which they are totally unfamiliar. In this open school setting of team teaching, open space, differing social values and diverse racial groups, extra pressure is often placed on an already stressful student teaching experience. The goal of the inservice coordinator is to provide a learning environment that is supportive and responsive to the student teachers' individual and group needs. This means that the open education philosophy of learning is not only observed by the student teachers but personally experienced by them.

Administrative Meeting

During the afternoon, the principal and I meet with the new police liaison officer to discuss his changing role and responsibilities. How to establish a more positive relationship between the students and teachers of the open school and the police department is the main topic of the meeting. Each person agrees that it is important for the staff to meet the new liaison officer and hear more about his new role and the services that he can provide for both the teachers and the students. A staff meeting time is established for that purpose.

Conclusion

The inservice coordinator in this open school is a facilitator of continuing teacher education. To do this job effectively, I need to be able to counsel, to organize, to teach, to listen, to lead, to influence, and to guide. Assuming that I have a modicum of skill in each of these areas, I must be at the school site interacting with the students and staff in order to meet my responsibilities. Yet, perhaps the most important characteristic of a school-based coordinator is to enjoy learning. She/he cannot impact inservice teacher education without recognizing the need for continual job-embedded learning experiences.

Chapter 4:

A University-Employed Teacher Educator: A Week in the Life of a Field-based Teacher Educator

Gwen P. Yarger

When I was contacted to develop this chapter around the question, "How does a field-based teacher educator spend his/her time?," I was immediately intrigued. In the past, I have been contacted about isolated responsibilities of my role such as facilitating collaboration between university and school district, developing programs conducting evaluations and needs assessments, supervising preservice teachers, and involving secondary inservice teachers. But this was the first time that I had been asked to provide an overview of the total role played by a field-based teacher educator.

I hold an appointment at Syracuse University as an Assistant Professor in the School of Education, Division for the Study of Teaching with a specific appointment as Coordinator of the West Genesee/Syracuse University Teaching Center. The funding for the teaching center and my salary are shared by Syracuse University and the West Genesee School District. As a field-based teacher educatior assigned to a teaching center, my responsibilities include the following:

- Teaching undergraduate, graduate, and inservice courses/workshops.
- Supervising and coordinating student field placements as well as staff assigned to the center.
- Developing programs for preservice and inservice teachers.
- Promoting public relations.
- Acting as liaison between the university and the school district.

- Sharing new ideas and materials.
- Gathering concerns of all constituents and responding appropriately.
- Initiating and conducting research as well as encouraging others to become involved.
- Matching resources with perceived/stated needs and interests.
- Pursuing personal/professional development interests.

My involvement with the Syracuse Area Teacher Center exerts influence upon responsibilities of this position as well. Three teaching centers are sponsored by Syracuse University: Jamesville-DeWitt/Syracuse University Teaching Center, Syracuse Urban Teaching Center and West Genesee/Syracuse University Teaching Center. They joined in a collaborative effort by forming the Syracuse Area Teacher Center, which is federally funded. Two major goals of that group include:

1. Teachers will be instrumental in developing and guiding programs sponsored by the Syracuse Area Teacher Center.
2. Collaborative efforts between the three centers: West Genesee Teaching Center, Jamesville-DeWitt Teaching Center and Syracuse Urban Teaching Center will be emphasized.

These goals require teacher involvement in the development, brainstorming, and promotion of all new activities. Such emphasis greatly influences my behavior as a program developer in that the needs and interests of all constituents must be taken into account.

In attempting to focus and share with readers the responsibilities of this field-based position, this chapter will be organized by providing a list of daily activities for a typical week and will include background information for each of the *italicized* events. The conclusion will present my perceptions of this role as a field-based teacher educator.

MONDAY

8:15—*Success Interview*
9:00—*Teaching Center* (notes, letters, calls, etc.)
11:40—Go to Campus
12:00—*Lunch with Peer*
1:30—Drive Back to Center
2:30—Meeting with One Teacher at High School
3:45—*Faculty Collaboration*
4:00—*Policy Groups* 7:00—*Policy Groups*

Success Interview

This morning's Success Interview, which started at 8:15, is with an elementary teacher about her conceptions of success in the classroom. Forty-five teachers are being interviewed as a second step in a research study which was begun about a year ago. At that time over 200 teachers were asked to list events which they consider to be successful classroom experiences. The results from that study were just reported at the 1980 American Education Research Association in Boston. Of particular interest in those findings was that, on the average, each teacher identified only four successful events. Elementary teachers were able to list a greater number of successful events than were the junior high teachers while the junior high teachers listed a greater number than did the senior high teachers and both were statistically significant. All three levels of teachers listed events that were primarily affective and events that were signalled from outside themselves, primarily coming from the child. Understanding how teachers define successful teaching may prove useful in developing and delivering more effective inservice programs (Harootunian & Yarger, 1980).

Teaching Center

I check my watch, it is 8:55—time to return to the teaching center which is located in an elementary school. Upon arriving, the first activity is to read the mail and make telephone calls. Items among the mail include: a note from a department chairperson at the high school asking for additional inservice training, a note from a teacher thanking us for a workshop she had just attended, a letter from a teacher thanking us for a workshop she had just attended, a letter from an educator in England confirming arrangements for a visit of English classroom teachers and administrators to our center, a note from the district public relations person responding to a request I had made for black and white photographs of teachers attending various center events, a note from a classroom teacher related to our preservice program and a memo from the district Assistant Superintendent about an inservice program which we are co-sponsoring. Telephone calls which need to be returned include: an official at the university requesting further information about some registration problems, a teacher requesting assistance he would like provided, three different presenters for upcoming workshops/courses, and someone from the Ontario Metal Company about some supplies.

This listing is typical of the mail and telephone calls which are received and returned on a daily basis. It will not be necessary to list such items Tuesday-Friday since similar contacts occur regularly. However, it might be useful to give a capsule explanation about some of these in terms of a typical response so that the reader will have a better understanding of my involvement.

Note from department chairperson. The request from a high school department chairperson asking for assistance is suprisingly upbeat and therefore most appreciated. I have just finished teaching a seminar for the department chairs of his high school on the topic of "Supervision for the Improvement of Instruction." This seminar had been designed after representatives for the department chairs had voiced a need for such training. After listening to their comments and concerns, a course outline was developed which was then sent to the representative group for approval. Once they approved it, the seminar was advertised to all the secondary department chairs in the district on a voluntary attendance basis. This procedure is a very common process in developing our inservice programs. I have found that teacher involvement in planning is very important if voluntary teacher attendance is to be achieved.

Even though this participation had been voluntary, a few individuals had great difficulty with the concept that supervision was being presented as a helpful and facilitative process rather than basically an evaluative one. Historically, these department chairs have focused more on judgmental evaluation rather than on cooperative supervision for the improvement of instruction. A few individuals voiced a strong need to continue performing an evaluative role and argued against a role which was in essence a cooperative and supportive role. Thus, when I receive this note, which is asking for additional help from one of these individuals, I feel very pleased that the content and ideas discussed during the seminars have apparently had an impact after all.

Letter from England. This letter is to confirm arrangements for a group of teachers from Crawley, England to visit the teaching center. Through a program at Syracuse University, preservice students spend eight weeks in England studying the English educational system and completing their student teaching. The teachers visiting us from England had worked directly with those Syracuse University students. We have in the past been able to house these English guests with school district teachers. The center assumes responsibility for transporting the guests and for developing their agenda which includes visits to American classrooms, conversations with the School of Education faculty, contacts with significant programs in the local school districts and trips to local landmarks. Exhausting, but fun!

The English guests are only one of several groups which visit the teaching center. Between September and April this last year, we hosted approximately 35 guests (10 groups) from the United States, Canada, England, and Puerto Rico who came to learn about our teaching center.

Memo from district office. This memo is announcing the date and agenda for an upcoming district administrators meeting. My name appears as an item on the agenda for later this week to discuss how the center might assist in meeting specific district curriculum priorities. Another step forward!

Call to Ontario Metal. You may be wondering why a teacher educator would be contacting a metal company. The reason is to assist a teacher who had been granted a Pet Project. The Pet Project is funded by the Syracuse Area Teacher Center to enable teachers to receive mini-grants to either enhance their own teaching skills or to buy products for use in their classrooms. This particular project has greatly enhanced the visibility of the center and has provided support for teacher projects not available from any other source. My conversation with the purchasing agent at the metal company is rather humorous. He needs to know whether or not a sheet of metal which is .08 of an inch thicker than originally ordered will be acceptable. In trying to describe to this agent the project the teacher desires, we decide that the substitute metal will be acceptable. I now know more about sheet metal than I've ever learned anywhere else. I'm not sure how many teacher educators find themselves in this position but I suspect that anyone trying to develop a comprehensive delivery system for inservice will indeed encounter diverse involvement.

Call to presenters. Making contact with potential instructors or facilitators for various inservice programs is a major on-going activity. On this particular day, I am contacting an individual who has already agreed to present at a one-day conference on the topic of "Career Planning" for counselors from a variety of high schools throughout the federally funded teacher center area. This workshop has evolved from a request by two counselors within my own teaching center area. In the anticipation that counselors from the areas served by the other two centers might want to be involved, interest was assessed by the other center coordinators. As it turned out, counselors from the other public high schools as well as parochial high schools were interested in pushing this topic. So the program was planned and scheduled. This type of conference typically requires the field-based teacher educator to order food, make arrangements for delivery of AV equipment, check out room arrangements, and even to arrange chairs, as well as obviously making sure that the program makes good educational sense.

A second group of teachers, representing secondary math teachers, has approached the center about the possibility of putting together a work session where they could design materials for students who are not at grade level in certain math skills. This need had been accentuated by the new competency-based requirements established by the State Regents in New York. After meeting with the teachers to enlist suggestions and concerns, I followed up by designing a Saturday workshop, contacted outside resource persons who would come in for the day and arranged for lunch and coffee to be brought in for the teachers. On this particular morning, I am contacting the consultants to finalize these arrangements.

Another telephone call has to be made to an individual about presenting a session at a "stress" workshop. A major concern of teachers in today's schools is a frequent sense of being overcome by problems rather than being able to enjoy their successes. As a result, a workshop sponsored through the Syracuse Area Teacher Center is in the design stage and speakers are being contacted.

Following these calls, I begin to rough out an evaluation form which will be used to gather suggestions and comments from participants at the completion of the stress workshop. Once this is completed I move on to the written correspondence.

Written correspondence. It is now 10:50 and time to dictate some letters. On this particular morning, I dictate a letter for principals and cooperating teachers to announce the arrival of a new group of student teachers and to schedule the cooperating teacher seminars. A second letter is dictated to the preservice students to welcome them to their student teaching experience at the teaching center and to establish dates for their seminars. Letters are also dictated to confirm starting dates and payment for course instructors; a memo is sent to a group of teachers that their request for funds has been granted. Finally, a letter confirming arrangements for the English guests is written.

The calendar indicates that the evaluation forms for the general programming at the teaching center need to be re-written and given to the secretary for typing and mailing. Once this is completed, I turn to the task of designing a flyer to advertise a testing workshop which is coming up within the next three weeks. It is also necessary this morning to take a look at the financial books and to make arrangements for current instructors to be paid for their teaching services. Payment vouchers are also written for lunches and other bills which have come in during the past two weeks.

Business/Social Lunch with a Peer

I drive the six miles into the Syracuse University campus to have lunch with a faculty member who has just completed a term on the Committee for Promotion and Tenure. I had received a letter about two weeks earlier announcing that, since I am completing my third year as a faculty member, I would be eligible for promotion during the 1980-81 academic year. It had been suggested that I investigate the process before I announce whether or not I intend to be considered for promotion at this particular time. After talking with this individual, I decided that I will continue to explore the possibilities by making appointments to meet with the Chairperson of the Division for the Study of Teaching and then, with the Dean of the School of Education.

Faculty Collaboration

Returning to the teaching center, I re-check arrangements which have been made for a campus person to meet with a group of art teachers from throughout the district. His reason for coming on this day is to share information with the teachers about the preservice training program and to answer questions posed by the teachers. As it turns out, he needs help in this task. The teachers also need help and I need help. We all need help! Communication between professionals with diverse backgrounds is a real problem.

Policy Groups

The next event in which I am involved is chairing the Directing Council which is the policy-making body for the local teaching center. The representatives are teachers, administrators, and university faculty. Meetings are used to keep the representatives informed about the teaching center programs, Syracuse Area Teacher Center activities, and to solicit their ideas concerning decisions related to ongoing events.

At 7:00, I go to the Policy Board meeting for the Syracuse Area Teacher Center. This policy board is comprised primarily of teachers representing different levels and areas as specified by federal guidelines. As an *ad hoc* member of this group (I do everything but vote), my main role is to share perceptions which I hold concerning upcoming activities. I intiate the discussion by asking members of the Syracuse Area Teacher Center Policy Board if they would be interested in helping to develop an innovative program for inservice teachers. Several individuals volunteer and many hours are spent brainstorming, hiring master teachers for children, selecting children, and designing flyers for advertising. We all find the notion to be very exciting and at the same time somewhat scary because we are trying to combine a number of proven educational ideas into a single integrated program. For example, we want each teacher participant to be able to develop and to follow-through on a contract to meet his/her own professional needs. At the same time an overall structure is desired so individuals will come together on a regular and purposeful basis and accrue the benefits of group interchange. I also want an enrichment program for youngsters which will be exciting and enjoyable. With the assistance of many fantastic people, including the teacher participants themselves, we were able to conduct such a program during the summer of 1979. One of the most exciting aspects of the program was that as the teacher participants worked through their contracts and began to develop new skills and materials for use in the classroom, they were then able to test those new skills with the children. Teachers were also trained to function as peer observers and they met in pre- and post-conferences in pairs to discuss and analyze the significant aspects and interactions which occurred during the "test teaching period." These individuals, some for perhaps the first time in their lives, were taking a hard look at their behavior in the classroom.

In designing the program for this summer, we have felt a greater sense of direction and much more confidence. My hope is that we remain flexible to the needs of the teacher participants so that the program will continue to be innovative and responsive.

TUESDAY

To the District Office

An all-morning meeting at the district office is scheduled with the assistant superintendent. After reviewing several minor issues, we turn to the main purpose of this meeting, which is to discuss the various training endeavors (i.e., a three-credit course, workshops, intensive building programs and teacher leaders) associated with a classroom management program co-sponsored by the center and the district. We review evaluation data collected to this point in time in an effort to assess progress and to guide us in planning new activities. We spend some time as well in reviewing *research questions* and discussing procedures for collecting additional data. We decide who will assume what responsibility for fol-

for following through on the next steps and decide to meet again soon.

I am firmly convinced that the success of a field-based teacher education program is directly related to the working relationship established with the school district. In this particular district, the teachers, the union, and the administrators have all been extremely supportive and willing to work together.

Luncheon Meeting

Lunch is spent with a superintendent from another local school district discussing an upcoming conference which we will be conducting jointly. The theme of the conference, "Teaching the Unique," presents us with a challenge in designing content which will meet the goals desired for the conference. We exchange ideas and develop a tentative outline. Each of us will assume responsibility for certain aspects of the conference and we make arrangements to talk by phone to exchange additional ideas and to mail each other materials which can be further distributed.

Preparing to Teach

I next go to the teaching center where I spend time reviewing materials which will be used in a class I will teach this afternoon. I also use this opportunity to begin reading and reviewing materials for use in future sessions of this course. I check my transparencies, position the audiovisual equipment, greet students as they enter and begin to teach a two-hour session.

WEDNESDAY

8:30—*Coordinators Sharing*
10:00—*District Administrators Meeting*
11:00—Teaching Center
2:15—*Meeting with Teachers*
3:30—*New Course*
4:00—*Dinner Meeting*

Coordinators Sharing

A meeting has been scheduled at the School of Education with the coordinators of the other teaching centers, so I leave home and head for campus. This morning we share information about upcoming events each of us are planning in our centers, discuss concerns about preservice field placements, and brainstorm strategies for improving coordination between the schools and campus, as well as among centers.

District Administrators Meeting

I leave the campus and drive to the school district to attend an administrators meeting. My primary purpose in attending this meeting is to discuss upcoming research I would like to conduct out of the center. One of my ongoing interests has been how teachers use various materials in the classroom. As a result, I have conducted a number of studies , looking at materials used by both teachers and children, and have related such use to different characteristics of teachers and to different types of training. In this new study, data will be collected through classroom observations and interviews. This will be done to determine both the types of materials being used by teachers and how they are being used. I am going to be allowed to use student achievement scores. This may not sound like much, however, having administrators and teachers trust you that much is important in this job. The administrators who have agreed to help facilitate the data collection have given approval to a letter which will be sent to teachers requesting them to participate in the study.

Teaching Center

After the meeting, I return to the teaching center where I make five telephone calls, review the mail, dictate several more letters, and handwrite five notes (often the personal touch is important). One of the telephone calls is to a colleague with whom I am working on a project, related to the use of materials in the classroom as discussed above. We have just completed a review of the literature related to materials use and are currently developing a training manual for teachers to use materials in more effective ways. We discuss our progress and set dates for future meetings.

Meeting with Teachers

Next, I drive to one of the junior high schools in the district to meet with a group of teachers who have expressed a desire for inservice assistance. At the meeting, I discover that the teachers desire assistance in working with gifted youngsters in social studies. We talk about various formats, desired content, and possible resources. It is agreed that I will develop a potential outline and format which will be sent to them for their approval.

New Course

A new course is starting at the center, so I drive back to the center to register the students and to answer initial questions. I am not involved in the instruction of this particular course but responsibilities such as this are shared by the center staff.

Dinner Meeting

I drive to a local restaurant to meet with other members of the Summer School in Action committee. This afternoon we are reviewing applications for the "master" teacher positions. The selection of these teachers is highly crucial to the success of our program. We not only expect these people to be outstanding teachers in a conventional sense, but we also encourage them to function with flexible curriculum materials and to develop opportunities for youngsters to grow in their attitudes about the entire process of learning. Additionally, the master teachers must maintain a flexible schedule so that the graduate teachers can be easily worked into their classroom schedule. Therefore, the selection of the master teachers is conducted thoughtfully and systematically during the next five-and-a-half hours.

THURSDAY

8:30—Meeting with Teachers
9:15—*Teaching Center*
10:20—Success Interview
11:00—Teaching Center
12:00—*To Campus*
1:30—*Dissertation Meeting*
3:45—Working in Office
5:00—*Student Meeting*
7:00—*Dinner Meeting*

Teaching Center

A meeting at the teaching center has been scheduled with the Associate Director of the Syracuse Area Teacher Center. Our task this morning is to develop a slide presentation which will be used for a series of Town Meetings. The Town Meetings are intended to familiarize parents of potential students in the Summer School in Action with the enrichment aspect of the student program as well as to inform them of the primary purpose of the program—to provide teacher training. Information is shared concerning the makeup of the classes, each of which is comprised of no more than 18 students with two youngsters designated as having a handicapping condition. There are youngsters from both the city and suburban school districts and from multi-grade levels.

Once the slides have been selected and the script written, the Associate Director leaves the center. I now turn to making my daily phone calls and answering correspondence.

To Campus

Once back on campus, I check my mailbox, respond to mail that requires immediate attention here, and again return telephone calls. Keeping current of messages and correspondence at separate offices, located several miles apart, causes one to be constantly concerned about whether or not he/she is responding *quickly* enough.

Dissertation Meeting

The primary purpose for coming on campus today is to serve as a member of a dissertation committee. I am meeting with other faculty members and the student to discuss the student's newest chapters. This meeting is rather involved since there are some differences of opinion concerning the progress of the student's work. Agreement is finally reached and arrangements are made for the future direction in which the student will work and a date is set for the next meeting.

Student Meeting

At 5:00, I head for a meeting with a group of preservice student teachers and university faculty to discuss student questions and concerns. The discussion is an active one as students are comfortable in expressing concerns about demands on their time and raising pointed questions about the purposes of several new requirements. Explanations are provided by various members of the faculty and the students appear satisfied with the responses and that faculty members are concerned about their welfare.

Dinner Meeting

Typically, there are one or two evening meetings each week, but there are a few weeks like this one where such meetings occur one right after the other! There is just time to drive to a dinner meeting, which has been scheduled with a group of teachers representing the Syracuse Area Teachers Center, to discuss the possibility of a research project which will focus on the teacher center itself. At this meeting, the teachers are initially ill at ease and minimally involved; perhaps because they are not sure exactly what is expected of them. Once it becomes evident that the center staff has no preconceived ideas about the direction of the research but is concerned with better understanding how a center works, the teachers become actively involved in discussing and sharing ideas. Eventually the teachers even volunteer their services for collecting data.

FRIDAY

9:00—*Teaching Center* (calls, letters, Annual Report)
10:30—*Staff Meeting*
12:00—*Cooperating Teachers Luncheon*
1:00—*Division Meeting*
3:00—Go to Bookstore
4:00—*Meeting*

Teaching Center

A bulging "Bills to be Paid" file indicates that it is time for further work in finances. Three teachers have sent in receipts for reimbursement through Pet Project funds, and two consultants and four instructors need to be paid, as do cafeteria bills and miscellaneous supply bills. Each of these items is processed and the financial books brought up-to-date. What amazes me is that I don't spend more than $10,000 per year.

Annual Report

As a university faculty member, I have been working on my annual report for the past few weeks and have just received the rough draft back from the secretary. I spend some time reviewing, editing, and making additions. Because there are so many different aspects to this position, the appendix to the standard form has become a rather involved process. I take time this morning to gather various materials, papers, advertisements, and statistics to substantiate various activities I share in the annual report.

In reviewing the annual report, I notice that I have taught two on-campus preservice courses, three graduate courses and one seminar. I have worked with two graduate independent studies, and taught/administered Summer School in Action. During this time I have managed the administrative functions of the teaching center. Twelve additional graduate courses have been initiated through the center. Seventeen workshops have been collaboratively designed around a variety of topics such as: Cartooning in the Classroom, Creative Writing, Making Metrics Work, and Classroom Conflict Resolution.

I have served on two standing university committees, three dissertation committees, four committees at our center, and two Syracuse Area Teacher Center committees. The report also indicates that 226 preservice university students have been placed in various classrooms. Professionally, I have presented at three conferences, including AERA, and published two articles.

Staff Meeting

It is now 10:30 and time to meet with the teaching center staff, two graduate assistants supported by the university, to discuss the preservice program. Although their primary assignment is to supervise the preservice teachers, they have also taken some responsibility for teaching the Cooperating Teacher Seminars and the Preservice Seminars. They are both in their third year with the center and have extended their skills in several ways. Today, we discuss the content of the upcoming seminars and evaluate the success of the most recent sessions. Some discussion is given over to problems that a few of the preservice students have encountered which involves probing for the possible solutions.

The three of us have also been designing audiovisual instructional materials. The first tape we produced, a 28-minute black and white tape based on Summer School in Action, used shots of planning sessions, interviews of parents and teacher participants, and sections of various presentations. Our next major project is the development of a training film. We wrote a proposal and received a grant from New York State Teacher Center Funds to develop a training film for teachers on how to use "direct" instruction in a variety of content areas. Classroom teachers have been filmed demonstrating the use of direct instruction in both social studies and math. One of the things that we need to do during this morning's meeting is to set a date when we can actually sit down and decide which segments of the film will be used in the final edition and to discuss the format of the manual which will accompany the film. As time grows short for the staff meeting, we wrap it up by reviewing the decisions that have been made and the dates that have been set for upcoming meetings.

Cooperating Teachers Seminar Luncheon

Part of the reason for bringing cooperating teachers together is so they can share their ideas and the progress that each is experiencing with their student teachers. The first few minutes of the luncheon is spent in sharing successful procedures that each has experienced during the past two weeks. Time is allowed for each to ask the others questions and to air any concerns. At times like this, negative comments are sometimes made about the students' university training. As a field person who strongly identifies with the university, I have to be extremely cautious about listening very carefully to what is being said. It is very easy to simply react by saying—"Well, I don't think you understand the program"—or by casually dismissing the concern being voiced. Instead, a field-based teacher educator must carefully analyze what is being said and respond appropriately. Many times the teacher is unaware of the actual training process, for example, which signals that we have fallen short in our previous explanations. Thus, this opportunity for sharing information is frequently used to clarify goals and processes in the preservice program. Sometimes the suggestions made by the teachers prove useful in strengthening the preservice program. Therefore, suggestions are needed to be carried back to the university faculty with full understanding that they may or may not be accepted. In cases where suggestions are carried back to campus, the field-based individual must be very diplomatic in how the information is presented to the faculty. On this day, this type of clarification is provided. As the staff begins to discuss today's seminar topic, I excuse myself.

Division Meeting

I leave the Cooperating Teaching luncheon early and drive to campus for the Division for the Study of Teaching monthly department meeting. At these meetings, I am brought up-to-date about concerns of the Division members, possible program changes, committee activities, and general announcements. Division meetings provide an opportunity to interact with the faculty as a whole and to make contacts with faculty members that I do not see often.

Meeting

After the Division meeting, I am off for a conference with another faculty member and an undergraduate student, who did not successfully complete her student teaching assignment. The discussion centers around ways that the student might successfully complete that assignment with an agreement being reached that the student will return to the center during the first summer session to complete student teaching.

Well, another week is all but completed. I am back at my office. I check my calendar book to see what is coming up during the next week and then collect materials which will be needed over the weekend and head for home.

CONCLUSION

Providing an outline of weekly activities has obviously been an enjoyable but relatively simple task. If this does not adequately communicate the role of field-based educator as I assume it, the reader should clearly feel short-changed. Few insights, cognitive understandings, or those funny feelings in the pit of one's stomach have been presented. Therefore, before I close, I would like to share just a few of my perceptions concerning the role of a field-based teacher educator.

Coming to Grips with the Role

It has been the perception of many that a *university*-based field-person will not be adequately recognized for his/her efforts by their higher education colleagues and that it is doubtful such a person will be promoted. It would have been very easy to accommodate such perceptions and to allow myself to become immersed in the more routine aspects of this role. Since I chose to come to grips with the general expectations for a university faculty person, I had to examine carefully my perceptions of what it meant to be a field-based teacher educator.

Time management. If there is anything I have learned over the past two- and-a-half years, it is that time management is of the utmost importance. Getting the letters out, designing and implementing advertisements, meeting for and putting together programs, hosting guests, and routine correspondence could consume one's time. I believe, however, that I am learning to put all these responsibilities in perspective so that sufficient time for teaching and professional growth is provided.

Committees. One of the things that I found especially frustrating during my first year as coordinator was the fact that virtually everything I did in this role was accomplished through committee. I was concerned that the value of my own work and leadership would somehow be lost in the total group. I have wrestled with that concern and have now reached a point where I consider joint effort an advantage rather than a liability. My perspective is that being *too* concerned about self-recognition is not advantageous to myself, to the university, or to the center. I have become very comfortable with group work since observing that such a process, when *thoughtfully guided*, can produce quality involvement and results for both school people and university faculty. I feel especially competent in being able to lead groups in deciding long-term goals which are highly important to the success of inservice teacher training.

Where does one belong? A second frustration was my inability to develop a strong tie with either the university or the school district. Having offices in both locations caused me never to feel really settled and to assume that others viewed me in the same way. I initially felt isolated from, even rejected by, both university faculty and school people because of my not feeling a part of either group. However, I am now able to focus on the service that I provide to both institutions and on the very satisfying aspects of this position which, I might add, allows me a great deal of independence and latitude.

A sense of direction. The field-based teacher educator must help to maintain a strong collaborative/working relationship between the school district and the university. At the same time, this individual must be able to conceptualize a holistic sense of programming which includes both pre- and inservice. As a field-based teacher educator, I consider that part of my obligation also includes looking to the future and anticipating outcomes.

In order for the center to be truly effective and to maintain integrity and neutrality, the center should be recognized as a *separate* yet *connected* entity. It is the responsibility of the field-based teacher educator to maintain this delicate balance. He or she must work to have others accept this role and to have the fortitude to say "No" when granting a request creates more problems than it solves. Each constituent group—teachers, administrators, and university faculty—are capable of making plans, however unintentional, that in some way infringe on another group. The center, with the stated purpose of working for the good of all constituents, cannot accommodate such plans.

Reality and Vision

I have shared with you a largely positive and quite upbeat attitude concerning my position as a field-based teacher educator. While I obviously enjoy the position and the many positive rewards I associate with it, writing this chapter has caused me to remember an event which occurred about a year ago. I was asked to make a short presentation to a group of university faculty from around the State of New York about Syracuse University's involvement with the teacher center. The presentation was well received and a number of very interesting questions were asked. As we were concluding the session, a faculty member from another university said to the group that he thought all of this had been very interesting and that he certainly enjoyed hearing about the university's involvement with the field. But, he continued, that at HIS university a field-based person would never be granted promotion or tenure. When pressed about the reasons for this he stated that, after all, this was not an "academic" endeavor. I believe this attitude is still typical and many field-based educators may reinforce the concept. This need not be the case, however. For the time being, I guess field-based educators such as myself will have to have tough skins due to comments and attitudes such as this. Nonetheless, it is my hope that this chapter has assisted in several ways to help others to better understand the role and variability of a field-based teacher educator. Specifically, I hope this discussion has presented evidence which indicates that field-based teacher educators: (1) can meet extensive demands placed upon their time and energies, (2) can meet academic expectations in higher education, (3) are able to contribute to a better understanding of teacher training, and (4) are able to provide a vehicle for bridging theory into practice. While there are those who may continue to protest the professional status of the field-based teacher educator, I will continue wearing my rose-colored glasses which provide a warm and optimistic vision of this role in the future.

REFERENCES

Harootunian, B., & Yarger, G. P. *Teachers' conceptual level and use of classroom materials.* Paper presented at the meeting of the American Education Research Association, Toronto, 1978.

Harootunian, B., & Yarger, G. P. *Teachers' conceptions of their own classroom successes.* Paper presented at the meeting of the American Education Research Association, Boston, April 1980.

Yarger, G. P. *Teachers' learning style and intended use of instructional materials.* Paper presented at the meeting of the American Education Research Assocation, San Francisco, 1976.

Yarger, G. P., & Harootunian, B. *Teachers' use of classroom materials.* Paper presented at the meeting of the American Education Research Association, Toronto, 1978.

Yarger, G. P., & Mintz, S. L. *A literature study related to the use of materials in the classroom.* Prepared for Exchange at the Teacher Center, University of Minnesota, 1979.

Chapter 5:

An Interview with Sue Brown: A Public School Teacher Assigned to Assist Other Teachers

Dick: If we could focus this discussion on your role as a "Helping Teacher," I think that would be most productive. I understand that much of your activity as a resource teacher in special education overlaps with your role as a "Helping Teacher." Can we talk specifically about the helping teacher role?

Sue: I am currently part of what we call the "Helping Teacher Cadre" in Lincoln.

Dick: How many years have you been in this position?

Sue: This is a one-year position only, for experienced classroom teachers.

Dick: And how were you selected?

Sue: I was selected on the basis of my experience in mainstreaming; applicants are asked to apply according to identified district priority needs. There were seventeen areas listed and I thought that I could provide inservice training for other teachers in the area of mainstreaming. So I applied and went to an interview where I was asked several questions by the selection committee regarding my current work and past experiences. I was then selected by the teachers and staff development personnel on the committee.

Dick: How are these various areas of emphasis in staff development identified?

Sue: Several diagnostic measures are used. One form is an individual teacher needs assessment. Also, district goals for that coming year are assessed by examining common themes at the building level.

Dick: So the district identifies areas of need and then recruits various teachers to fill these spots. How were you prepared to meet the mainstreaming need from the role of the helping teacher?

Sue: My academic preparation was in special education and I have had various experiences in the district working with mainstreaming.

Dick: Is there any further preparation that occurs after you become a member of the Cadre?

Sue: Yes. After the designated number of teachers are selected for the Helping Teacher Cadre, the staff development leaders provide us with some basic principles of inservice. In addition, we were offered a chance to come in and work with the Cadre coordinator this past summer to work on various inservice projects and to share some of our ideas. I also had the opportunity to attend a Tri-State Workshop on inservice for mainstreaming. I thus had the opportunity to review different inservice activities and curriculum materials that were available through the state departments of Kansas, Nebraska, and Iowa. Becoming familiar with these resources was very helpful. The district reimbursed me to do this.

Dick: What type of prior experience could you cite that particularly assisted you in this role?

Sue: I think the most profitable experience came from the fact that my job duties as a resource teacher in special education are very similar to this role. I do a lot of inservice with teachers in my own building. Also, as a special educator and as a resource teacher, I have been taking coursework at the university regarding the use of consulting techniques and working with adults in a consulting role. I attended a class on developing effective seminars and other instructional strategies, and many things I learned on my own. I have tried to focus on learning things that I felt I was not qualified to do yet.

Dick: If I may change the focus just a bit, is it an elementary school that you work in?

Sue: Yes.

Dick: And you serve only elementary level teachers?

Sue: No. I serve K-12 teachers. My Cadre position is a K-12 position.

Dick: Given this wide range of responsibilities, are there any formalized plans for your activities?

Sue: I develop written plans for the inservice I engage in. I always have a format to follow. It is expected that each Helping Teacher plan activities; we can bring in outside help if we feel it is necessary.

Dick: How does that planning relate to the activities that the other helping teachers are involved in?

Sue: There are specified inservice days during which the district offers a series of workshops. The Helping Teacher Cadre works with district staff development personnel in planning these workshops. Different types of collaboration take place here. For example, I did an inservice on a new mathematics technique that could be used with exceptional children in a regular classroom. I also did a workshop with another helping teacher on using community resources to benefit mainstreamed students.

Dick: Good. Are activities of this nature tied to any specific long-range inservice goals?

Sue: Yes. We would like to see all regular classroom teachers and the resource teachers become involved in some sort of joint inservice training to see how they could work better as a team in providing better services for the students. We offer a wide range of activities towards this end.

Dick: What kind of data sources do you use in identifying specific activities or in formulating the longer-range plan?

Sue: This past summer I was involved in some research which looked at adjusting or modifying curriculum to match teaching styles to learning styles and matching material presentation and format to learning styles. I have spent approximately 100 hours collecting materials and working with faculty at the University of Nebraska on this concern. I then used that research and the information gathered to both plan my workshops and also to develop a packet of materials that would list logical steps that a teacher could take in better matching learning styles and the instructional format.

Dick: Are there any other sources that assist in your planning for or

	providing inservice activities?
Sue:	Yes, I also did some work with the state department in looking at what expertise they had in my areas of interest. I also conduct ERIC searches to find other information that I need from time to time.
Dick:	Do you ever use any observations in the classrooms to obtain additional insights?
Sue:	I guess most of the observations that I make, and I do use them to plan my inservices, are made in my regular role as a resource teacher. I often see areas of unique teacher need during my classroom visits.
Dick:	Do you conduct any formal or informal needs assessments in addition to the district-wide assessment done by the Staff Development office?
Sue:	Yes. The Cadre sent out a needs assessment last spring to see if mainstreaming in fact should still be an area of emphasis. Also, I did a formal needs assessment of my own building staff to see what kinds of things they were interested in or concerned with. Finally, I visited with each of the consultants to see how they felt their teachers were functioning with mainstreamed students in their classrooms and what areas they still thought needed to be focused upon in our staff development activities.
Dick:	Very thorough. Obviously you have been working on this for some time.
Sue:	I actually started working on determining priorities about a year ago.
Dick:	Have the plans that you formulated at that point undergone any modifications or changes?
Sue:	Yes. At first I concerned myself with working largely with regular classroom teachers. I did this because in the past most of my work had been done in rather formal inservice presentations or on an "on-call" basis where I would work with one teacher in a building or perhaps a small group of teachers in that building. Since then I have decided to provide inservice by working with the consultants as well as with the teachers. Right now consultants are in the process of writing curriculum for many areas in the district and so I have been working with them, using principles that I have found in my research on learning styles to assist them.

They in turn have worked with other curriculum consultants giving attention to these concerns. My basic objectives have not changed but my "delivery" format has.

Also, I have done more coordination with personnel in the special education department. I have provided inservice training for their people to work with the classroom teacher in facilitating mainstreaming. Right now I am involved in planning inservice training for the special education staff which involves 200 people. We have also just completed a very brief assessment to see what kinds of needs these resource people have.

Dick: How do you inform, or gain support, for your various activities among the teachers?

Sue: That is a big problem. Mainstreaming is a difficult concept for many. Lots of times I am called into the schools by the resource teacher; that makes it easier. Really, the teachers have to realize a need before I can be very effective. I guess I do a few things to advertise my skills. At the beginning of the year, for example, each helping teacher cadre's name, picture, location, and code number is listed for the teachers. It is up to me then to write a description of what I have available and what I can do and what kinds of inservice I would be able to provide. That brochure goes out then to every teacher and consultant in the district. However, after that initial publication, we are on our own to sell ourselves.

Dick: To what extent are your inservice plans communicated to the general community?

Sue: I would say, just speaking from my own area, that it is not actually extended to the community very well at all. I do have a series of inservice activities that are designed for parents in the mainstreaming process. However, I have not felt that many people think that is needed at *this* point. I have made it practical. I have also tried to make resource teachers in their buildings aware that certain community resources are available to them. (Currently we have quite a large parent group involved at our school.) In fact, I have developed a packet explaining community resources available to the people in charge of planning but as yet it really has not been used.

Dick: Let's continue talking about the community but switch focus just a little bit. In the plans that you have developed, are general community concerns taken into account? That is, are there some major issues that the community feels are important, and are they taken into account in any way in your planning?

Sue: I would not say we sit down formally and look at those concerns.

Dick: Do you do this informally?

Sue: I think so. I can only speak for my area again, but I did look at the concerns that the parents and communities have regarding such questions as, "Is my student being cheated because the teacher has this 'retarded' or 'handicapped' child in the classroom?" Right now, that seems to be a major concern. I try to sensitize teachers to look at community concerns such as this.

Dick: Can we move a little further in this area and discuss the notions of collaboration and coordination. Do you involve any other agents or agencies in the implementation of inservice activities?

Sue: Yes. I have called on the State Department to help with some of the workshops. I have also done some inservice training that was open to anyone in the state, for example, at teachers conventions with the teachers' organizations. Also, I have gotten some help from the University and incorporated that into my inservice classes. I have given some presentations in the university classes as well. I have used some community agencies as information sources in the planning. Some of the programs for the retarded citizens and special education in Lincoln are quite active and I occasionally use them as a resource. As I stated, I put together a brochure on how these community agencies are able to help the parents and the schools with the mainstreaming problems. I got fairly good cooperation. Most of the agencies gave me a contact person that I could list in the book so people would have someone to deal with directly when they called. They were very helpful in providing me with further elaboration of the services they offer.

Dick: It sounds as though you do then employ a variety of individuals, agencies, and community resources within the context of meeting your goals. How do you involve your principal in this network of resources?

Sue: I am on call for principals or any administrator, just as I am for teachers. One example of the work that I have done for principals was to offer a "growing teacher" workshop geared for administrators as well as teachers on how mainstreaming might be most effectively implemented. After that workshop, I was contacted by some principals looking for further resources to facilitate mainstreaming. I have also had some administrators from outside the district contact me on how the mainstreaming concept can be implemented. I have been out to visit several principals and their staffs. Some of these contacts are made by the principals, others by me. I visit with the principal and see where he or she is on the mainstreaming issue. If there are requests for instruction or materials I try to accommodate those requests.

Most of the principals that have called me have had as one of their building goals the improvement of the special education program or the improvement of management systems in the classroom. In most of the cases I have worked with the principal in helping him or her spread ideas throughout the school. In one situation, the principal contacted me to work with a specific new program where mainstreaming was not very effective. First, I worked with him. I invited him with me to what I thought was an effective program. Next, he brought staff members with him to observe: to watch us work. The following week I brought in another team of observers from his school. Finally, I did classroom demonstrations in his building with his teachers. They eventually decided that basically this approach would work in their school. I reviewed materials and assisted his staff in modifying materials to meet their particular situation.

Dick: Tell me how the Staff Development team and the rest of the Cadre members operate in terms of decision-making.

Sue: Okay. The Helping Teacher Cadre members meet monthly. In addition, there are specific inservice dates set up where Cadre members are required to provide inservice training for other members on that day. As far as scheduling of the inservice activity, that is all done by the Staff Development team. For example, I will submit a plan of what activities I wish to provide, and then the Staff Development team does all the scheduling. They get me a room and they provide me audiovisual equipment or whatever I will need. The physical setting and the registration, and all of those things are taken care of for me. Sharon, the Cadre Coordinator, oversees these support functions, Once I submit a plan, she is in charge of making sure it is ready to be implemented. Sharon also provides psychological support. If you think that you are going to be involved in a very controversial workshop or one-on-

one inservice with someone, she can be very helpful here. Sharon serves as a go-between; she does do a lot of publicity for the Cadre people with those in the schools.

Dick: Is there anything you might like to change about your role?

Sue: I guess I would like some more training in dealing effectively with adults in the school setting. I have sought out training on my own; however, it is not enough. Much is learned by trial and error. Thankfully, I had some training and had given seminars. I think without these experiences, I would not have been comfortable to even apply for this position. I think there needs to be some training given to all Cadre people including Cadre Coordinators. Much of this training should be provided before they start. My own personal feeling is that it just puts an extra burden on you when you realize that your planning is not quite what it should be. I just think people like myself need more on general principles of effective inservice.

Dick: Who might offer that training? How should it be provided?

Sue: I feel that it should be presented as a beginning skill prior to the year you are going to serve on the Cadre. The Helping Teacher Cadre is picked in May; your first meeting is in June; and then you have the summer off. There would be time here for more extended training. The coordinator did say, "You may come in and work with me." I did. But it was a *choice* and I feel it should be mandatory.

I know that some people think just because they have an area of expertise and they have a lot of knowledge to share, it will be easy. They don't realize that they are lacking in skills such as planning and organizing, and of doing a "sales" job. They are unaware of the various formats inservice might take. They have the expertise, but they have not been able to sell their product because they did not have the back-up skills needed to go out and have people accept their ideas.

Dick: You see yourself as a salesperson?

Sue: I think a lot of the Cadre's position is a sales job. You have to sell *yourself* first and get yourself in the buildings. You cannot just send out flyers to remind people that we are available. I am in constant contact with most of my resource people so that they can refer me to the classroom teachers. It is a big sales job. As a member of this district, I was unaware that the Cadre even existed the first two years I was here. No one ever contacted me; the brochure came out but I was not aware really of what kind of functions they could perform. You have to make sure not only that everybody knows that you are out there but that you *will come* when they call.

In summary, I would say I need personnel skills, relating skills, basic skills of getting along with people. I need to know how to present them with some expertise, without making them fearful of me or threatening them.

Dick: Do you feel that you have those skills now?

Sue: I feel that I had some to start out with, and I feel that is why I have been contacted so much this year. I see myself as having developed quite a few of them over the years I have been working in a resource or consultant position. But I feel I still have much to learn.

Dick: From what you have shared with me, I suspect you have learned a great deal. You have helped us better understand a relatively new and complex role. Thank you very much for sharing your insights.

Chapter 6:

An Interview with Fred Baker: A College Teacher Educator with a School-focused Role

Ken: Can you provide me with a brief overview of your role as a school-focused teacher educator who works with both pre- and inservice teachers?

Fred: I have been in this position approximately eight years. I was selected for this position through an affirmative action search process. Experiences which qualified me included public school teaching, previous administrative experience, overseas teaching, both as a Peace Corps volunteer and working for the United States government as an educational consultant. I had also worked with both beginning and experienced teachers. I presently work with four rural school systems ringing the city of Mt. Pleasant which houses Central Michigan University where I am employed. These are small, by Michigan standards, class B, class C and class D schools. I do have an office on campus but my position means working almost entirely in the public schools with my student teachers and experienced teachers. I am in each school system weekly. This ability to spend a considerable length of time in each school system, I think, is mandatory in order to be an effective school-based teacher educator. I think some background experiences like I have had are also essential.

It is extremely difficult to take campus-based professors, especially after a few years' of teaching on campus, and plug them into school-based teacher education activities without a tremendous amount of retraining. I would recommend pulling public school people in to work with would-be school-based educators. Sabbaticals could be used to orient people in this direction also. Teaming with school personnel would seem to me to be essential especially in initial contacts. I realize not all university teacher educators should pursue this type of role but more effort in this direction is certainly needed, I think. I recommend some faculty who specialize in this role—teacher educators who can spend most of their time with public school people, both in team situations and inservice situations.

Ken: How do you plan for inservice in your role?

Fred: Inservice planning in my schools occurs at many different levels. Much of it however revolves around a mini-teaching center that was constructed in the schools that I service. This center was the result of a cooperative effort between three school systems: Chippewa Falls, Shepherd, and Veal City. We took the Chip out of the Chippewa Falls, and the her out of the Shepherd, and Veal out of the Veal City and came up with a new term called Chipherveal which gives us joint identification in this center. The planning for inservice in this center is done entirely by the teachers and administrators in the school systems. I serve in an advisory role. The primary purpose of this mini-teaching center is to *share* information, ideas, skills, and feelings among the teachers and faculty of the participating school districts. It operates on the principle that teachers themselves must be centrally involved in deciding what types of activities will help them strengthen their teaching abilities.

The focus of this center is on the practical. We provide teachers practical classroom strategies through activities basically planned for and provided by their own peers. It is not so much a place but a moving resource of people and ideas. It is comprised of nine different buildings in these three school systems. Thus most planning is very much an *ad hoc* cooperative venture in response to perceived needs.

Ken: Is there any formal decision-making body?

Fred: This operation has a nine-person teacher council. As a university supervisor, I am a member of that council. There are three administrators on that council and six classroom teachers. Participation in this council is strictly voluntary; all the representatives, whether they are selected or elected by their peers, serve on this council only if they so desire.

Our responsibilities are several. We select workshop leaders in center activities. We decide on possible dates and times for workshops and meetings. We decide on sites for activities. We help advertise workshops and other events. I also act as a liaison between the college and teacher center council. That is part of my responsibility as a "linker" between the school systems and the college. I am also the only person who can get to all of the school systems so I'm the runner, the "gopher." I help disseminate and distribute information. I am often the follow-up person and the initial contactor. A student teacher is also selected to this council and performs the same duties as the experienced classroom teacher. However, this person does not have a vote in decisions.

Ken: Do you ever use any formal types of assessment or diagnosis in your planning?

Fred: All of us on the council take the responsibility for evaluating the effectiveness of the teacher center activities and for assessing the professional needs of the teachign staff. There are no extensive written plans but we do go over assessments that are conducted in each of the schools. This is very much a *teacher* centered activity and the majority of the planning is done by the teachers with input from the administrators and myself. It is pretty much their ball game. It should be underscored that there is no money involved in this. No inservice monies are generated by this activity. We work as creatively as possible to put our own resources to best use.

Ken: Fred, elaborate for a minute on what contributes to your success in this cooperative venture.

Fred: This is a difficult question. Again, being in touch with these people on a continual basis is a mandatory requirement for this job. We have very few people in the school systems in Michigan who have this kind of a function. Some curriculum directors do this and perhaps some support people in special programs (Title I, Title II, etc). Some of them are able to go from system to system and be a linker. If you don't have a good linker, however, it is going to be difficult to pull this type of inservice off. I also think that the interpersonal dimension in this process is extremely important. This person not only has to be known by the teachers but perceived as a friend that they can trust; someone that they can talk to. It has to be someone they don't have to worry about as far as creating tension between the administration and the faculty is concerned.

The person has to visualize both long- and short-range goals. However, it is kind of funny when you engage in a seat-of-the-pants inservice program like this. You would think you would start to run out of things to do. It is like a process of elimination—you do one thing and something else is left, you do another and there's something else left and so you do something else. We have done everything from art, to science, to creative reading, and to math, whatever, but we can see where additional things are going to have to be done between ourselves, the teachers, and the administrators. It is one thing to work yourself out of a job in terms of starting new things but it is quite another thing to get by the initial teacher need and into the classroom with kids and follow up to see if it is working or not. So, these are some things that have to be done. This is very much a grassroots kind of a cooperative process that we're talking about.

Ken: What are some specific examples of cooperation you can recall?

Fred: Collaboration generally exists between the three parties I talked about—the university, the teacher, and the administrator. At this point we are really pleased with this process; it has been very open. I think part of the reason for this success is that teachers are doing it with their own resources. There are no "turf" problems. The recent social studies activities are a good example. Grade-level sharing sessions were created in K, 1, 2, 3, and 4-6 and staffed entirely by the teachers of these three school systems. The basic format is one of sharing ideas with their peers. We meet in the afternoon and then usually have dinner followed by a second session. There might be specific presentations, or we might have a "make it and take it" workshop where materials and supplies are brought in and teachers design instructional activities for the duration of the evening.

Let me share another idea where cooperation is involved. We have sessions where one needs an "entrance idea" to get in. This is part of your registration for the workshop. You must come with, say, a science idea or a social studies idea, depending upon the particular emphasis of the workshop. Then we type all of these ideas up, run them off on a ditto, and distribute them to the 50 or so people that came to the workshop. We've averaged this number of participants for the past three or four years now from the three districts. Teachers bring in one idea and take away 50 activities that they might possibly use with kids. This multiplier activity is fun and hopefully, it is providing teachers with a broader repertoire of classroom activities.

Ken: You say, "hopefully." Do you formally evaluate specific inservice activities?

Fred: We do evaluate each workshop as to what was done, as I said, and we have engaged in initial needs assessment to find out what teachers want to be done. However, the basic benchmarks of our success are the general attitude of those involved and the amount of time and effort they put in. These teachers feel good about themselves, they feel ownership in the program, they are willing to spend considerable time, and they work hard without remuneration. I basically rely on these as indicators of our success. I suspect that some inservice projects may possibly run too fast, too strong, too hard, and with too many guns. Teachers often feel pressured. Our teachers do not. I think they enjoy their participation. I also think the personalities involved help to make our center work—they care about what they are doing. They are excited about what they are doing and they are doing what they want to do. I cannot stress how important this is. No one comes with any lay-ons. No one is saying you have got to fill out these forms; you have got to do this or do that. We try to maintain an aura of informality and volunteerism in organizing activities for teachers by teachers. I have a sneaking suspicion that the more formality that is introduced, then the less effective the process will become. That goes for "evaluation" as well.

The people know each other well within their own small systems. In the other two systems they share with, barriers, when there are barriers, are being broken down. There is a tremendous amount of sharing going on across school district lines. A good example of this is the "battle-of-the-books" activity where the students come in and engage in this contest related to reading. Teachers from one school system conducted this activity in front of the other two. Within a year a second school system picked up the battle-of-the-books idea. It is now incorporated into their system as an innovative way of approaching reading.

Ken: Do you ever review the decision-making or planning activities relative to what transpires later?

Fred: Decision-making and communications processes have not really been a problem. Activities have largely not been seen as inappropriate or the timing has not been off because the people that engage in these activities are always involved in planning them. I think the key here is rather than an outsider being the driving force, the outsider (me) is only a member in the process and has no more authority than anyone else. Also, the impact of our programs in the school is easily seen. We are small. When a good thing happens it gets around by word of mouth. Any information generated is fed back directly into our planning. I should add that we not only give attention to the academic areas that they may wish to explore, we also discuss techniques as well. We might decide on team-teaching, a workshop format, teaching/learning centers, whatever they believe will work best. If they want a large group session or small group sessions, whatever they want to do to get ready or follow up is decided by them; it is their ball game. We have yet to construct an inservice activity where we told anyone what it was they were going to do; it's always been the other way around. They have told us what they want and it has been relatively easy to set this up and run with it.

Ken: It certainly appears that a great amount of enthusiasm has been developed for your mini-center concept. What do you think the distinct advantages, if any, are of your being school-based in your assignment?

Fred: I think there are unique advantages to a school-based or school-focused approach. The frequent number of activities I have worked on *in* these schools has generated a real sense of camaraderie. I very seldom see this in inservice presentations where the university engages in the more conventional model of a consultant coming in and doing a two-hour presentation and then galloping off again into the sunset. The "guru" coming out of the east or out of the west (I've never met a guru in the great plains but I'm sure they are there) serves a limited function. In our school systems teachers are leery of this approach. I do believe that they like a day off, and often like the presentation, but an on-going follow-up is essential if a school system is really going to change. A presentation by a national or a local consultant who knows his/her stuff is most helpful when that person is able to come back to visit that school system and actually work in the classroom with teachers and kids on the matters the initial presentation addressed.

Ken: Are you ever perceived as an outsider?

Fred: Not really. the on-going ability to meet with these people and to observe in their classrooms, to work with their kids, and to share overcomes this perception. I think I operate much more informally than formally. There is quite a bit of agreement in our ranks about "visiting" as opposed to "supervising" in the classrooms. The more one is seen as a professional friend, colleague, or a facilitator of work, the better off you are when you desire to provide direction or supervision. You cannot turn on and off the comfort level of teachers which is achieved by working continually in the schools. You just cannot be a "drop-in" and "drop-outer." School-based, means *school-based* and if the majority of your time is not school-based, then you simply are not seen as school-based.

Ken: What specific changes in classrooms and schools have you seen as a result of your efforts in these schools?

Fred: There has been a good deal of material development coming out of our inservice work at the individual teacher level. Materials produced by individual teachers have been initiated in "make it/take it" types of workshops and also through ideas generated in quality inservice presentations. New learning centers are continually being developed. Many of our teachers use learning centers. I do not see the classical open classroom approach but there are many center activities where children are able to work in a math corner or reading loft or in social studies or science areas. The materials needed to operate effectively are obviously important. Our teachers are very hungry for new ideas and will use every opportunity in our workshops to scrounge for new ideas. They "steal" what fits. If it works, they use it and if it doesn't, they throw it away. They try a lot of new ideas. We have created a good atmosphere for experimentation. Thus, in visiting almost any classroom, I can see a variety of ideas and techniques that are being tested out. There are not major role or organizational modifications. Basically we're talking about materials and reordering the classroom structure.

Ken: You are apparently very successful and well-received in the schools. Talk to me about your relationship with the campus faculty.

Fred: I am definitely perceived as being different than a "traditional" college professor. I am difficult to find on campus and this can lead to some definite problems in the academic community. I am not seen as an integral part of the university community and this type of "outsiderness" can restrict my influence on campus. It is a trade-off. It should be noted, however, that at my university we have centers throughout the state of Michigan and so there are only a few of us who work in these centers housed on campus. We have many situations where professors are housed in the public schools in certain areas of the state. They have full-time faculty appointments, but they are 100 percent field-based. Thus, the problem is not one of rewards or priorities. This is supposed to be my job. It is more one of respect and identity in a relatively new role. It's hard to maintain an identity with the university in this way. Colleagues see your role as not only being different but often less academic. There is this tendency for superiority/inferiority connected with on-campus/off-campus. This is a challenge. I would have to say that universities have not as yet, as a total academic community, begun to really accept or understand the responsibilities of a field-based teacher educator.

We need specialists in this role. Obviously not everyone on campus can or should be field-based. For example, professors in other departments such as biology and math who try to follow up their students in the field, both for support and for feedback, find it very difficult to do this. It takes a "pound of flesh" from these people to leave the campus for extended work in the field. Time and money commitments are often not there. Public school teachers know this and this continues to build barriers, not a bridge, between the two institutions. Again, fortunately, our student-teacher supervisors are entirely field-based and we don't have to fight that organizational pattern. We can also devote considerable time to inservice matters as a trade-off for preservice assistance.

As I said, I also think the public school people understand and appreciate the role. Even in the schools, problems can arise when it comes to one's academic credentials. When you spend so much time in the schools as a colleague, it is not always easy to assume an "expert" role. Perhaps, you will be listened to but perhaps not. There may be an underlying problem—a prophet is not easily accepted in his or her own native language (to mix a metaphor). Often one has to go someplace else to get information rather than from a colleague or a perceived "equal." Being a linker, I think, has that drawback. You become seen not so much as a resource person but as an access to resources. It takes a special kind of person to assume this role. I think the strength of the individual facilitator as a *resource* definitely has to come into play at times. If you get yourself wrapped up in just a linker role, that can become hollow in a hurry. You have to take the responsibility to share, to make decisions, to behave the way you believe, to extend your belief system, and also to grow academically and intellectually. I think there's a balance there that has to be maintained and one has to be a resource as well as a resource facilitator. One needs intellectual interchange with colleagues on campus as well as in the schools.

Ken: Has your role impacted other more conventional district roles responsible for staff development?

Fred: I think I have impacted other school support personnel in how they approach inservice. They see the success of what we're doing. They—at least many of them—try to plug our class in the programs that they're involved in at other levels. There is growing attention to inservice. Districts in Michigan now have inservice dollars attached to the heads of students and there's a lot of competition for inservice now. Most of the time, however, a system decides it wants a program on such and such. Teacher stress is big now, so they find a "stress expert" and that person comes in and does his or her thing and that's it. Other staff developers are beginning to acknowledge that you have to live with the people the next day that you're doing this with. School support personnel see this organic kind of inservice as successful and they can't help but say that maybe the one-shot things they have been doing are both costing a lot of money and having very little impact on the people that we are supposed to be supporting. They are beginning to examine their efforts more critically.

Ken: Do you ever use data on students or actual observations in

	classrooms to build activities for inservice?
Fred:	Definitely. Being able to work in the schools, it is very easy to come into a classroom and use specific diagnostic instruments both with student teachers and experienced teachers. I often focus on the children working in that classroom. I'm able to do a lot of this kind of thing. Often this activity is initiated by teachers who wish to receive some specific type of information. Then I can select a specific interaction analysis scheme to chart their teacher-to-student verbal behavior or whatever. Sometimes a teacher is working on a degree program and needs to generate a research project in the classroom, and I help them with this kind of project as well. I am able to do that quite freely.
Ken:	How do you tend to work with principals in the buildings?
Fred:	Counseling is an area that is easy to become involved in. I think being a university person definitely helps here, especially with administrators. Administrators find themselves caught many times with no place to turn. They often don't have a professional relationship with a person, outside of someone in the teaching-bargaining unit, that they can really sit down and talk to and say, "Here's a problem I'm having. Just listen to me." As a university supervisor who frequents their schools, I'm pulled almost weekly into one office or another to listen and that becomes a major function of my job. Again one has to be a very good listener. I also share at an administrative level among principals and superintendents similar problems that others are having. I am there to let them bounce a program or an idea off a different ear. Being in tune with administrative perspectives helps in working with teachers. I think I can help teachers be sensitive to the problems of others.

I should stress again, Ken, that my relationships are built in many informal ways. Trust develops from time spent over a lunch hour, attending a carnival after school with my wife and children, and going to other social functions with the teachers and their husbands and wives. |
| *Ken*: | While I expect you have addressed this implicitly in your approach to inservice, I wonder if you would say a few words about what you think are the most important inducements for teachers to continue to invest in their professional development. |
| *Fred*: | One of the incentives for teachers in our approach is that it is cheap. They may pay for their dinner but that is about it. In addition, our university has a small budget for each of the university |

supervisors that work with student teachers and I open up that budget to the teachers to support them to go to inservice programs. I also have a few dollars for lunch occasionally and I get a very large pay-off from that as far as I'm concerned. Also, at the university level, there is incentive to participate in the two classes taught off-campus by university supervisors. One is concerned with the supervision of student-teaching and a second with problems in student teaching. We are able to offer tuition reimbursement to the teachers that work with our student teachers. These classes become inservice since we work with the same group of people but in a graduate class atmosphere, academically sharing ideas and talking about supervision skills. We offer it off campus and I have found that the same games are not played off-campus as on-campus by teachers. The atmosphere is more relaxed, resources and materials are often easier to come by. Also, in a seminar situation each person has to be responsible for a portion of the course. The course has to be very pragmatic or people are not going to put up with it. They're not going to stay after school for three or four hours to talk about supervision skills if it has no meaning to them personally. While giving them some ownership and direction in the class, we still focus on the process of supervision. There is a balance between our needs and theirs.

The primary inducement, however, in our mini-teaching center are that activities are based on *their* needs; activities are relaxing and fun, and they are on-going. I think we attend to the needs of different types of teachers because we have all types involved in planning. The council, for example, is comprised of first-year teachers and teachers with ten years of experience and teachers that have just moved into the district. There are teachers on it that are tenured and teachers that are non-tenured.

Ken: Could individual schools or small school disticts support school-based or school-focused teacher educators?

Fred: This might be difficult. As a university-appointed person, I am able to get an inservice foot in the door because we have student teachers in all the buildings. If there were no student teachers in the buildings, then the money that would be necessary for gasoline, for driving between buildings and all the time I expend in these buildings would be difficult to come by. In our situation, by using student teachers as the means to link a series of buildings and school systems together, we have been able to generate an on-site person. It would be hard to do this from a school system point of view, especially in small systems, unless they saw fit to take their inservice dollars and translate most of it into a salary for a person that might perform this roadrunner role. I do not think this part of Michigan would be any different in this respect than Nebraska or Wyoming. I believe that it is very difficult for small systems to provide adequate field-based inservice if there is not an external institution to help support it.

This is not to say that there are not several personnel involved in inservice in the schools: support persons, teachers, and principals. Several people take some responsibility for inservice. A principal may be one of the session leaders in a particular area (for example, we have some teaching principals). Various curriculum specialists can be most helpful but in specific areas only. I should add again that while the university person can assume much responsibility, we still see teachers themselves as being the main impetus for inservice.

Ken: How might we prepare someone for your type of role?

Fred: I do not think one becomes prepared for this role in a traditional academic model. It is almost like the stereotypes of elementary classroom teachers and secondary classroom teachers. At the elementary level, teachers and their teaching role are seen as being more student-oriented and holistic; they have to attend more to the social-emotional development of their students. Secondary teachers tend to emphasize subject matter. They are more academically-focused and trained; although they can also have a deep concern about the social-emotional matters that tend to get in the way when they are teaching subject areas. If a person is going to be an inservice facilitator, he/she is going to have to go more beyond academics like the elementary teacher and work on such things as interpersonal skills, valuing, empathy, and listening. They will know how to create necessary support systems and how to *evolve* inservice. The ability to work effectively on-site calls for experience and a person willing and able to share responsibilities, to work cooperatively. I hope your efforts will continue to better prepare people like myself.

Ken: Thank you very much, Fred. It is our hope that sharing the many insights people like yourself have gained will be of help to others. I appreciate your taking the time to share with us.

Chapter 7:

An Interview with Frank Lyman: A public School Teacher Educator with Joint Responsibilities with a University

Ken: Give me a brief overview of your role, Frank.

Frank: Since 1970 I have been Coordinator of a Teacher Education Center in Howard County and am employed jointly by them and the University of Maryland. I am responsible for both pre- and inservice. I've an average of, I suppose, 25 preservice students, to place in five schools and I do have an inservice budget for the teachers of around $6,000.00 for the five schools.

Ken: How were you selected for your position?

Frank: I was selected by a joint selection committee, composed of twelve individuals; six from the University and six from the public schools. At the time, 11 years ago, I was working as a teacher.

Ken: What kind of selection criteria were used?

Frank: Well, you had to have at least a Master's degree, some experience with staff development, and prior work with student teachers. I had coordinated the field experiences for previous students from the University of Maryland, Baltimore. I had also been a master teacher in the Harvard summer program in which I supervised student teachers for their graduate program. That background and ten years of teaching in elementary classrooms were my primary credentials.

Ken: Were there specific characteristics or traits that the selection committee was looking for in selecting a coordinator?

Frank: Yes, they wanted someone who could easily move among different role groups, a liaison, a catalyst. They wanted an individual who was both personable and knowledgeable and would have credibility with teachers.

Ken: What gives someone credibility with teachers?

Frank: Repertoire, for a starter. I do have a lot of teaching ideas. They're practical and they work. It was also important, I think, to have materials and the ideas in a form that they could use. I had collected over the years several materials. I also believe credibility with teachers comes from a certain amount of humility which I attempt to communicate both verbally and nonverbally when talking to teachers. This is important and yet you still have to be able to help. Finally, being there is critical. Being a person who is on site, a person who doesn't just say they're going to come occasionally and supervise but actually is in there working with teachers.

Ken: How many schools did you say you are working with?

Frank: I have five. I had three in the beginning, but I have five now.

Ken: Can you tell me a little about these schools?

Frank: The general population in three of the schools is middle class to upper-middle class with some in the lower economic strata. They are somewhat diverse in terms of race. I'd say there is about a 20 percent black or nonwhite population in Columbia. In the schools about one out of every five students is black and I would say that over half of those black children are fairly well off economically. There is, however, a subsidized housing situation in two of these schools that I work in. All the schools are elementary, grades K-5.

Ken: What is the typical size, or does that vary?

Frank: I would say that in four of the schools, there are between 400 and 500 students. Originally, there were more. One of the schools, the smaller one in the poverty area, is down to five classroom teachers and some special education teachers. I suppose I work with around 100 teachers total.

Ken: Are you located in one of those schools?

Frank: Yes, my office has been in Bryant Woods School. I have a half-time secretary, an office, and I maintain a small professional library in that school.

Ken: Do you have some kind of scheme where you rotate through the schools?

Frank: My style is to adjust to what's necessary each week. I promise the preservice students that I'll see them every week in the classroom. I keep that promise! In fact I usually see them twice a week, especially if somebody is having trouble. I saw three students last year nine days in a row, near the end of the year. I tell them to expect me anytime unless they schedule a specific time. I work with the experienced teachers in the same way. I spend most of my time with individual teachers. In addition, I have a half-time assistant this year for the first time. She does a lot of visiting in schools, approaching teachers with, "What are you doing?" "Can I share that with somebody?" We work with teachers just as we do with student teachers. A lot of inservice evolves from discussions right there on the spot.

Ken: What is your academic background or preparation?

Frank: Well, my Master's was in Elementary Education from Harvard. My doctoral studies were interrelated around how teachers learn, which is what I am most interested in in my current job. My thesis focused on how teachers continue to learn once they begin teaching. This research helped me in my job, and I also took ideas from my job for that study.

Ken: Were you able to find courses that were concerned with teacher education?

Frank: In my doctoral studies I had several seminars in supervision. There were also some curriculum courses which helped. The projects undertaken were all related to teacher education and I wrote several papers on teacher education.

Ken: Let me sort of shift gears. One of the areas that I'm interested in, Frank, has to do with planning for inservice. Since you have five schools, I suspect there is considerable coordination. There are often at least three levels of planning for inservice. One would be district level, or at the county level in your situation; another level is the specific school level. I know that Montgomery County, for example, develops plans at the all-school level. And third, there is the kind of planning which occurs between individuals. What type of planning do you engage in relative to staff development or inservice?

Frank: The school district employs a staff development supervisor who plans for the needs of individual schools. There are a few days provided each year for inservice education in the county (district). He is primarily responsible for this planning, but I have input. For instance, today there is a county-(district) wide inservice activity in which all teachers at the elementary level are going to what we call "Make and Take." Here they create their own materials. There are also themes at individual schools. The staff or I will facilitate getting a consultant to come and work with everyone at the school. A second aspect of staff development in the county is the activities offered through different universities in the area. The county staff development supervisor conducts needs assessments to determine who needs or desires certain courses. The staff development supervisor also has a limited number of substitute days to be used by teachers to go for conference and workshops. The staff development program also provides funds for various kinds of workshops.

Ken: Is there a planning group in your center?

Frank: I have an advisory council. We discuss the needs of the teachers and what kinds of activities we want to offer. We examine the responses to the questionnaires we send out. We select and build courses. For example, this year we have one in leadership. Sometimes the initiative for the activity or the idea for the activity will come directly from the Coordinator and sometimes from the Advisory Council, and sometimes from the questionnaires. We are rather "coursed out" after all these years. The courses have been tuition-free and are held after school on site. Usually 15 to 30 teachers attend. However, attendance is starting to dwindle.

Ken: Are there written plans of any kind?

Frank: Yes. Each school has to have written plans for every inservice day. They have to submit them to their director, so that activities for any inservice day in the county are formally written up. Each year I also go to the principals and write down the general kinds of needs that have been identified and then follow up with a variety of activities. As I stated I also meet with individual teachers. If I see a teacher very interested in something, I'll try to provide some options on those topics of interest. We also have forums open to the whole county. I will usually organize these. The most recent one was on conserving teacher energy. I advertised it for the whole system. The teachers did conserve energy! Only about six people came to this forum, but we generally average about twice that.

Ken: What other kind of sources do you use in planning for inservice? Are tests used? You also mentioned questionnaires.

Frank: Most often priorities are set by what the county feels should be done. For instance, there is currently a lot of concern about mainstreaming and that has become a focus for inservice.

Ken: Are actual observations of teachers ever used in terms of deciding what should happen relative to their staff development?

Frank: Each building has a supervisor who, with the principal, could plan activities this way. It would not necessarily be announced; it tends to be informal through the process of observation.

Ken: Tell me about these supervisors. When you say each building has a supervisor, what kind of person is that?

Frank: Well, their job is to see teachers a set number of times each year, regardless of whether they are tenured or not. The principal also has to see these people a set number of times a year as well and conference with them. There is a standardized form for every supervisor and principal to use while observing. There is a lot of controversy about this process in the system. The Teachers' Association is quite concerned about it and they are trying to come up with a process that is a little more open-ended.

Ken: It appears that the supervisors are there primarily for the purpose of teacher evaluation, especially of non-tenured teachers.

Frank: Yes, although they work with the tenured teachers quite a few times, as well. They are there primarily for that purpose, but some of them free lance—getting teachers involved, getting clusters together for different projects. They come in with ideas on their own and try to get some spirit of learning in the situation. Also, each supervisor has to provide special workshops for all non-tenured teachers in the building. That is another aspect that is mandated.

Ken: Does the community ever have any input into what they think might be good for teachers to pursue in the way of education?

Frank: They have a lot of input in terms of their general level of satisfaction with the school. For instance, one of the reasons that there is regular supervision of teachers is, supposedly, because parents are concerned about so-called "dead wood" in the system.

Ken: How does that opinion get expressed—through the school board?

Frank: Yes, through the school board and through letters from parents. The superintendent conducts what he refers to as a "listening post." He listens to parents' concerns about specific topics. He picks up on all kinds of things. A lot of community input is through the district office or district administration but some schools also have what's called an advisory council. That council might come with suggestions to the principal or to the staff such as, "Here's what we see as needs for the school instructionally." The school then can decide or not decide to take that advice. There is also a county advisory council made up of representatives from all the PTA's.

Ken: Will they get into the inservice matters very often, or are they primarily concerned with other matters affecting their children?

Frank: Inservice matters usually only come about as a result of dissatisfaction but occasionally there are ideas from the councils.

Ken: What kind of coordination exists relative to inservice? You have a center, the district provides inservice, you are joint-appointed with the college of education, and the state promotes inservice as well.

Frank: The staff development director in the county is my immediate supervisor in the county. Anything that we do in terms of course or workshop, after-school forum, or non-credit workshops, goes through him. However, he generally accepts everything we suggest. He does not necessarily attempt, however, to make them thematically connected to the total district program. In the case of the teacher education center, the schools work together so that there is more coordination in terms of the activities provided. County-wide, there are, as I stated, some priorities which we can relate to. Another kind of coordination occurs at the central office level. When a certain activity is well received, such as a particular teaching strategy, that office will assist in providing the activity or materials for others. This helps the teacher center. We have at least two major teaching ideas which have spread county-wide with the help of that office. In addition, district curriculum committees occasionally incorporate our ideas. So there is an idea spreading function at the district level that happens when people are very much caught up with an idea.

Ken: Do you involve people on the University of Maryland faculty?

Frank: Yes. For instance, a principal will call and say he needs somebody to assist with problem-solving strategies; who can I recommend? I will then get in touch with a faculty member and get her or him together with the principal.

Ken: Is there an understanding in the college of education that if you request someone to go out and help in Howard County, the faculty member will do that?

Frank: Yes, they almost always do it. I should add we usually pay them to do it. We don't pay them much, however.

Ken: How do those in the college view you? How do they see your role? A common concern is that people like yourself in a joint appointment are in a role not fully understood or appreciated.

Frank: I think it varies. If I am involved in college activities, it helps. For some years I have gone to faculty meetings at Maryland. I often assume special functions with them, for the preservice teachers and supervising teachers. They begin to see me as serving an important function. If they only do occasional consulting and do not see you on campus, then they just see you as a kind of recruiter from the schools. Also, several ideas I helped develop in the center have started to spread in the university.

Ken: Give me an example of something that you have done in the center that has had an impact on people in the college.

Frank: We have a technique that we call "think links." This technique is a graphics medium for children, where children actually diagram their ideas and use those diagrams as blue prints for composition in writing. It has been very well received. It is now in a cirriculum guide and we have had two masters papers done on the topic. It is probably used in every district in this state because the University of Maryland Reading Clinic has picked it up.

Ken: Do you have rank in the college?

Frank: I am an adjunct member, but I definitely perceive myself to be a member of the elementary faculty. I taught a course for them, for example. I also know they respect me, because I have been asked to make presentations in a number of other courses on campus. I just did a presentation for the reading clinic.

Ken: Let's go back to the center itself. Could you elaborate on governance or decision-making structures in your center?

Frank: I have a representative from each school on an advisory council. The council meets for a half-day three to four times a year; and they serve in an advisory capacity. We don't have a formal system of Robert's Rule of Order—that type of thing. Rather I say, "Look, we have this much money and resources; what do you suggest?" They provide feedback on how people perceive the way the center is operating, how supervisory strategies are working, and how various inservice projects are progressing. They are an excellent feedback group.

Ken: Are these advisors always teachers?

Frank: Yes, they are always teachers or specialists in the school and almost always very good teachers and most interested in teacher education. They also report to their faculties as a contact person for me. They provide information at school staff meetings. If I have any kind of problem, I will call them. They also receive all data, all instruments we use to get teachers' reactions to inservice. They then disseminate that information.

Ken: Let me see if I understand their role then. One function is to advise you on how to spend the budget—to set goals; a second function is to give you feedback. And a third function is to serve as a communications link with their colleagues. Are they reimbursed in any way?

Frank: We subsidize their expenses for the meetings.

Ken: What are some current priorities?

Frank: There is some interest from the college in more action-research in the schools and I am interested in teachers being able to publish their ideas.

Ken: How will you facilitate that?

Frank: That's what I am thinking about right now: how to promote action-research so that at the end of the activity a teacher would have a publishable piece of writing. We just had a workshop in which it was expected a teacher would produce something for publication. The trick is to make it appealing, to make sure that the instructor is competent, and that the time is a good one.

Ken: The time issue is a critical one. How often can you accommodate teachers' concerns for when, where, and how often? Do they want a weekend activity? Do they want the activity in their

	school?
Frank:	We have pursued this in a couple of different ways; one is to have the course after school. What I've done is have the courses run anywhere from four to six o'clock. They are tight, well-planned and organized, so that teachers don't go into it late in the evening. We also encourage one or two sessions where the instructor will just come out and visit the teachers in their classroom setting. We also have had independent studies situations where they meet on their own with other teachers to do certain projects. Thus the course has some variety and a school-focused nature. We have also had some weekend retreats. We have varied a bit according to their wishes.
Ken:	How about evaluation. Tell me what you do here?
Frank:	One thing we do is issue client satisfaction questionnaires; one is for student teachers and one is for cooperating teachers. The student teachers are asked to respond to a number of items on a Likert scale related to how satisfied they are with the coordinator's job, the cooperating teacher's job, and the teacher education center as an organization. I discuss the results of this with the advisory council and attempt to do something about the areas that are weak. We do the same with the teachers.
Ken:	Do you engage in follow-up activities? Do you ever go into the classrooms and take a look at some of the results of courses or workshops?
Frank:	Yes, one type of evaluation we have for courses is that every course includes a follow-up project which has to be done with the children in the classroom—at least one project. I also keep a copy of all the papers I can from these courses. The teachers give me a copy even though I do not usually teach the course. I believe a number of those projects have made a lasting change in teachers' classrooms. I can actually see the difference in the classroom setting.
Ken:	So you do observe in teachers' classrooms.
Frank:	Oh yes.
Ken:	How do teachers feel about this?
Frank:	It's a matter of showing them from the outset that I am not dogmatic about teaching. If I thought something could be done better, I surely would state this opinion directly. I might wait two years before I say something.

Ken: Do you keep a file on teachers, as such?

Frank: We keep a record of specific teachers' strengths where they might assist others. If somebody asks for help, we can go through this resource list and hopefully find an appropriate teacher to help and put them together. A lot of that file is also in my mind; a lot of it is just knowing the teachers.

Ken: Do you keep a record of various inservice activities? For example, do you have some profile of the types and variety of inservice activities that various people have been engaged in?

Frank: We have a record of everything we have done, but we have not built any type of profile, as such. That is an interesting idea.

Ken: Is there any effort to evaluate the decision-making or administrative aspects of inservice as well as the actual inservice itself?

Frank: By way of example, it may well be that what was offered accomplished less than it could have, not because the activity was not well-conceived but because the activity was not really a priority and I missed the boat in terms of what really should have happened. I am able to ascertain this from our formal evaluations. In addition, this type of feedback comes from the teachers themselves.

Ken: Let me ask you specifically about our inservice person on site. What are the advantages or disadvantages of being school-focused as opposed to college-based or a district staff development director?

Frank: Frist of all, I think it was best expressed in a recent publication by the Far West Laboratory. The article addressed the role of the advisor. It talked about the need for a person who is not in a judgmental role. I think it is necessary to have somebody who is basically a helper and who can put people together with other people and resources. A person who is not evaluating you, and yet *is* powerful, is needed. I believe an advisor can influence people much more than he or she could if they were in a supervisory role.

Ken: What do you do differently because you are on a school site as opposed to having teachers come to you? How might we make a case to the legislature to get funds for people like yourself?

Frank: One of the advantages is that I am there at the "teachable" moment. If somebody needs something, and if I am on site, I am more likely to recognize that need. We trust one another and the teachers are more likely to share problems and concerns. They see me as a helper. Therefore, the direction of the inservice is more likely to come from the teacher to me, rather than from me to the teacher, and actual problems are confronted more often. I think that is important. Another thing I do, for instance, is teach. If the teachers want a model, an approach, I often actually can demonstrate. Teachers will watch. Currently, we are making videotapes of certain teaching strategies. Another advantage is providing praise at the right time. I am able, by being on site, to have credibility in my praise. For example, I can say specifically, "I like that, it is an impressive idea!" I have an enormous amount of power in a praise-starved atmosphere. Also, if there is an idea that is being discussed by the teachers and I am involved, I can do something to implement the idea, and provide feedback. If I am a person that they see only every four weeks, I am not a significant person in their teaching life.

Ken: Frank, one of the reasons I am interested in this concept of school-focused inservice is that, from my vantage point, there are times when the total school or at least a number of teachers within that school need to be brought together to work on problems. In most district or college courses and workshops, you cannot do that. Do you work with a total school as a group, or teams of teachers within the school?

Frank: I do this in a gradual way. For instance, we are now working on a discussion strategy technique, called "multi-mode-teaching." This strategy is aimed at enhancing academic learning time for kids in a discussion. It is an idea that spreads easily. We have lots of teaching aids or teaching tools used by the teachers which quickly spread among the teachers. I would suspect that over the next two years one in every three teachers in the county will use this approach. So rather than the idea of meeting often with the whole staff, I work more through a ripple effect. I try to put teachers in touch with other teachers around good ideas and common needs and interests. As a coordinator I can also make suggestions to a principal regarding the whole staff. In fact, I have suggested that a recent "levels of questioning" activity be followed up with the whole staff. This cannot be mandated, however. In some cases the principal will try to force it, but teachers will go through the motions at best. The power available to the on-site person is that he is able to do more "fifth column" kinds of activities. Teachers know when they are using and/or doing something that they weren't forced to do. They have a tremendous resistance to being forced.

Ken: Sometimes there is a curriculum problem that has to be coordinated across grade level or age levels, for example. An ideal way to attend to this is to have at least one person involved from each grade level. Or, perhaps there is a problem in the school that has to do with general communication among the faculty. It seems to me that those types of concerns call for coordinated faculty involvement. Do you think that a case could be made for an individual staff development person at a given school site on a full-time basis?

Frank: I do, but I do not think that is the total answer. Certain topics might be difficult for a person who lives with these people to handle. For instance, just recently the center paid for a consultant to come and talk about teacher burn-out. For me to have dealt with that topic would have been detrimental. It is a too highly politicized area. The more overtly political I become or the more I take sides in any kind of a problem within a school, the less credibility I have. For certain problems it is best to bring a person in from outside. In terms of a school-wide curriculum problem, the school-focused role would be ideal.

Ken: Even though you work with five schools then, you can see a need for a person full time at a school site, although you wouldn't have that person get in the highly political issues which divide a faculty.

Frank: Absolutely. If the public schools are going to move away from custodial kinds of care and crisis management, there must be a competent individual in the building to be a resource to teachers and to have good rapport. If a school is ever to get anywhere in terms of moving beyond bare survival, that kind of person is needed not only for the teachers, but also to recognize talents in kids. To say, "Those kids are super, have you noticed this?" I am talking about that kind of individual. Principals and vice-principals do not have that responsibility. They want good administration to enhance their precious time to teach. I also think this person should have some tie with a university.

Ken: Allow me to shift gears a minute. Can you recall when inservice, conducted at a school site, has resulted in any changes in the physical environment or in teacher roles, or in any changes in organizational structure?

Frank: Here is one example. Recently I was requested by a school to provide help with multi-mode teaching (switching modes in the discussion). In this particular situation, in order to make the multi-mode teaching operational, physical cues are needed. Now I go in every room in that building and see abstract symbols of the different levels of thinking in different places in the room where teachers can refer to them like cue cards. I also see in most of the classrooms some kind of device for assisting the children to change from an individualized approach to a pair to a share mode in the discussion. In the schools where we have done science process approach, I now see the materials much more in evidence. I also definitely see it with the children's graphics project because their work is up and all around. I am not satisfied with inservice until I can actually see examples of it.

Ken: Excellent. Have you ever gotten to the point where teachers are assuming basically different teaching roles, for example, team teaching, as a result of inservice?

Frank: I don't know. Maybe in a formal sense inservice doesn't affect their role but I think definitely in an informal sense it does. A number of our preservice graduates are team leaders, and so our preservice program has an impact in that respect.

Ken: What do you think are the primary goals that a good continuing education program accomplishes?

Frank: One goal is improvement of professional self-concept. The teacher must see himself as one who is effective with kids and who can invent. I really think that the teacher's ability to invent ideas is underrated and I think that it is an important area. In many cases, we assume a basically remedial approach to inservice. I turn it around and try to enhance their stature and status. In the main, what I am interested in, is bringing out in them what they already know and getting it better organized. I am more interested in taking something that they have discovered and showing how that relates to other ideas, than I am with filling them with new notions. For example, teachers are often fearful; they are afraid to be caught not doing some of many things they are asked to do. They are always trying to decide what it is that is being wanted by the system. Therefore, they forget the kids at times. A major goal is to reduce anxiety and enhance professional (self-)

image.

Secondly, I am also interested in the idea of practiced theory. In the course that we hope to teach next year in publishing and action research, we will focus on this. For example, a teacher might notice that a child can't spell a word, and then asks the child how would it look in a book. In many cases, the child can spell the word. Take just that moment, to think about what theory is related to that notion. Then try to expand it into a general teaching idea. I work from the teacher's example, from concrete to abstract. This does a couple of things. It shows the teacher that he is a creator of theory and in a sense a creator of his or her profession.

Ken: I applaud your goals; they appear to go beyond a focus on pedagogical skills. What about the personal development of the individual?

Frank: This is an important function. People are always coming to me with "What will I do now in my career?" Once the person is in my role and has a reputation of being trustworthy, a lot of personal questions are raised about career goals. Many times a year someone will come and talk about his/her career with me, so that I think that a person in my role could do much to enhance personal development.

Ken: Do you think there are career-related and age-related kinds of concerns or issues which confront teachers?

Frank: I will go right to an example. I have been working with a teacher for the last four years. I have been telling her she really is a middle school teacher. She is around 35 years old and she has taught about ten or eleven years, at the elementary level. She is beginning to get itchy for a change. She finally did move to the middle school and told me, "I wish I'd have done it four years ago." Some of this has to do with personality and some has to do with her career pattern. She taught in elementary school and she was a "superstar." But she was bored; it was time for a change.

There are other people I am trying to counsel back to graduate school. I see people who are college professor material, excellent. I tell them, please start studies now, because if you wait too long, you won't be able to afford it. Of course, some of that relates to their stage of teaching as well. This type of insight comes from getting to know the people over a long period of time. It takes a couple of years for even the most personable kind of individual to provide that kind of advice.

Ken: Do you think that there is a lot of "plateauing out" at one point or another with teachers?

Frank: Yes, I think right now, that the most talented teachers that I know want to get into something else, either quit teaching or work with other teachers. It's tragic because there are very few jobs like the one I have. I believe there would be a lot of interest in my kind of role. For example, the woman I rode here with this morning was in my first group of student teachers; she said, "I want your job." She has the ability. I think there are a lot of people that want out. We have to devise ways to rotate teachers in new and challenging roles.

Ken: What are the primary reasons behind this disenchantment?

Frank: Well, right now, there is not enough appreciation for what teachers are doing. The appreciation is much less than the pressure (stress) that they are feeling from various sources, even from principals they like. Colleagues can see the pressure.

Ken: As you suggested earlier, not just general plaudits but specific and meaningful praise is needed. Praise from someone who understands how difficult the task is and specifically what they are doing well.

Frank: Yes. If you ask a person, "Let me take that idea and share that," that is an implicit kind of praise. They need that, both implicit and explicit. They get very little specifics. Perhaps their real support comes from children (and parents) and once that glue between them and the children starts to break down, they begin to have more and more problems. They are losing the real intrinsic motivation for teaching. I think this is now happening especially to experienced people. They are the ones it hurts the most if they see they don't have the rapport.

Ken: Let us review one of the major themes I have heard you speak about, Frank. I do not want to put words in your mouth, so correct me if I did not understand. First, a large part of your function is to be sensitive enough and skilled enough to draw out from teachers things they know but perhaps aren't doing for a variety of reasons, to rekindle sparks, to reinforce them as competent people.

Frank: Related to that are my efforts to distract them from their unhappiness by what I call teacher "tool" or "toy" ideas. These are ideas that they can "play" with which take on a life of their own. Teachers are often the inventors of these ideas.

Ken: I like that. Let us talk about incentives a little bit for participant in inservice. This is related to teacher attitudes. A lot of teachers may have shut the door to staff development or continuing teacher education because they have more than enough to do; they are very suspicious. "Do not tell me anything more; I have more than I can use already."

Frank: Yes. I have heard people who have that sentiment lately.

Ken: What are specific kinds of things that you do, both initially to get people involved in various activities and also to sustain the effort?

Frank: The secret is—and I have not perfected it—to show them that what you are doing often can save them time and energy, as well as help the children. That is why I am so interested now in energy-saving devices, devices which allow more teachers to be more focused and to spend less time in peripheral activities. The children's graphics approach and the "think-links" approach facilitates writing and the organization of writing in a way that nothing else seems to. Teachers can actually see the results. I encourage them to change. I show them the children's work and show them samples of children actually doing it, so that the "proof of the pudding" is the eating. Time-saving and better results are themes I stress. Teachers will buy your theory if you imbed it in practice.

Ken: Part of the problem has been that continuing education is often "additive". It can make a difficult job more difficult, if you will.

Frank: Right. Things with organizational power are more likely to be pursued seriously right now.

Ken: Going back a bit, do you think that different kinds of incentives or inducements are needed for people at different stages or ages?

Frank: Yes, definitely. For instance, college course credit is not a positive influence for most of our teachers any more. Many teachers have master's degrees. Three credits just are not doing it. However, if these teachers are first- and second-year teachers, there is a larger demand. They often need the structure of courses. I also think the experienced teachers need the incentive of recognition for what they are doing. On the other hand, the first- and second-year teacher needs answers to desperate questions. I think once an experienced teacher is reinforced for what he or she does well, he or she will come out of the shell and confront the difficult questions.

Ken: Do you work with principals and teachers helping other teachers?

Frank: I do a lot of this. Often, suggestions go to the principal. I can say, "Why don't you go over to this school and see that person; you won't believe it—it's fantastic." In the forums we try to have teachers teaching teachers. One of the biggest advantages is the fact that the teachers gain more respect for each other. I gain more respect for the teachers myself. I hear them ask excellent questions and respond to these with good ideas. Teachers generally come out of these activities feeling better about each other and feeling less competitive.

Ken: Can you talk more about the role of principal in inservice? What happens in your various schools? What ideally do you think it should be?

Frank: Well, some principals are very direct and say, "We are going to do this, and I want to see the evidence of this on the wall tomorrow!" Obviously, there's a lot of grumbling about this type of approach. It's funny however; where there is a lot of grumbling, sometimes the approach is still effective. Sometimes you have to taste the ice cream flavors before you know what you like. I think a blend between being direct at times and my type of approach is what the principal ought to employ. It depends on the staff, too. But, generally speaking, mandated change does not work well.

Ken: What primary role do you think the principal should play in inservice? Instructor? Needs assessment? Creating conditions?

Frank: Well, it depends on the principal's talent. If the principal is a person who's inventive and can bring out other people, then he ought to invent and bring out invention in other people. If he or she is a person who basically isn't that, but is able to go around and is pretty good at putting one teacher together with another, he or she ought to do that. The important thing is that the curriculum and the instruction improve. The personal characteristics of the principal are an improtant consideration.

Ken: Do you work with principals in trying to bring out their strengths?

Frank: Yes, I do a lot of reinforcing of principals. They are often somewhat paranoid about their schools, and they too need reassurance. For instance, I try to provide them with ideas about documenting good practice in their building. I am concerned about how they feel about their school.

Ken: How do the principals perceive you?

Frank: In various ways. In some sense, I play a jester role. Another principal calls me the catalyst for improvement of instruction. When she introduces me to people from the building, she says, "Here is our catalyst." She sees me in that particular way. They do not identify me with administration. There is a little mystery involved in my role but they know that I'm there if they need something. They know that I will suggest ideas. I have a habit of bringing materials in the building. Usually the principal likes this. In fact, the other day the guy actually took pictures—he got his camera out. It is knowing what will appeal to each one of these individuals.

Ken: There haven't been problems in terms of you treading on their responsibility?

Frank: It can be very delicate.

Ken: Summarize for me what the *ideal* school-focused or school-based teacher educator person would look like. What would they have in the way of resources? It might be a nice way to close off since we have been talking mostly about the realities of your situation and it is quite obvious to me that you do an outstanding job. Another way to put this question, if you could improve upon your own current situation, what suggestions or recommendations would you make?

Frank: Let me think about it. First of all, I will talk about areas that I would like to improve. Then I will talk about some ideal characteristics of the person in a school-focused role and what they ideally could do. I think that in any kind of improvement or instruction situation, you need video tapes on basic ideas on teaching that are very dramatic and which show children's work. We do not have enough of those. We have some, but they are not well organized. Ideally, in my role, I would like to have more of these. I would like to also have a "museum" of children's work and of teaching aids or teaching tools that teachers could have access to. I think that could be very effective. I would like to see better publications. We have one now and I would like to see it expanded so that more teachers' ideas would be in print. I would like to see better school-to-school liaisons. I do not think the Teacher Education Center does a very good job of that in a formal way. People should be able to come from one school to another to see each other and each other's work. Principals from those schools should communicate on more dimensions. I would like to see a better dissemination system for materials and ideas. We are working on that now. That is extremely important.

I would like to be able to reward people more. It is important to recognize teachers for being serious about teaching and the improvement of it. I would really like to have more ways in which they could get recognition for their inventions, for their work with student teachers. Those are a few ideas for improvement.

Basically, I think that a person in this role has to be able to do demonstration teaching. Either by putting teachers together with other teachers or to see it on video tape, or do it yourself. My research brought that out pretty clearly. There also has to be a way for people to see the products of children's work. There have to be the incentives for teachers to apply new or different ideas. That means you have got to be there. You have to follow up, you have to see them do it, you have to praise them for it. This person has got to connect people with other ideas and people and their personalities, their problems. You have to be a link. And you can do this through writing, through a publication, through forums, workshops, and courses. But it just has to happen.

The person in this role has also got to be able to distract teachers from the problems of their work, through humor, through helping them laugh with each other—looking at the light side of things. The inventing of ideas and the development of gimmicks is important in this role. Gimmicks can be profound when the theory embodied within them is understood and spread. I think that a person in my role has to work at building "support systems" within buildings. Particularly with beginning teachers and older teachers, the whole business of bringing teachers together and helping them with their problems is critical. Breaking down competition and encouraging cooperation is the idea. A person in this position has to be concerned with teacher repertoire and with the sharing of a teacher's repertoire with others. It is not an easy role, but it is a challenging and rewarding one and one that is most important.

Ken: I could not agree more with the importance of having competent persons like yourself to assist at school sites. The ideas you have shared here have been most helpful. We thank you very much, Frank.

Chapter 8:

Variant Approaches to School-focused Inservice

Richard Bents

There are many approaches to inservice education. Herbert Hite (1977) noted that:

> Unlike the preparation of beginning teachers, inservice education has no tradition of what constitutes a basic program. Different perceptions imply different sets of values—what ought to be *the way* to undertake professional development. Because values do not lend themselves to technical criticism, each different definition may be legitimate for its supporters. The way inservice is perceived seems to determine the activities and content of programs. Thus, there are very different perceptions of inservice education which lead to equally different programs in operation. (p. 2)

The following discussion is predicated on the notion of *school-focused* inservice—as articulated in Chapter 2 of this book. The underlying assumptions of this school-focused notion are outlined in the book entitled *The Education of Experienced Teachers: Implications of P.L. 94-142* (Corrigan & Howey, 1980). Succinctly stated, the authors posit much of what takes place in staff development and teacher inservice education should be focused not only upon increasing knowledge and skills which enhance teaching practice, but also on addressing the conditions in which the teacher is expected to perform—schools and classrooms. Further, it is assumed that activity can best be planned and coordinated by an inservice leader who spends the majority of his/her time engaged in these activities at the school site.

Given these assumptions, various school-focused inservice education programs were reviewed to better discern the training and practice of school-focused teacher educators. This chapter provides a discussion of three prototypical programs for training leaders in school-focused inservice programs. One, the Vermont Consulting Teacher Program, presents to the reader an example of a state-wide network of consulting teachers who provide inservice leadership in their local schools. Two, the University of Southern California/Lynwood Unified School District, exemplifies a College of Education's coopeative venture to design a flexible and regenerative inservice approach for an urban school district. Three, the Lincoln Public Schools Helping Teacher Cadre is one example of the efforts of a public school district to provide staff renewal activities for experienced teachers as part of a larger staff development effort.

These programs were selected as *examples* of school-focused inservice. While the inservice is focused at the school level, it emanates from three different sources: a state-wide network, a University/public school cooperative scheme, and a public school district approach. Further, these three programs were selected as examples because they have implemented many of the principles of school-focused inservice outlined earlier.

As this chapter proceeds be remined of Louis Rubin's (1978) comment:

> Professional development is an exceedingly complex phenomenon that can be approached from many different vantage points. Because little is known about the subtle interplay among various factors involved, an open-minded attitude is essential if only to ensure that significant matters are not overlooked or ignored. (p. ix)

Therefore, the following framework is used to present the descriptions of current fuctioning school-focused inservice programs.

Teacher instructional behavior, organizational development, and adult growth and development are the three major dimensions which school-based teacher educators are asked to address. It is, however, a rare occurrence to find an inservice leader trained in all three areas. Typically there is an emphasis on pedagogical skills in inservice programs, at times organizational concerns are attended to, and on rare occasions a developmental approach to teacher growth is undertaken. In each of the following descriptions one of these three dimenisons will be highlighted. It will be obvious, however, that concerns for all three aspects exist.

Vermont Consulting Teacher Program

The Vermont Consulting Teacher Program is designed to train learning specialists, who, in turn, work toward enhancing classroom teachers' instructional behavior in working with a wide range of students in regular classroom settings. These learning specialists are experienced teachers who are offered additional training and practicum experiences, and then certified as consulting teachers.

The primary focus of the consulting Teacher Program is special education but this inservice model has general applicability to all of inservice teacher education. Thus, while the emphasis here is on school-focused teacher educators who enable teachers to work with handicapped children, it should be obvious how this program might translate to the training of school-focused teacher educators in general.

The Consulting Teacher Program is a collaborative effort of the Vermont State Department of Education, the University of Vermont, local school districts, and the U.S.O.E. Bureau of Education for the Handicapped. This united effort has resulted in a unique state-wide resource network which provides special education services to handicapped learners within regular classrooms through the training of classroom teachers, school administrators, and the parents of these eligible learners. This training-based approach is designed to provide direct assistance to classroom teachers so that they are better equipped to provide special services within their classrooms.

The training of the Consulting Teacher conists of learning activities conducted by the staff of the special education department at the University of Vermont over a period of a summer and one academic school year. During the spring, a recruitment and selection process is conducted. Each year approximately twenty-five consulting teacher trainees are selected. Selection is based on successful teaching experiences (minimum of three years), leadership capability, and academic promise. Each trainee submits a portfolio of previous and current work experience and indicates how these competencies will relate to the curriculum of the Consulting Teacher Program.

The initial summer training program is comprised of four components: 1) service to eligible learners, 2) peer training, 3) curriculum development, and 4) dissemination. The first component, service to eligible learners, stresses such aspects as observation and measurement, recording systems, testing procedures, instructional design, alternative instructional strategies, and behavioral analysis. Here the Consulting Teacher trainee is given the requisite knowledge base and opportunity to apply the learned skills in a controlled clinical setting. The limited number of children in the summer program enables the Consulting Teacher trainee to work with individual students or small groups under the guidance of an instructor or professor. This experience then becomes the basis for further discussion and extending the knowledge base.

The peer training unit, in which the Consulting Teacher trainees work with one another, familiarizes the trainees with techniques of adaptation and application of new technologies to specific district settings. In addition, the training of educational personnel and parents in the use of applied behavior analysis skills and individualized instruction is stressed.

Curriculum development includes aspects such as modification, design, adaptation, change and evaluation. The emphasis here is on curriculum revision to meet the needs of the special learner. The Consulting Teacher trainee is taught how to make special curriculum provisions for handicapped students. At times it is appropriate to make curriculum changes which will eliminate all of the nonessentials in each curriculum area. At other times a parallel curriculum must be developed, and at yet other times some areas of the curriculum will be eliminated. The Consulting Teacher trainee is taught to determine the appropriateness of various changes and how to make the changes when deemed appropriate.

Dissemination competencies include the basic sharing skills such as public speaking, listening, writing and publicizing to inform others of the relative merits of a given change or innovation. [Included here are aspects not only of providing information to a generalized audience of parents and professional educators, but of techniques for reporting to parents and students.] During this initial summer training, the potential Consulting Teacher works in a tutorial arrangement with students who have special needs. This provides an opportunity to immediately apply theory in a relatively controlled environment and to report and reflect on the acquired learnings.

The first semester of the year as a Consulting Teacher consists of an internship during which the trainee has an opportunity to test new skills in a school setting, but on a limited basis (i.e. one-half time spent in the schools and one-half time spent at the University). Coupled with this practical application of skills, ample time for refinement and guidance is provided through structured time at the University.

After completion of the aforementioned components (service to eligible learners, peer training, curriculum development, and dissemination), an additional component is added: district development. This component engages the Consulting Teacher with the salent principles of incorporating improved instructional practice in the public schools. The uniqueness of school organization, socio-economic status, curriculum focus, general school climate, and the like must be taken into account. The district development aspect of the Consulting Teacher program, then, stresses the identification of the unique characteristics of a school and equips the trainee to plan appropriate strategies to address these characteristics. This focus on the particulars of a *school* prepares the trainee to work effectively *in situ* with existing resources and constraining factors. Since the trainee spends the majority of his/her time on-site, the specifics of the setting are used to provide an appropriate reality base for study.

This district development aspect is bolstered through the Consultant Teacher Trainees' work in the designing of workshops and training sessions for the local site staff, parents, volunteers, and paraprofessionals. The trainee is expected to tailor learning activities to the needs of a *specific school constituency.*

The second semester the Consulting Teacher works in more detail with the school stafff. Again the program components of service to eligible handicapped learners, peer training, curriculum development, dissemination and district development are addressed. However, an additional dimension is included: planning. At this time, the Consulting Teacher has responsibility to plan, design, implement, and evaluate the various services delivered. Follow-up services become an integral portion of the Consulting Teacher's activities. These follow-up activities not only provide programatic continuity but also speak to the site specific nature of the effort. That is, by remaining in one setting for an extended period of time an expression of commitment to change is made.

The Consulting Teacher is also involved in garnering school and community support for various programs. Again, the placing of a Consulting Teacher in one site for an extended time period provides an excellent opportunity to nurture the acceptance and support necessary for substantive change.

The successful completion of the Consulting Teacher Program makes the trainee eligible for a Master of Education degree and Vermont certification as a Consulting Teacher. A number of Consulting Teachers continue their education and become adjunct instructors who are able to offer inservice activities for university credit.

The Consulting Teachers are then employed by the local Vermont public school districts. The precise role is a negotiated aspect. In many cases the Consulting Teacher returns to the district in which he/she had been previously teaching to orchestrate the special education inservice activties. At times the Consulting Teacher is in a "resource teacher" role. In some districts the role is cast in an administrative posture. In almost all instances the role evolves to include more inservice functions than the original special education focus.

USC/Lynwood Staff Development Program

In his book, *The Socialization of Teachers*, Colin Lacy (1977) reinforced the concern both for the development of the school as an organization and for the individual teacher. While the teacher indeed has degrees of freedom to manipulate and change his or her situation, he/she is at the same time being constrained to adjust to it. The University of Southern California Trainer of Trainers concept attempted to build the internal capacity of the Lynwood school district to plan and deliver its own inservice program that addresses both organizational development and the enhancement of the teacher.

An inter-disciplinary team from the Department of Education at USC collaborated with Lynwood Unified School District in the design of the Trainer of Trainers Program. The Lynwood Unified School District, after an assessment of inservice needs and goals, identified specific "how-to" inservice training in motivation and discipline, with a focus on reading. The multi-cultural inter-disciplinary team from USC cooperated with Lynwood to meet not only the identified needs but also to initiate a flexible and self-maintaining staff development program. This program trained a cadre of thirty inservice leaders, which was then responsible for *onsite* training of the approximately 400 teachers in the Lynwood District.

The general goal of the USC/Lynwood Inservice Staff Development Program is to:

> Develop, through a collaborative, participative model, a viable, self-maintaining, humanistically oriented resource storehouse wherein teachers can learn to teach themselves and others new concepts and processes or adaptations of older concepts and processes to meet the needs of the emergent population. (Brizzi, 1978, p. 5)

More specifically, the USC/Lynwood Inservice Staff Development Program is designed to develop a selected group of teachers into trainers and facilitators of inservice. A cadre of resource teachers from the Lynwood district were selected to be the participants in this trainer-of-trainers program. They were selected on the basis of their expertise in reading, which was to be the core target area, and their potential and interest in providing leadership in staff development and inservice education.

These leaders were initially trained to assist teachers in improving reading skills of students in the areas of decoding, vocabulary, and comprehension. By meeting definite, concrete, felt needs in the specific manner of providing direct instruction and practice time, the inservice leaders established positive rapport upon which more extensive staff development could be nurtured.

The inservice leaders were also trained to identify and organize instructional approaches designed to improve reading skills in various disciplines of the student curriculum. In addition, the identification and replication of multi-modal and multicultural instructional materials and activities was addressed. This aspect continued to provide concrete technical assistance and moved beyond the initial dimension of reading instruction.

The inservice leaders were then trained in systematic needs analysis. Emphasis was on the identification of local school strengths and needs for the successful implementation of the aforementioned curricular and instructional strategies. *Organizational assessments* were included to determine not only program needs and dimensions, but also to determine program roles, goals, and objectives and to define advantages to be gained by all role groups associated with the school. Planning models were also addressed here to enable the inservice leader to plan meaningful activities to increase teacher competency as determined by the needs analysis. The inservice leaders then identified appropriate leadership styles to meet the needs of the local school and designed procedures to obtain feedback and commitments from staffs for ongoing inservice and staff development.

The inservice leaders were trained to identify and implement procedures for teachers to use in conducting staff development for *total* schools, small groups, and parent and community groups. The creation of this type of communication-dissemination-support system is intended to assist school staffs as they begin to implement various changes or innovations. Collaborative assessment and planning, the use of community resources, and motivation are all highlighted in this phase of training for the inservice leaders.

The developmental aspects of this program are obvious. The program starts with a delimited area of need, building through comprehensive staff development to obtaining support and commitment to school renewal from a wide constituency including teachers, administrators, parents, and community agencies. It is also of interest to note the collaborative process of developing and tailoring this program.

A dual focus trainer of trainers program was developed. One phase of the program concentrated on intensive training sessions which required that every participant understand the concepts (i.e., of reading as well as the process of systematic needs analysis) and be able to present or implement them. Since the trainees represented different school levels and contributed different skills and abilities, a wide range of training strategies were modeled. This collaborative approach promoted effective sharing and communication skills.

The final phase involved on-site follow-through. This phase was designed to assist district resource personnel (i.e., reading specialists, special education staff, and administrators involved in staff development) as they developed their own *participative* staff development programs with their individual school staffs. Although the original model was identified as USC, the entire process was collaboratively plotted. Thus, the program design, plan, implementation, and evaluation involved the trainees. Therefore, the participative strategies that the trainees were to learn and employ were modeled for them during their training. Then as the trainees worked with teachers, on-site follow-up was provided to ensure support and continuity. This localized interactive approach is captured by the project director Elsa Brizzi (1978) when she wrote that the program "*provided* the trainees *the content* they needed for their role, *demonstrated the use, modeled the way, supported in the delivery,* and *involved all role groups* in the total effort" (p. 11, emphasis added).

Helping Teacher Cadre

The Lincoln Public Schools, Lincoln, Nebraska, have instituted a school-focused inservice program entitled the Helping Teacher Cadre. This program was designed to 1) implement a broad range of training needs specified by district needs and goals, by 2) maximizing the internal resources of the school district in meeting their own ongoing inservice needs.

Each year the Lincoln Public Schools conducts a district-wide needs assessment to determine the areas of focus for the upcoming year. Based on the identified areas of need, teachers who have demonstrated excellence in these areas are selected to serve as resource persons to their colleagues. For example, the 1979-80 needs analysis indicated a desire for additional support in the following areas: Education of the Gifted, Health Education, Social Studies, Mainstreaming, Individualization of Instruction, Personal-Social Growth, Teaching/Learning Styles, Interdisciplinary Planning, and an Educational Equity Resource Center which includes advocates for the handicapped and school/community relations.

Teachers with experience and expertise in each of these designated areas were selected to assist their peers in addressing these issues. These 'helping teachers' then represent expertise in an area which is emphasized by the district. For example, mainstreaming was identified as a high priority of the district. Those teachers with particular expertise in educating the handicapped in regular classroom environments were solicited. These teachers then work with their fellow educators by responding to various requests for assistance. The response is through presentations, demonstration teaching, modeling one-on-one activities, serving as a resource person, or developing materials.

In this way the Helping Teacher provides on-site inservice training and serves as a liaison between the school and central office regarding staff development activities, needs, and wants. It should be noted that the Helping Teacher Cadre is only a portion of a large staff development effort. Another portion of the Lincoln Staff Development, highlighting the total school effort, is discussed in Chapter 14 of this book.

The Helping Teacher fulfills two basic functions: 1) that of service, and 2) that of advocacy. The service function consists of responding to the unique needs and demands of individual teachers and groups of teachers with common concerns. The bulk of the training provided for the Helping Teacher involves techniques which better enable them to respond to the various needs of their constituents—the teachers as learners. Concepts of adult growth and development are discussed, and problems unique to the teacher are confronted. How adults learn is stressed. The needs of teachers in different settings such as regular classroom, multi-aged classroom, primary aged, and the like are taken into consideration. The most appropriate delivery strategies are discussed by the Helping Teacher Cadre. Then, presentation styles are worked out, small group skills, tutorial strategies, and one-to-one communication skills are honed. In addition, dissemination skills are developed. Writing brochures, word processing, and advertising courses and skills are discussed.

In further preparation for the service function, the comfort level of the Helping Teacher is considered. Self-identity and self-renewal concepts are introduced, thereby placing the Helping Teacher in a position to help him/herself while assisting his/her colleagues. The Helping Teacher role itself is designed to serve a regenerative function. By placing a teacher in a leadership role and providing necessary support, the individual benefits and is placed in a better position to serve his/her students and peers.

The Helping Teacher is also an advocate for a specified concern. The individuals in the Cadre were selected because of their expertise and experience in a given area. Building on that expertise, the theoretical foundations underlying practice are stressed during the training of the Helping Teacher. In addition, tuition for graduate course work is available to the Helping Teachers in extending their knowledge base.

The training for the Helping Teacher is conducted during an intensive orientation which occurs prior to the start of the school year. The training then extends throughout the year at regular monthly meetings of the Cadre. If an individual Helping Teacher is enrolled in graduate courses the training is thus extended further.

The Helping Teacher, then, responds to various calls for assistance during the monthly release days (2 per month), during regularly scheduled staff development activities, after school, or whenever it can be arranged. The Helping Teacher maintains the normally assigned responsibilities of his/her teaching post while being released the two days per month and receiving a modest stipend.

The tenure of a Helping Teacher is generally one year. Although program development needs and individual teacher expertise may indicate that it would be productive to extend the one year responsibility, as many teachers as possible are encouraged to participate as Helping Teachers.

The training of the Helping Teacher indeed develops new competencies for each individual. Beyond the training, the year as an advocate for a given concern, peer recognition, and the differentiated role provides a unique renewal function.

Another role-taking experience is provided in the coordination of the Helping Teacher Cadre. Three teachers (one representing each area - primary, intermediate grades and secondary) are selected to coordinate and support the Cadre. This managerial or administrative function provides role-taking experience for the participating teachers.

The Helping Teacher Cadre, then, provides a unique dimension to staff development. The Cadre offers an opportunity for individuals to share their expertise. Concurrently, the cadre serves to meet the identified needs of the school district. Most importantly, the Cadre provides a *school-focused* perspective in addressing over-all district policy.

Summary

The Vermont Consulting Teacher Program was reviewed to give the reader a glimpse at a statewide network that trains learning specialists to work with the professional development of their peers. The University of Southern California/Lynwood Unified School District presented a collaborative approach to train inservice leaders. Finally, the Lincoln Public Schools Helping Teacher Cadre identified a public school's strategy in staff renewal.

References

Brizzi, E. N. *Staff development program: Trainer of trainers.* ERIC Document ED151337. 1978.

Brizzi, E. N. *Trainer-of-trainers: A collaborative approach to inservice staff development.* Los Angeles: University of Southern California, 1978.

Corrigan, D., & Howey, K. R. *The education of experienced teachers: Implications of P. L. 94-142.* Reston, Va.: The Council for Exceptional Children, 1980.

Hite, H. Inservice education: Perceptions, purposes and practices. In K. Massanari (Ed.), *Higher education's role in inservice education.* Washington, DC: American Association of Colleges for Teacher Education, 1977.

Lacy, C. *The socialization of teachers.* London: Abbey Press, 1977.

Rubin, L. *Inservice teacher education.* Boston: Allyn & Bacon, 1978.

Chapter 9:

A Discussion of Issues Relating to School-focused Teacher Education

Fred Baker

Tom Kromer

Michael Wolf

The three discussants are all very much involved in the professional development of teachers and the school-based teacher educator process throughout the state of Michigan.

Fred: The first thing we would like to talk about is our general perception of frustration and the difficulties involved in professional development while working as *field-based teacher* educators.

Tom: A primary area of frustration is the *seeming* lack of support from the university. I have a very distinct feeling that, particularly at the administrative level, there seem to be few people who understand the multi-faceted role of school-based teacher educators. Tenure and promotion are based primarily on one's ability to publish in refereed journals. There is very little mention made of service provided to teachers in the public schools, which is the primary role of the school-based teacher educator.

Another area of frustration I would term "time commitments." The time that we devote to the various aspects of our role, such as accommodating a full load of student teachers, which in many instances numbers 20-25 students, really constitutes a full academic load. When you deal with that, in addition to providing some input and assistance for professional development, you are talking about a 70-80-hour week.

I would just summarize by noting that the university does not perceive or fully appreciate the importance of the role of school-based teacher educator.

Fred: Probably this difficulty the university has in understanding our role may be because we give insufficient information to the university community about what we do. The student teaching supervisors, as field-based educators, are scattered around the state of Michigan; they are in centers around the entire state. Because of that distance factor, there are many things that go on at the university that the school-based teacher educator is not involved in. They can easily be a forgotten minority. On the other hand, this situation gives them a certain bit of freedom to possibly do some things that the university might not even know about. That could be both positive and negative. Either way, it can be a lonely situation if you think you are going to become a member of a university community and then find yourself 200 miles away from the university, yet having to assume all the responsibilities of the spokesperson for the university. That could become frustrating to many school-based teacher educators.

For example, the distance factor does not enhance our ability to provide resources to the teachers in our schools. If you are a school-based educator 200 miles from campus, you are still seen as being a university resource, yet you may not have the physical resources at hand from that university itself to provide for people. The provision of resources, then, either entails a long car trip or lots of phone calls.

Mike: I think, in addition to that, the way the role is defined can be very frustrating to both the university community and to the school-based teacher educator. I mean, does one choose to, a) spend the majority of his or her time working with the public school teachers in professional development, or b) spend his or her time with supervision of student teachers and working with supervising teachers and administrators, or c) make it a 50-50 proposition with 50 percent time working with the teaching staff to update their teaching skills and competencies, and 50 percent with student teachers? To me, that can also be very frustrating since the role has not been *clearly* defined. Thus, one seems to work at what seems to fit best.

Tom: Compounding the role definition problem is the fact that programs develop differently depending on what part of the state they are in and what schools you are working with and what the expectations are of particular administrators or teachers. I work in a rural area. I have three MEA-affiliated teacher groups that I work with, and one AFT-affiliated group. Their expectations are all quite different, especially in time of MEA quorums and restrictions on the number of student teachers that we are able to place.

Mike: So you are saying that part of the frustration is not being able to operate consistently from one district to another.

Tom: Yes, my role changes and my set of expectations changes from school system to school system, and sometimes even within a school system. These differing expectations are based on whether I work with a secondary person and, of course, the degree to which the community education people are involved. And when the community is highly involved, that is an entirely different set of problems altogether.

Fred: What kind of advice would you give to a person just entering the role of a school-based teacher educator?

Tom: Get as involved as humanly possible with the teaching staff in your schools. Spend a lot of time with the supervisors and teachers that you are initially working with. But spend time in the lounge and get to know the other people. It is critical to be perceived as a helping person by the staff, especially by the administrative staff. You have to be able to somehow work with both groups without alienating either.

What I have tried to do is to get to know the staff. The more opportunities that are available for them to ask you questions and to give you chances to respond, the better position you are in. This is, in effect, the underlying premise for the role of the school-based teacher educator.

Mike: I think building the level of awareness is also very important. What I mean by that is as a person goes into a new environment, a new school system, a group of schools, whatever, it is necessary to do some type of research or resource search to find what types of resources are available in that environment, community, or system. It is necessary to identify different kinds of groups and people to work with. Identify the individual resources from plumbers to carpenters to whatever, to determine what kinds of resources are actually in that environment that may be useful in the education process. Get to know the community as well as possible. For example, we may do things with our student teachers that may sound silly, such as having them ride the bus route just to find out where the kids are coming from. It may not be a bad idea for an on-site supervisor to ride that bus route too, and really understand the depth of the community and to appreciate the kind of involvement and the kinds of questions that the community is in turn asking the public school people. Therefore, to know that community as well as possible and to understand the resources that can be elicited from that community, I think, is very helpful.

Fred: I think what both of you have been saying is that the role of the school-based teacher educator is not what one would perceive as a normal professorial role on a university campus. Our colleagues who work exclusively on campus perceive their role as teaching three or four classes per week and having set number of office hours. I see the school-based teacher educator as working in a role that is conceivably a five-day week operation with some days from 7:30 in the morning until 8:30 in the evening. I guess if there is any insight to be given to teachers it is that the role of *the school-based teacher educator is different from the usual role of the university professor. The role is definitely unique.*

Tom: The uniqueness provides many advantages to our job as well as liabilities, I think. Not since I taught in a self-contained classroom have I had this kind of a setting in which to work with student teachers. Now I am assigned a group of student teachers and I am totally responsible for a semester's worth of their education. This gives me an opportunity to get to know them in ways that people on campus never get to know their students. I see this as a distinct advantage.

Fred: And yet on top of that you also have a responsibility for working with building level staff in identifying professional development needs, conducting surveys, interacting with staff to design innovative professional development programs, working in evaluating them, and in fact, delivering the service. It is a multifaceted role that we play.

Tom: I think a good thing for a person just entering this kind of business, assuming you are a great distance away from the university, is to try to create some kind of mini-center that would provide some material resources to the people you are working with. It is helpful even if it is just a storefront office, whatever, something that is identified with you, your position, and the university. Then modules, program materials, books, movies, and the like can be housed, and a place for teachers to convene can be established. I think knowing your limitations in this respect is really important because, unfortunately, one is perceived as being able to deliver things that, in fact, he or she can't always deliver. I think the school-based teacher educator should know that and know where to turn to get additional resources.

I would also recommend that, if it is possible, develop some kind of an advisory committee, wherever you happen to have your base. If it is a one school system base, then have that school help you by appointing a committee of teachers, administrators, maybe even non-instructional personnel, to help give suggestions on how to develop the program. Therefore, the support base for the school-based teacher educator can be both programmatic and material.

Mike: Are you seen as belonging to or being a part of the sites in which you work? Secondly, do you have any problems of being viewed as an outsider in the kind of job that you are doing?

Fred: I am not viewed as a part of the staff. And yet, I am pretty much accepted as being an integral part of the systems in which I work. I am asked a lot of questions and I am expected to give a lot of answers, and yet I do not have any line authority.

I think going the extra mile is really helpful in being accepted by the people you are working with. For example, out of the four school systems that I work with, I was in at least three of them for after hours activities including a school carnival, a fair, a pot luck supper, and a pancake supper. All of these activities were designated for the teachers of the school system; because I was working there, I was invited. So I would either take the family and involve them, or take a bowl of potato salad and roasted chicken. I was then viewed as being part of that group. That is really important. And the more you are involved in that type of informal sharing, the more you're not only accepted but the more you're probably listened to when questions of seeming consequence or substance come up. Then teachers will come to you and say, "Hey, I've been wanting to know something about interaction analysis. I want to code the behavior of what I'm doing with my kids in the classroom. I don't know how to do it. I don't even know if it's a good thing to do or not. What do you think?" I then have an excellent entry. That whole thing might have been triggered by the fact that you had a brew at the local pub after school one night and were sitting down and rapping with people where they see you in a little different light. Generally, I think most of us are accepted at the local sites. However, we are on that cutting edge where we walk the line between going in to the principal's or the superintendent's office one hour and really sharing things that aren't meant to be shared with teachers as far as the principal and the superintendent are concerned. We then turn right around walk into the teacher's lounge going through the exact same kind of thing but on the teacher side, where things are said that shouldn't be shared with the principal and the superintendent, as far as the teachers are concerned. So we're kind of outsiders that way but effective outsiders in that most of the segments of the population we work with accept us and probably trust us. Because the school-based teacher educators do not have an ax to grind, we can sit down and we can talk with both administrators and teachers and we can listen and share and that's okay.

Tom: I think being viewed as an outsider, as you're suggesting, is not at all bad. I think it provides us with access to all parties without being a threat. We belong to a variety of sites and there are some school-based teacher educators who, I am sure, would perceive themselves as being outsiders on the university campus—even though the university is our employer. We are separated from the campus life and some of our colleagues by many miles and are on campus at the most two days per month. So in terms of being outsiders perhaps we are viewed more as outsiders on our own campus than we are in the school district and buildings that we're working in.

I think that we agreed to get involved in extracurricular things at all schools. I have, for the last three or four years, played basketball with a group of middle school teachers.

Another thing that I found to be really helpful, but in a more structured way, is to offer teachers a course in supervision of student intern teaching and also a seminar on student teaching. I recommend that if you have the opportunity to provide a service, like teaching a course off campus in the site itself, do it as soon as possible. This is one way people can really get to know you as an academic personality, as well as your belief system and the things that you feel are important, what you think about kids, and what you think about your working relationship with the people in the schools. Those kinds of things done early can really help build the base in a working relationship with people. You have to remember when you're on the circuit and travelling from school district to school district that it takes a lot of time—quality time—spent with the individual in those schools, be it student teacher, principal, or classroom teacher. The time will be minimal and if you can relate to your peers at all ends of the spectrum within the school system and sit down with them and work on the issues of professional involvement, student teachers, whatever, that will go a long way in making you a more integral part of that academic or school community.

Mike: At another level, as far as the university is concerned, let us talk a minute about changes or conditions that might be needed in higher education to make this role work from a college perspective and what a trainer of school-based trainers program would possibly look like.

Fred: I think the first thing that comes to mind is, in our own state, that the legislature must view the role of a school-based teacher as educator differently in terms of the initial funding to the university. The current funding model is based on the number of student credit hours generated. That is what ultimately determines our student teacher ratio. If part of our job is to provide inservice to public schools, then that somehow has to become part of the funding model. One cannot provide services to public schools and at the same time work with 25 student teachers (which constitutes a full load). I think that's probably one of the most basic kinds of changes in working conditions that needs to occur.

I think, along with the changed funding base, someone within the school of education must make a decision that this role is important and unique enough to fund it in a different manner than other roles within the school. Instead of looking at a 25 to 1 student ratio, which occurs in most departments in the school of education, we may be looking at several individuals who play a school-based teacher educator role having a ten to one student-teacher ratio with the understanding that the other part of the role will compensate for this reduced student to teacher ratio.

Tom: Also, the currency of professional development in school-based teacher education has to be made respectable. In other words, with the academic community and the game one has to play for promotion, tenure, there are certain things you have to do, such as publish your creative research endeavors and serve on various committees, and the teaching act per se, the working in the field, is not acceptable currency in and of itself. If I were to be an outstanding teacher educator, or an outstanding school-based teacher educator, that, in and of itself, currently would not insure promotion. I would still have to play the same academic games as anyone else on campus. Yet I do not have the same type of time commitments as people on campus. I do not have a Monday-Wednesday-Friday classload with two or three classes. I have an 8:00-4:00 public school position. Until the university accepts the fact that a school-based educator operates under certain constraints and also possibly very difficult objectives from the traditional professor on campus, there are not going to be very many people that want to buy into the model. They know that that is not the way to get promoted, it is not the way to get salary increased, it is not the way to earn the respect of your colleagues on campus. The case must be made for school-based teacher educators. Administrators and deans on campus have to take a stand and say, "Hey, these people are respected members of our faculty. They are doing a service for the community, and for our institution, and we respect that and we support that." The instutition is going to have to make that kind of commitment or these programs are not going to work, or they are going to work at minimal level.

Fred: What about the program itself? If we are going to train people to work in the schools, what would a program look like?

Tom: I think the school-based teacher educator needs to be a so-called expert on teaching, what it is, how to do it, how to convey that information to others. I think we do about as much counseling as we do teaching. Much of my work is done on a one-to-one basis and it is done basically within a problem solving model. It seems to me that the crux of the training program ought to evolve around a counseling type of internship. Therefore, a person wishing to become a school-based teacher educator ought to work with a school-based teacher educator so that the counseling skills required in teaching, in planning, in supervision, in curriculum development, in inservice education, can be learned on the job as an apprentice. I'm not sure that in any Ph.D. program one can develop all of the necessary skills that one will need in order to successfully operate as a school-based teacher educator. But it seems to me that a basic core can be identified, those things that we perceive as commonalities. I would include counseling and an internship as common factors.

Mike: I think there are two pieces to that one. One, you have to provide time in a training program to allow a person to cultivate something that they are really good at. In other words, the program would have to be open-ended to allow the person enough freedom to develop some idiocyncrasies, whether it be a strength in the areas of self-concept, a strength in the area of teaching skills, or a strength in the area of whatever. The other phase would be more structured in putting the person through his/her paces in relation to the teaching act, in relation to styles of teaching, in relation to empathy, listening skills, and communication skills. I think those kinds of things should be included.

But also there should be that time for *people* to run with whatever strength they have really developed. They should have an opportunity to practice those vehicles they use to get close to their district and close to the people *they* work with. If you are seen as having a strength area in a particular field, and again I will use self-concept as an example, if you are seen as a self-concept person and you can do your own inservice on self-concept, you can be a spokesperson for that area. I think you are seen and respected as having that particular strength. But then you have also got to have the basis as a clinical professor, as a school-based educator, which is more generic, which has more of the, in the acceptable jargon, whatever philosophy, whatever teaching style, whatever a teacher educator is supposed to know about. I think the generic things have to be dealt with; you should have a specific skill that you are comfortable with, that you can run with, and then you have the generic skills necessary to communicate with a wide range of people.

Fred: Moving to another area, could we explore the kind of people we generate ideas with, get personal support from, and solve problems with? How do we keep abreast of research and get feed-back on what we are doing and how do we avoid teachers resenting a possible differential status?

Mike: I can't speak for all of us, but it seems to me that the exploration of ideas in our own support system is built pretty much with each other as school-based teacher educators. Obviously the people we work with in the schools also are a support system, but I think not at the same professional level. I think the conferences we attend, the professional readings that we do, are shared among ourselves.

Tom: I think we all belong to a variety of networks. I have a network of people within a building that I am responsible for in which support is gained, research is shared, and ideas are discussed. I have another network at the university, and then there is another network nationally, with our active involvement in national teacher education organizations; ATE for example. There is also a network within the state that, I believe, is becoming much stronger. There are people working at other universities who also support the role of school-based teacher educator who are just now beginning to feel the need to spend more time together. And I see more and more conferences at the state level dealing with the whole networking business and the need for a strong support system.

Fred: I think this is a frustration for school-based teacher educators. Although you have many contacts and so many possible support systems and even though you come in contact with many different kinds of people, you still know that it can be a very lonely position. The fact that you are doing things differently than most of your colleagues back at the university, the fact that you are on the move a lot, you always feel that you have your foot out the door ready to go someplace else, ready to do something else. You find that time becomes really an essential commodity and that you may not feel like you are spending a tremendous amount of time doing any one given thing. And that support system, your colleagues that you are working with, sometimes you feel you are not spending enough time with them. So you really have to feel strong, in and of yourself, in where you are going and what you feel good about because it is going to be lonely. You are going to feel like an outsider at times and it is difficult to continue in that kind of a system.

Mike: As far as feedback is concerned, I try to arrange that in several different sectors. I always ask student teachers to fill out a student opinion survey. I always ask for the supervising teacher and principal to fill out a more formal evaluation on a semester basis. Because I am in the schools, I am always asking for and getting suggestions on changes or just ideas that people want to see tried.

I think the more time you spend in the school, the more honest people tend to be with you. They will let you know if they feel you are spending enough time, if you ought to do more observations, if they need some resources or whatever. There is both a formal and an informal system of feedback that you set up when you are in the school and it is usually culminated at the end of each semester with the formal feedback forms.

Most of us interview our students the semester before they come to us formally for their student teaching experience. And it is amazing what you can learn from students that you have not even heard yet. I often ask the question, "Well, why did you pick one of the four districts that I work in to do your student teaching?" And oftentimes they will cite an instance they have picked up from either other student teachers that they have talked with, former student teachers, or from administrative or teaching personnel in those districts, and will give that to you as the reason for their choosing one of the school districts in which you work.

As far as avoiding possible differential status with the teachers we work with, I think very few of us have that kind of a problem. One of the reasons we do not have that problem is we see it as a collaborative effort, a team approach. In all of the inservice activities that I'm involved with, teams in the schools provide the direction that we are to take. I am just a member of that team—another resource, another body, another spokesperson. But because it is a team and because it is collaborative, they do not see any differential status. I do not run the meetings; I do not tell them what the inservice is going to be; and more likely than not, I do not even do anything in the inservice itself. The teachers will produce what is important to them. I will try to plug in resources to help them. By having the team approach I think we get away from that kind of problem.

Tom: I think one thing that makes a real difference is that I am there. I work in one district where two colleges place student teachers. It is getting to the point now where most of the teachers are refusing to take student teachers from the one college and are asking for my student teachers. The reason they keep citing is that I am there; they can depend on me. They know that if a problem develops, they can get a hold of me quickly, and that I will respond to the problem and that in a collaborative way it will be taken care of. And I think that is a good way of getting over that feeling of differential status. If they see me in the schools approximately the same amount of time that they are in the schools and we have basically the same objectives, that difference in status is gone.

Fred: As an extension of that, priorities and the juggling of priorities are important. I think the school-based teacher educator reflects a combination of three possible models. One is an administrative model, another is the teacher model, and the third a student model. Any given school-based teacher educator may spend more time with one of these three role groups than another. Administrators are obviously important. They are important in a placement process, they are important in the overall aura of the schools, and some of us may spend a great deal of time working with them and let the other pieces fall where they may. Others of us spend a great deal of time with teachers and see that as the base for our work. We then deal with the classroom teacher and the student teachers as they come and go, but the classroom teacher remains the focal point. The third model would focus on the student. This model deals with the student as an individual and sets up the conditions that allow the student to receive the skills and experiences he or she needs to be a good teacher. I think I take the student model first, and possibly the teacher second, and the administrator third. However, I am working toward, and I think a good school-based teacher educator should be working toward, a balance among the three. You cannot leave any one of these three role groups out. Most of my time now is spent with the students themselves, but I think we have to realistically deal with all three groups at some kind of an equal level, involving them all in the entire process.

Mike: I guess I concur. You listed my priorities as well as yours. I find that I deal most with principals and superintendents. I find that one of the best roles that I fulfill for them is that of a person who will come in and will listen to their problems and act as a sounding board for ideas. I'm accepted as a person that will do that. But I need to balance my priorities among teachers and students.

Tom: As far as who I respond to, whether teachers, administrators, or students, I feel much like a fire person. I respond to whomever needs to be responded to. If it is an administrative problem and a principal comes to me, that's who I respond to. If a student has a problem, I go straight to the student. If a teacher has a problem with a student-teacher, then collaboratively we set down and try to work out that problem.

Fred: How about working toward getting inservice teacher education more job-imbedded, that is, how can we find time for teachers to get involved, deal with reluctant teachers, involve teachers with different ownership, assess and obtain fiscal and other resources, in a more integrated way?

Tom: I think, to a large degree, it depends on their contract. We do a lot of inservice work after school. The teachers put together the model they want, the kinds of things they want to do, and they do it themselves. There is also the possibility of release time with the more traditional models of inservice days.

Mike: The limitations within the teachers' contract are a factor, but I also think it is important that, when you are conducting a needs assessment, you have got to do more than just a paper needs assessment. You also have to do an interactive needs assessment. You spend time talking with people and you get a feeling of what life in the classroom working with kids is like, and you get a pretty good feeling about a direction the building staff is taking, the kind of support system existing in that building, and the kinds of things the teachers are interested in. Conducting the traditional pencil and paper assessment is one way, but also being a good listener and sharing with teachers and talking about problems and the kinds of things they are working on help to elicit some directions to go in. That provides insight for more job-imbedded inservice.

For example, in one of my high schools, we have been very successful in presenting what we call "mini-topics." These 20- to 30-minute inservices are planned and conducted by either an administrator or a committee of teachers. They are offered many times during the day and the teachers attend during their free period, or on their conference hour, or whenever they happen to be free. About 8 to 10 teachers attend each session, which does not use the entire amount of their free time, but it does give about 20 minutes to a half hour for intensive inservice. This has been a very successful approach.

Obtaining funds is another matter, however. There are some district monies and there is some state professional development funding as well. There is also a good possibility that you do it off the seat of your pants and that a group of teachers in the school system can implement fine programs without external funding and they make it go. Funding is a tough issue.

Fred: This has been helpful. As we summarize and give credibility to what we are doing as school-based teacher educators, should this role be recognized as a formal role in the school? And, if so, what would you think of certifying this role?

Tom: I do not think that is a bad idea. I think the formal role could be beneficial. But I would not be in favor of certification. I think we are probably seen as formal school-based teacher educators, at least partially, as we work with student teachers and certainly when it comes to doing major inservice programs. We have a kind of professional development arm at our university. We frequently are called to travel around the state and do presentations in the areas of our expertise.

Mike: Obviously when you are seen as a expert in a particular field there is a certain status attached to that. The fact that you are informal in the schools in which you work also gives you a certain status. The more comfortable teachers are with you, the more they see you as non-threatening and a good listener (and also resource), the more credible you become. I do not think these notions need to be "certified." I would be against that. I would push for a formal definition of the role. I think that should be shared with people and publicized, but I do not think you have to certify the process or the individual.

Tom: Right. I do not think you can sit down informally in a teachers' lounge for the first time for more than 20 minutes without having someone sit down and say, "Who are you? And what do you do?" You very quickly have to give them your background and so on. I do not see where a formal certification would help that process out at all.

As far as it being easier to train and employ school-based teacher educators, if certification were required, on one hand one could say that that would increase the credibility of the position. However, I do not believe that just because the person goes through a certification program means that he/she is going to be a successful school-based teacher educator.

Chapter 10:

The Advisory Approach as a Form of Professional Growth
Robert P. Mai

Renewing the Practice of Teaching

Renewal in the Classroom

Leon Lessinger has noted that teaching is the only profession that talks about its "practice" as something that comes before being licensed to teach. Doctors practice medicine, laywers practice law, but teachers, we might infer, stop practicing once they get their degree and their certification. Most teachers, of course, don't really feel this way. Many seek to grow as professionals through the traditional means that teachers use to upgrade their skills and credentials: the college course and the inservice workshop. It has yet to be convincingly demonstrated, however, that amassing credentials in these ways has any significant effect on the actual practice of teaching.

Teachers also differ from other professionals in that they play little or no role themselves in training and supporting the growth of other teachers. There are no "teaching hospitals" to speak of in education (except, perhaps, certain "portal schools"). Teachers have relatively short preservice internships, with little chance to work over a period of time with a master teacher who sees this role as a serious undertaking worthy of some thought and preparation. Since there is no vital tradition in education for professionals sharing and reflecting about their practice, or solving pedagogical problems as colleague staff, it is not surprising that the effectiveness of the occasional inservice workshop or course usually stops short of the classroom door.

It is, in fact, our common experience that new ideas and good intentions fail to be realized as successful practice for lack of the *in situ* encouragement and technical support necessary to adapt and incorporate them into workable classroom programs. The Rand Study on change in schools makes the same point in concluding that though "new educational technologies are undoubtedly important to improved practices, they cannot be effective unless they are thoroughly understood and integrated by the user" (McLaughlin, 1976).

The Rand Study, as well as other studies in educational change (see Zaltman, 1978, for a good summary), have called attention to the need for a process of "mutual adaptation" between innovative programs and their users. School professionals *need to* reinvent the wheel themselves, despite all the good offices of curriculum developers, management consultants and behavioral psychologists to develop "adoptable" new technologies in their behalf.

What would be useful, these studies argue, are strategies to help teachers adapt new ideas (or old ideas, for that matter) to their own unique settings, and to the very real circumstances their children, parents, school rules and policies, etc., dictate. Conspicuous in the failures of most staff development and school improvement programs has been a disregard for this need, as well as for the ways in which adaptation, implementation and growth are most likely to occur with professionals. Instead, unsuccessful programs showed a tendency towards opportunistic, short-term approaches to problems that typically sought solutions in new accountability systems, expensive educational hardware, or slickly packaged curriculum models.

In contrast, the characteristics of the few successful programmatic efforts at school change noted in the Rand Study included:

—continuous, on-line planning and evaluation involving teachers and principals;
—training whose objectives were determined by those to be trained and which reflected the real needs and issues of the particular school setting;
—training resources that were consistent and ongoing—available over time to support extended growth;
—local adaptation and experimentation with commercial curriculum, along with development of "homemade" approaches to learning materials and activities.

Common to those successful efforts was a focus on professional renewal, and upon the organizational climate and resources necessary to support such renewal.

The Advisor Role

> What we need are great groups of generalists who specialize in resource utilization, and among the critical resources which they must know how to utilize are blends of other technical skills drawn on as appropriate in given client situations. (Crandall, 1977)

In our experience as teachers and teacher educators in several New England towns, in New York City, and in St. Louis,* we have seen some headway being made in the matter of professional renewal leading to improved teaching practice. We have watched small groups of resource persons, or *advisors,* function effectively in each of these locales, and we have seen teachers willingly, albeit cautiously, examine various aspects of their practice, and work through some changes using the advisor for support and assistance.

Advisors are typically master teachers with strong human relations skills. They work primarily in the classroom alongside the teacher, as facilitators at school meetings, and as workshop leaders. Advisors are "linking agents" who help others "engaged in problem-solving by connecting them to appropriate resources" (Crandall, 1977). In particular, advisors help teachers plan and manage their own professional development. They do so by focusing on the total practice of the teacher as the theater for renewal.

The advisor's impact on the implementation of new ideas is largely a consequence of how he or she relates to teachers. Unlike more programmatic approaches to staff development, the advisory view is not founded upon a formal change model of goal setting, planning, implementation, and evaluation. While this sequence might in fact characterize a given teacher-advisor relationship, it does not have to. Advisors offer their assistance as resource persons without a predetermined agenda, picking up on specific requests and invitations to help as they are made.

While the most common pattern of advisor-teacher collaboration starts with a response to personal and practical needs, then graduates to more extended and articulated problem-solving, the key to the advisor style is that it is heuristic. The general tactic of the advisor is to support questioning and thoughtfulness in the teacher as the most legitimate determinants of innovation and renewal—and then be available to connect the teacher with whatever resources are necessary to follow through.

---

*As participants in the University of Massachusetts Integrated Day Program, the Open Corridor Program in New York City, and the Educational Confederation in St. Louis.

To be able to do this, the advisor needs time to develop relationships with teachers that allow for active periods as well as dormant ones. As Manolakes (1975) argues,

> ... the advisory system takes a long view of time in the educational process. It assumes that real growth on the part of people is a generally slow evolution, and that direct efforts to bring about dramatic changes often result in a cosmetic effect. Advisors recognize that the process is continuous, but not even-paced in terms of when steps are taken.

Corollary to this view is the need for an advisor's schedule to be flexible in order to accommodate a variety of requests. A basic assumption governing the scheduling of the advisor is that different teachers will use the advisor in different ways, that the amount of help given by an advisor will probably vary from teacher to teacher, and that both the focus and the amount of resource provided through the advisor will probably change with each teacher over a period of involvement. Thus, while maintaining a fairly regular schedule is important, the advisor needs to be flexible enough to devote extended time to a teacher when certain realizable gains are in sight, and to capitalize on unplanned-for opportunities like special projects, calls for help, or two or more teachers with a similar problem or a convenient match of resources.

Motive for Renewal

The authors of the Rand Study observe, apropos their findings, that the most common school improvement program is a "deficit model," wherein teachers are presumed to require further training to develop requisite new skills and insights. In these typically top-down, standardized-across-the-district programs, the major incentives for participants were often cash stipends, credit on the salary scale, or fulfillment of relicensing regulations. Teachers frequently found that these courses were

> ... irrelevant and, moreover, that the district cared little about the staff development program. Teachers in these systems felt that the administration was participating in a ritual—that staff development was not a priority for the district. (McLaughlin & Berman, 1977)

The matter of motive for professional renewal is a complicated one. Most teachers have ambivalent feelings towards "staff development," since it is usually tied to both their own desires to learn and to grow, and their contractual obligations to improve their skills. All too frequently, the work that qualifies for salary steps and recertification is that very sort of impractical session or demeaning experience alluded to above. Teachers, like most professionals, seek increased knowledge (and credentials that so testify) for myriad reasons. Curiosity, need to deal with particular problems, job security, advanced salary and status, peer or superordinate pressure, and dissatisfaction with current practice are some of the common ones.

The conclusions reached in most studies of change strategies employing staff development (including the Rand Study) suggest quite clearly that most efforts to induce or support teacher renewal will fail unless they acknowledge the teacher's need to determine what takes place, and what its focus should be. A priority to these considerations is, of course, a determination that a teacher is indeed wanting to engage in such activity.

Teacher Choice

An advantage that both teacher centers and advisors have here is that they are not, by definition, programs with formal objectives and schedules and a mandate to produce certain prespecified results; the advisor is patently a *free agent*. Advisors can be attached to a "program" or a project, but their effectiveness as a resource for renewal varies in direct proportion to their being identified with some set of packaged goals. As Manolakes (1975) puts it, "The advisory view places control of help to be received with the individual teacher and assumes that he or she will use, in a support system, those elements that are of most benefit at a given time."

In our experience, this view—essentially an argument for teacher choice in matters of self-renewal—has raised some interesting issues. On the one hand, many school system administrators feel that if the choice is left to teachers to seek assistance, the ones who "need it most" will be the last to ask for it. Another allegation concerning the practicality of staff development inventions like advisories and teacher centers is that they tend to be elitist and clubbish: they appeal only to certain progressive types and are usually not used by the "profession at large" (Kemble, 1977).

We can only note in response that advisors with whom we've worked report requests from teachers firmly in control of their various programs *and* from teachers who are struggling. Sometimes, it is true, the latter will wait until they are quite certain that inviting an advisor in is not testimony to weakness and failure. Most advisors, however, advertise themselves as resource persons for professional renewal, not as trouble shooters, and as such are available to serve everyone.

The other side of this issue is of course the question of how much help an advisor (or anyone else, for that matter) could be if forced upon an unwilling and unreceptive teacher. And to the charge of elitism, it is sufficient to respond that advisors in this country and in England have by now a track record for working effectively with all sorts of teachers: urban, suburban, and rural; probationary and veteran; "open and traditional."

Qualities of Advisors

Most accounts of advisor work inevitably call attention to what should already be apparent here: that advisors need to be fairly special people, possessing a mix of skills and talents not necessarily prerequisite to either teaching or administrating, but crucial to advising. There is naturally no one recipe for a good advisor, just as there aren't any for teachers or principals. However, after several years of observing and talking with advisors at work, I would like to offer this brief attempt at characterizing them and their skills.

The most important quality in an advisor, I feel, is not curriculum expertise, nor a dynamic personal presence, but a combination of *enthusiasm for teaching* and an *unobtrusive style* in working with other professionals. Advisors also combine solid teaching skills with a kind of professional humility. They have the capacity to put people at ease, while at the same time challenging them to accept real responsibility for their own renewal.

We have found that a key characteristic of successful advisory work is patience and an appreciation for the individuality of self-renewal in professionals. Many of the advisors I have worked with are familiar with Carl Rogers' "Characteristics of the Helping Relationship" (1970), and have found it useful to think through their role in terms of them.

Advisors we have observed also conveyed a self-confidence that typically drew people to them rather than repelled, and a willingness to question and explore, as well as to reflect and talk about teaching practice. Advisors are by necessity personally strong and mature people who can operate within vaguely defined job structures, and who can find rewards for their efforts in the protracted gains and incremental growth of other professionals (this, in comparison to the relatively more easy-to-see development of school children). Lastly, advisors need to be able to "set up shop" in a variety of places, and under a variety of circumstances (occasionally tinged with elements of apathy or hostility). They need, then, to be resourceful, if not ingenious, "field agents," working to renew the practice.

What Advisors Do

What do advisors do that makes them advisors, and not principals or curriculum specialists or supervisors? Since each of these latter positions have responsibilities in common with advisors (insofar as they all be considered to work *in support of* teachers), it is perhaps easier to draw a distinction between roles in terms of what advisors do not do. This in fact is what happens when advisors are described as being not patently curriculum focused (instead, they are more people-focused), and not involved in performance evaluation (instead, they contribute to a self-critiquing and growing process).

The range of specific functions that define the advisor role still needs further articulation, however. Lillian Katz's (1974) list of types of advisor activities is a helpful start, and has served as the basis for the advisor job description in the St. Louis Public Schools program:

1. Providing inservice assistance to teachers only when such assistance has been requested by them;
2. Providing assistance in terms of the requestor's own goals, objectives and needs;
3. Providing such assistance *in situ* rather than in courses, institutes or seminars exclusively;
4. Providing assistance in such a way as to increase the likelihood that teachers become more self-helpful and independent rather than helpless and dependent. (p. 154)

In reviewing our own experience with advisories in St. Louis, New York, and in New England, as well as articles and other written accounts (Alberty & Dropkin, 1975; Bussis, Chittenden, & Amarel, 1976; Katz, 1974; Mai, 1977; Manolakes, 1975; Sproul, 1978; Thomas, 1979), it has become evident to us that there are several useful approaches to describing the advisor role. I have chosen to discuss three: the *content* of the advisory assistance, the *mode and locus* of advisory work, and the nature of the *problem solving relationship* between teacher and advisor. This discussion needs to be preceded, however, with mention of that aspect of the advisor role upon which all other functions are built.

Advisors as Listeners and Observers

> The advisor becomes a listener to the teacher, creating an opening wedge to break down the teacher's isolation by providing a supportive and non-judgemental atmosphere in which the teacher can struggle with problems. (Alberty & Dropkin, p. 25)

Advisors begin as listeners and observers. In one respect, this is an obvious stance for advisors to take: their need to be helpful in terms predicated by the teacher demands that they know something about the teacher, his class, and what's on his mind. Less obvious, perhaps, is the advisor's need to be responsive to the fact of isolation as a condition of the teaching profession. Those who study the schools as social systems (Lieberman, 1977a; Lortie, 1975; Sarson, 1976, for example) have regularly cited this condition as a significant and overlooked factor when considering such issues as professional growth, cooperative planning, and innovation in schools.

Teachers in general don't feel they are much listened to, at least as individuals. Most professional contact within the normal course of business is characterized by one-way communication. Principals dealing with administrative and policy matters at staff meetings and curriculum specialists explaining new programs and materials are the norm here. If problem solving and reflection are professional expectations of teachers, the context within which they will have to occur is typically one of isolation.

Advisors, then, represent in many cases the means for professional dialog to take place, and perhaps the possibility for a problem solving dynamic that is so rarely present in teaching. Equally important—as both advisors and teachers have testified—is the advisor's role in facilitating teacher monolog. Teachers, like anyone else in a challenging and often perplexing job, need "someone to be a sounding board, to whom they can just express frustration over a situation they haven't been able to resolve or concern over a child they're having difficulty with. Sometimes you can help directly and sometimes you just commiserate" (Alberty & Dropkin, 1975, p. 26).

While it is true that principals and fellow teachers could also perform this "sounding board" function, the social reality of most schools is that this just doesn't occur. Not wanting to admit to "having problems" and not trusting a collegial situation that is frequently more competitive than cooperative, teachers are frequently left with isolation as the most prudent—though still unsatisfactory—recourse.

Listening, Observing and Needs Assessment

> People need to learn to talk about their needs, and they may require help defining their needs and putting them in a form to be acted upon.... The current phrase 'needs assessment,' we suspect, makes a mechanical process out of a well developed skill. (Lieberman, 1977a, pp. 163-164)

When various agencies, both within and outside of school districts, undertake to assess the needs of teachers for the purpose of determining staff development strategies, the result is more often than not a rather sterile tabulation of so many checklists. Needs assessment in this case is not really responsive to how needs are most likely to occur, or how they are most naturally expressed by the teacher. To survey every six months or so the staff development needs of teachers, and then to mount a programmatic response several weeks (or perhaps months) later is at best a way of addressing only those "needs" which have no temporal context, and which can be dealt with as ideas apart from the reality of the classroom.

The advisor role, on the other hand, represents a different perspective on needs assessment, one that acknowledges both the element of skill alluded to above and the need to make this activity a vital and continuous part of professional practice. Because they regularly consult *the teacher* for direction and because they work in the classroom, advisors are agents for a needs assessment process that is organic and spontaneous. This process is also more valid than the exercise of using externally set checklists because the categories and terms for stating needs—or subjects for inquiry, or problems to solve—are set by teachers themselves.

Furthermore, this kind of needs assessment, involving ongoing observation and dialog and on the spot analysis and reanalysis, can evolve to keep pace with needs determined by teacher growth, changes in students, new classrooms and school conditions.

Needs assessment here becomes a dynamic process, a joint endeavor where advisor and teacher try to become more astute and more skillful in pinpointing directions for problem solving, and then, for follow through.

Being a listener and observer is therefore both a door-opener and an ongoing prop for supporting reflection, experimentation, and assessment in a professional growth relationship. It is also a primary condition for building and sustaining trust. Advisors who are willing and ready to listen are imparting value and respect for the teacher's point of view against a long contrary tradition.

This crucial aspect of the advisor role should be considered then as both overture and refrain to the following descriptions of what advisors do.

1. CONTENT FOCUS

One way of describing an advisor's activities is to talk about them in terms of their substantive focus, or which aspects of teaching practice they are addressing. Broadly speaking, advisors have helped teachers both with curriculum and with "technique"—strategies and tactics for working with people in the classroom (and the school). It is this latter focus that usually distinguishes the advisor from the subject specialist or the curriculum supervisor, and which makes the advisor's approach to professional growth and development more holistic and truer to the reality of the teaching situation.

Figure 1* **Content Focus**

CURRICULUM		TECHNIQUE
Goal Setting	Diagnosis	Counseling
Provisioning	Questioning	Discipline
Scheduling	Didactic Instruction	Behavior Management
Grouping	Group Routines	
Record Keeping		Reward & Recognition
Room Organization		

*While curriculum is frequently defined more broadly as to include social and emotional development, here it refers primarily to the academic side of learning. Neither of the three lists are meant to be inclusive.

Figure 1 is drawn to show this broader province of the advisor. It is also meant to convey how integrated the advisory approach to staff development is. Because the advisor can actually take part in the life and routines of the classroom, he can be a useful staff development resource in all aspects of teaching practice, and can deal with them as the interrelated subjects they truly are. For example, if a teacher wants some help in creating some curriculum alternatives in math, there is often a need also to replan activity scheduling, and perhaps alter classroom organization and rearrange space.

The classroom is a "system," and innovations and alternatives are never just matters of simple adoption, as the Rand Study pointed out. There must be an adaptation process taking place, where both the teaching environment and the new element are reshaped somewhat to accommodate a systematic change. It is the *complexity* of the growth and renewal experience that makes the advisor role such a logical and appropriate staff development resource (and which, in turn, makes the single subject workshop and course approach so limited in its effectiveness). One natural advisor service within this complexity involves functioning as "the intermediary playing a translation role relative to potential resources" (Crandall, p. 204).

Curriculum Development

Building curriculum, or developing alternatives, or just adapting commercial materials to fit particular needs, are some of the most common tasks advisors are asked to assist in, and they deserve special mention insofar as they bring out an important dimension of the advisor role. Teachers' center director Amity Buxton has noted quite rightly that advisors (and teachers' centers) have the capacity to help teachers *think of themselves* more as curriculum developers and innovators, and that this might be the most important service they can provide. By working alongside the teacher and encouraging and supporting thoughtful experimentation and assessment in the classroom, advisors have been quite effective in helping teachers assume more responsibility in making curriculum responsive and suitable to their students. The payoff here is of course a considerable one: teachers who see themselves as curriculum developers are more likely to feel a need to know more about their pupils and how they learn; they are also more likely to think and reflect about their teaching in general and to be more self-sufficient and self-initiating as professionals.

2. MODE AND LOCUS OF WORK

Where advisors function and how they operate as staff development agents within a complex of professional needs and resources suggest another way to examine the role. Figure 2 is drawn to emphasize that advisors carry their staff development efforts beyond the classroom, and see themselves as linkers and resource brokers as well as in-classroom helpers. It is also meant to illustrate the wide repertoire of advisor tactics and the many ways advisors can act as teachers, as colleagues, and as problem solvers.*

When the advisor works in the room with a teacher, he affirms both the collegial status of their relationship—he *is* indeed, another teacher—and the position that problem solving ultimately needs to be worked out right there, in the reality of the class routines and with thirty-odd children. Dealing with professional issues in the classroom also makes the advisor and teacher more likely to ground their problem solving strategies and their curriculum buildling on the actual needs and capacities of children. The result, not always a common one in education, is to derive

Figure 2   **Mode and Locus of Advisor Work**

WITH INDIVIDUAL TEACHERS		
Listens		
Suggests Ideas		
Critiques		
Shares Experiences		
Explains & Interprets		
Provides Support & Encouragement		
WITH CHILDREN		**WITH OTHER PEOPLE AND AGENCIES**
	Demonstrates	Leads Workshops
	Models	Arranges Professional Visits
	Co-teaches	
		Convenes
		Liaison with Administrators and Specialists
Observes & Takes Notes		Works with Parents
Tests and Diagnoses		Gathers Resources
Works with Individuals & Small Groups		Collects (and Translates) Information
		Works with Student Teachers & Paraprofessionals

pedagogy as much from what we know about the child (or a group of specific children) as from the dictates of subject matter and broadbased curriculum guidelines.

Demonstration and Modeling

Other benefits can accrue from the advisor's presence as a colleague teacher.

> The advisor helps the teacher by working with children in her classroom. By what she does with children and by how she uses materials with them, the advisor models some of the possibilities for the teacher.... A significant, often subtle aspect of this help lies in modeling relationships with the children. Such modeling can sometimes open a next step for the teacher. It is a particularly important part of the advisor's role in helping a teacher who has reached a plateau in her own development or who has opted for a 'pleasant' but limited use of the advisor. (Alberty & Dropkin, 1975, p. 16)

We have confirmed this observation several times over. Some teachers have admitted they "just didn't think kids were capable of doing that." Others didn't feel they themselves could afford to risk trying a certain way of behaving, or a very different way of relating to a child. If an advisor is able to convey in modeling that he is not modeling *himself* as an extraordinary teacher, but rather an *approach* to a given situation, this tactic more than any other can help some teachers move beyond that "plateau."

Modeling is also an activity that advisors should be very open-eyed about, for its desired effect requires skill and the right occasions. Katz has rightly noted two dangers in modeling. The possibility of undermining the authority of teachers—as well as perceptions of their competence—in the eyes of their pupils is one. Another, already alluded to, occurs when an advisor's virtuosity leads a teacher to respond "I could never be that good" (p. 155). Since this response might be a fairly natural one with many teachers, the advisor needs, then, to be a confidence-builder as well.

Advisor as Broker

Typically, working with several teachers in the same building, and needing to maintain close contact with the principal, advisors are inevitably "linking agents" within a school. Often advisors have formal connections to district offices of curriculum or instruction, or are tied into a system-wide staff development structure, thus enabling them to span the formidable institutional boundaries that so effectively separate the "field people" from the central office. Advisors may furthermore serve as connecting links between school systems and university (or institute, teacher center, etc.).

Because of the role's unique mobility, advisors can take an active part in helping to reduce the traditional isolation (and loneliness) of teachers, and perhaps have an impact upon the patterns of cooperative problem solving and collaboration that exist within and beyond school systems. In our own experience, for instance, advisors invariably helped to draw the principal closer to a joint problem-solving relationship with teachers, or at least provided him with more information about how teachers were organizing to cope with specific teaching concerns. Advisors working to build "corridor communities" in several New York City public schools also tried to involve principals as active partners, and were in turn seen by principals as having a strong influence on professional sharing and group problem solving.

Advisors have also worked in New York City and St. Louis schools to develop greater collegiality and cooperation between classroom teachers and ancillary staff. Urban schools especially have many subject matter specialists (as well as special education staff) who all share children with classroom teachers, but who do not always have an opportunity to share opinions and concerns about the children and about instruction. By arranging small, impromptu meetings—frequently focusing on a single child—or just by modeling a collaborative problem solving style in relating to teachers, advisors have been able to bring together different teachers, as well as school nurses, social workers, and custodians—to work through specific issues and tasks.

One of the most obvious consequences of the advisor's mobility is that he can become a means for information exchange between teachers. Advisors are excellent cross-pollenators, picking up an idea in one classroom and dropping it in another. Frequently this kind of exchange leads to teachers getting together to help each other. Advisors also act as professional travel agents, arranging classroom visits between teachers who the advisor knows have similar concerns, or suggesting and arranging visits to outside resources (teachers' centers, museums and other cultural institutions). This brokering function operates within individual schools and districts, and between like and unlike institutions. It acts always to build networks of support for school professionals seeking, in Matthew Miles' phrase, "low energy access to trusted competence."

---

*For other related descriptions of the advisor role, see those of Bussis, Chittenden and Amarel (pp. 144-7) and Katz (p. 155). Also instructive are the "School Based Teacher Educator Competencies" (Cooper et al., 1976) and the descriptions of linking roles by Havelock and Jung, cited in Lieberman (1977a, pp. 179-180).

3. PROBLEM SOLVING ORIENTATION

Despite their different strategies and logistics, all the advisory programs shared the goal of helping teachers assume a more thoughtful and active role in influencing the educatonal environment. It follows, then, that their ultimate aim was not to provide isolated services or singular solutions to a particular problem, but to provide a range of support that would enable teachers to analyze situations and arrive at their own decisions about problems and solutions to them. Thus, the advisor's long-range goal was to perform an educative function. (Bussis, Chittenden, & Amarel, 1976, p. 157)

Advisors respond to many kinds of requests, and focus their problem solving efforts at as many different places. With some teachers, advisors will start out as provisioners and then later be used more as partners in a joint project. Being a broker of resources and a stimulus and support for a teacher's own resourcefulness are the two basic dimensions of an advisor's problem solving function.

In any working teacher-advisor relationship, there will be certain initiatives taken by each party to address specific problems. Sometimes the advisor is the primary initiator, with the teacher observing and perhaps following up. Advisors can also provide an important service as reactors to teacher initiatives, perhaps by supplying appropriate resources for the teacher to carry through on some action plan.

Usually the advisor's role as an initiator can be seen as a direct function of the teacher's own posture towards introducing new ideas, experimenting with curriculum and teaching technique, and reflecting on their consequences. The following schema is an attempt to show how the advisor's tactics are determined by the potential for initiative-taking by the teacher, and by other, corollary factors discussed below. Four basic kinds of problem solving situations are suggested by the intersection of two axes, each representing, as a continuum from low to high, the degree of "initiative-taking" for teacher and for advisor in a given problem-solving relationship.

The advisory functions in each of the quadrants are meant to characterize four different categories of the advisor-teacher relationship. As with any schema, there is a degree of artificiality to the clean separation of categories. In fact, advisors will quite possibly use their full repertoire of tactics and services in any of the quadrants, and over time, will *probably* have occasion to use them all with a given teacher. The schema is more an attempt, then, to acknowledge that just as client teachers make different kinds of requests and suggest different inclinations to growth, so

Figure 3   **Advisor Problem-Solving Orientation**

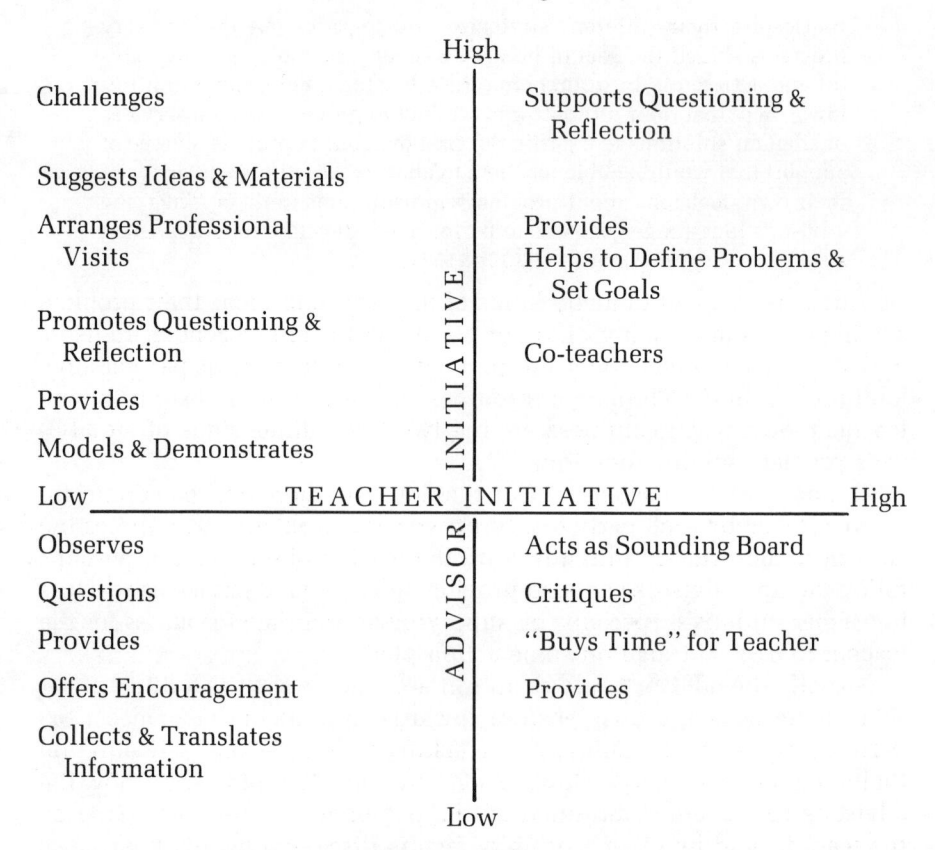

```
                                High
Challenges                       │  Supports Questioning &
                                 │     Reflection
Suggests Ideas & Materials       │
                                 │
Arranges Professional            │  Provides
   Visits                        │  Helps to Define Problems &
                              E  │     Set Goals
Promotes Questioning &        V  │
   Reflection                 I  │  Co-teachers
                              T  │
Provides                      A  │
                              I  │
Models & Demonstrates         T  │
                              I  │
Low_____N__│_____High
                              I     TEACHER  INITIATIVE
Observes                      R  │  Acts as Sounding Board
                              O  │
Questions                     S  │  Critiques
                              I  │
Provides                      V  │  "Buys Time" for Teacher
                              D  │
Offers Encouragement          A  │  Provides
                                 │
Collects & Translates            │
   Information                   │
                                Low
```

must advisors analyze a potential problem solving situation carefully so as to make a response that is appropriate and useful to the teacher at that time.

The lower left-hand quadrant describes situations where neither advisor nor teacher takes any active problem solving initiatives. This quadrant often characterizes the beginning stage of an advisor-teacher relationship, where advisors, not wanting to run ahead of teacher requests, or force their role, or set themselves as "solution givers," will restrict their activity to drawing the teacher out and establishing rapport and familiarity with the classroom. For obvious reasons, this is a situation that needs to develop somehow for any real problem solving to take place, and for the advisor role to be well-used beyond a rather superficial kind of service. It should also be noted, though, that in our experience, such a situation can remain static for quite some time, and only after some months will a teacher make a move to really address some concerns, and use the advisor accordingly.

When an advisor is asked to take a more active role by a teacher who still prefers to hold himself back, the resultant advisor activities can include those listed in the upper left-hand quadrant. At a minimum, advisors can contribute to a problem solving collaboration here by helping teachers expand their arsenal of learning activities and materials—and by helping them become more active consumers of ideas and alternatives.

Requests for materials, and suggestions, as well as for demonstrations and modeling, are sometimes invitations to be quite didactic, and do not necessarily lead to teacher reflection and growth. Advisors do want to be responsive, first because the teacher has asked for something, and secondly because being a provider and a modeler has frequently led to other requests, out of which can develop some thoughtful problem solving. As merely a dispenser of advice, however, the advisor role can "serve to increase teachers' tendency to see themselves as consumers of 'answers' and 'solutions' rather than as generators of them" (Katz, 1974, p. 155). Over time, as Bussis, Chittenden, and Amarel (1975) point out, "advisors would hope to see teachers who entered . . . with a consumer orientation toward support move to a more active role in mediating their own development" (p. 158).

Advisors' services characteristic of the upper right-hand quadrant more often play to a teacher's own resourcefulness with an insight about children, or new ideas for the classroom. Once shared, there is less of a tendency for the teacher to request demonstrations, and more likelihood of incorporation into that teacher's practice. There is also more likelihood of some joint problem solving through co-teaching. For example, after the advisor has introduced an idea for diagnosing how particular children learn best, advisor and teacher might proceed to develop strategies to accommodate "visual learners" and "aural learners" differently.

Advisors have occasionally encountered teachers who were active experimenters and importers of all kinds of new teaching paraphernalia, but who were not quite sure where all these initiatives were taking them. Their motive for such action was in fact less often a response to a well-defined problem than to a desire just to be "innovative." Such teachers manage to acquire a lot of educational trappings, but don't always incorporate them into viable teaching strategies, or integrate them so that they truly enrich a teaching program.

The situation created when this kind of "high-initiative" teacher invites an advisor to play an active problem solving role marks a special challenge for advisors. It represents, in effect, what Bussis, Chittenden, and Amarel (1975) have called going "beyond surface curriculum." Advisors here find themselves working with teachers more to question why specific materials and activities might be appropriate for specific learning needs, and to develop this kind of questioning as a strategy for using educational resources. Sometimes, in response to a statement like "I've tried so many different ideas but they don't seem to work," advisors will suggest a house-cleaning process so that a teacher can get out from under what might have become so much innovative debris. Sizing down a problem as well as establishing a suitable direction for problem solving are also ways an advisor can help a teacher think through more effective resource utilization.

The lower right-hand quadrant, defined by high teacher initiative and a less active role played by the advisor, is often the hardest to describe in terms of what advisors actually do. Stan Chu, a teachers' center director and former New York City advisor, once said in conversation that, as an advisor, he sometimes wasn't providing any new materials or suggesting innovative techniques, but just helping a teacher try out what he already knew. Here, the advisor acts almost as an accessory to a self-directed growth activity.

In both the quadrants defined by a high degree of teacher initiative in problem solving and growth, advisors often find themselves in collaborative enterprises of an extended, evolving nature. Again, what advisors *do* is not always easy to pinpoint or isolate. Rather, as part of an ongoing, problem solving task relationship, frequently defined by broad goals (e.g., integrating the arts into the general curriculum), advisors are more like colleagues engaged in a joint project. At other times, advisors can be useful in simple, short-term ways: securing a hard-to-get resource, being a sounding board for new ideas or just random, fugitive thoughts, or buying time for the teacher to try out a new small group activity by "taking over" the rest of the class.

In this connection, Linda Welles, a former advisor in New England and a consultant to our St. Louis advisory, noted how important it is to acknowledge that advisors do not have to know more, or be visibly more expert or experienced than the teacher they're serving in order to make a useful contribution to professional growth and renewal. Merely by being a thoughtful and sensitive colleague, able to provide appropriate assistance on request—or just to be a listener—an advisor can be a valuable staff development resource.

The most rewarding advisor experiences are not necessarily confined to any one of these quadrants, but can instead trace a developmental pattern across all the lines of this schema. They can occur over a long period of time, as really significant professional growth often does. Adelaide Sproul makes this point about her own work as an advisor in the Boston schools.

> The real work which gets real results is only accomplished by quiet, persistent effort that stays on schedule. Over a stretch of several years this kind of commitment is more fruitful than any number of quick attempts. My memories of situations that have been continuous are full of the imagery of growth. Getting to know a school is a growing, evolving process and I am constantly startled at the changes one's perceptions go through. It is this process which helps make advisory work so satisfying. (p. 119)

REFERENCES

Alberty, B., & Dropkins, R. (Eds.). *The open education advisor.* New York: The Workshop Center for Open Education, 1975.

Bussis, A. M., Chittenden, E. A., & Amarel, M. *Beyond surface curriculum.* Boulder, Colo.: Westview Press, 1976.

Cooper, J. M., Houston, W. R., & Warner, A. R. Specifying competencies for school based teacher educators through task, conceptual, and perceptual analyses. Paper #7 of Improving the Competence of School Based Teacher Educators through CBTE Training and Credentialing Systems Project. Houston: University of Houston, 1976.

Crandall, D. P. Training and supporting linking agents. In N. Nash & J. Culbertson (Eds.), *Linking processes in educational improvement: Concepts and applications.* Columbus, Ohio: University Council for Educational Administration, 1977.

Katz, L. The advisory approach to inservice training. *The Journal of Teacher Education, 25,* Summer 1974, 154-159.

Kemble, E. At last, teacher centers that are really for teachers. *Teacher Centers* (Commissioner's Report on the Education Professions, 1975-76). Washington, DC: U.S. Department of Health, Education, and Welfare, 1977, pp. 141-150.

Lieberman, A. Linking processes in educational change. *Linking Processes in Educational Improvement,* 1977a, 149-188.

Lieberman, A. The social reality of schools. *Teachers College Record, 77* (Dec. 1977b), 259-267.

Lortie, D. C. *Schoolteacher: A sociological study.* Chicago: University of Chicago Press, 1975.

McLaughlin, M. W. Implementation as mutual adaptation: Change in classroom organization. *Teachers College Record,* 77 (Feb. 1976), 339-351.

McLaughlin, M., & Berman, P. Retooling staff development in a period of retrenchment. *Educational Leadership,* December 1977, 191-194.

Mai, R. P. Inservice in the classroom: The advisory approach. In K. Devaney, (Ed.), *Essays on teachers' centers.* San Francisco: Teachers' Centers Exchange, 1977, 123-130.

Manolakes, T. The advisory system and supervision, In T. J. Sergiovanni (Ed.), *Professional supervision for professional teachers.* Washington, DC: ASCD, 1975, 51-64.

Rogers, C. R. *On becoming a person.* Boston: Houghton-Mifflin, 1970.

Sarason, S. B. *The culture of school and the problem of change.* Boston: Allyn & Bacon, 1976.

Sproul, A. Selections from an advisor's notebook. *Essays on teachers' centers.* 113-121.

Thomas, G. The advisor: Emissary from teachers' center to classroom. Occasional Paper #6. San Francisco: Teacher Center Exchange, October, 1979.

Chapter 11:

Staff Development Via Colleague Training

Willis D. Copeland
University of California

"Darleen just can't do the work! She gets frustrated and angry yet, because of mainstreaming, she's in the class with other kids that are moving right along. What should I do?"

"How can I get Eddie to raise his hand instead of shouting out answers all the time?"

"My kids can't work alone. If I don't keep them together and ride close herd, they never get anything done."

"I need something to do for music instruction. I can't carry a note in a bucket. What should I do?"

These questions, and hundreds of others like them, are being asked each day by teachers who must face the formidable task of educating youngsters in our public schools. As professionals, these teachers are aware that their task is difficult, that they have problems as well as successes, and that they need help. They want to solve their problems and do their jobs better.

Most of the problems faced in their day-to-day work have, from the teachers' point of view, two interesting characteristics. First, these problems emerge largely from each teacher's own classroom. They tend to be particular problems related to particular children. Though teachers are concerned with broad educational issues, they occupy most of their time and energy with concrete problems specific to their classrooms. Second, many problems that trouble teachers don't go away easily. If they did, they would not remain problems, for teachers are normally good problem solvers. Successful problem solving is prerequisite to survival in today's classroom.

Notwithstanding this problem-solving experience and the fact that most teachers have been educated beyond the bachelors degree level, they still face problems for which they alone cannot generate solutions. There are problems that persist, that are troublesome and for which teachers seek help.

What does a normally successful and well-intentioned teacher do when faced with such an instructional problem in his or her classroom? Neither district nor, for that matter, building level inservice training programs focus on the particular problems faced by individual teachers. This is not to say that such activities cannot lead to some improvement in classrooms. They generally are not able to focus on the diverse problems faced by each individual faculty member in a school.

Turning to the principal or another administrator does not appear to be especially helpful in many cases either. Teachers have repeatedly reported that school administrators are ineffectual in helping them deal with classroom level instructional problems (Blumberg, 1974; Croft, 1969; Goldstein, 1972; Osborne & Burlburt, 1971; Young & Heichberger, 1975). Again this is not to say that principals are not helpful in other aspects of inservice or that all principals are ineffective in this regard. It would appear administrative training and priorities often lie elsewhere.

Variations of clinical supervision have been advocated for helping individual teachers (Boyan & Copeland, 1978; Cogan, 1973; Goldhammer, 1969). This process normally includes concentrated and focused in-class observation. It is usually preceded by a conference aimed at problem identification and definition and followed by feedback of observation results and generation of strategies for change. It is a process which seems to be an attractive vehicle for helping teachers improve instruction. Teachers with whom clinical supervision has been consistently used report satisfaction (Eaker, 1972; Reavis, 1977; Shuma, 1971). Further, there is evidence that its use is related to changes in actual teaching behavior (Garman, 1973; Krajewski, 1976; Reavis, 1977; Skarak, 1973). Its advocates see it as purposeful, humane, and able to focus on individual needs.

Yet, despite its apparent attraction, the clinical supervision model has not been widely adopted as a method for staff development. There are various reasons for this lack of adoption. First, clinical supervision requires a considerable investment of time—a most precious commodity—by both the teacher and the supervisor. Teachers are often reluctant to invest valued preparation time especially when past work with administrators has been less than productive. On the other hand, supervisors, who often have district-level responsibilities, often do not have the time required to establish and carry through a comprehensive supervisory process with individual teachers. Further, the very nature of their administrative role, which can include functions related to staff evaluation, may also inhibit establishing a relationship conducive to improvement.

There is also evidence that the perceptions held by the teacher of the supervisor's expertise in classroom instruction is a strong variable influencing the teacher's acceptance of the supervisor's intervention (Paulin, 1980). When the teacher doesn't perceive that the supervisor who is implementing the clinical supervision process has expertise in teaching a particular subject or grade, the results of that process will often be less than satisfying.

Finally, to engage in fruitful clinical supervision, the supervisor must have a clear and workable understanding of the process of clinical supervision and its various components. Further, he or she must be adept at using the variety of specialized skills required for successful implementation of this process. Unfortunately, many college and university programs which certify today's administrators do not offer extensive training either in the related skills or the process of clinical supervision.

In summary, though the process of clinical supervision appears to be an attractive vehicle for inservice or staff development, it appears to be infrequently used and then not always effectively. In this chapter an approach to inservice which adapts the process of clinical supervision in the hope of avoiding some of these problems is proposed.

Teachers as Resources

There is a potentially powerful pool of resources for helping individual teachers solve instructional problems—other teachers. Within normal school faculties there resides a variety of experiences and expertise which can be used to help improve instruction in classrooms. Yet, these potential resources go essentially untapped. The teaching profession has not been characterized by a significant amount of conversation among teachers about substantive issues related to classrooms, instruction, or learning. Dan Lortie (1975) has described a "closed door" mentality which characterizes many teachers. The teaching act, often confined by four walls to one adult and 30 youngsters, is largely a private affair. In a profession characterized by such wary isolation, the conversation in teachers' workrooms only rarely turns to substantive issues of learning and instruction at a level that will allow one teacher to help another solve an instructional problem.

There has been much speculation as to why teachers, professionals in many ways, lack consistent interaction with one another about their work. Lortie has pointed out that, unlike students preparing for other professions such as law, medicine or engineering, potential teachers move through the average college or university credential program without relying on their fellow students as lab partners or study group fellows. They begin their training as "independents." Certainly, once in the profession, there is little formal structure in most schools to encourage communication among teachers. Channels rarely exist for the referral of specific problems to other colleagues who are expert in particular areas.

Given the above picture—the frequent individual nature of instructional problems as perceived by teachers, the expertise potentially available from within most school faculties, the lack of professional interactions among teachers, and factors that can mitigate against successful intervention with individual teachers by administrators—a strategy for staff development begins to emerge. That strategy would attempt to break down the walls, both literally and in the psycho-social sense, which currently separate teachers. It would give teachers the experience and skills required for successful collegial interaction and would establish a climate in the school in which teachers would utilize the expertise of their peers to solve problems and improve instruction. It would have as its central purpose the further development of individual faculty member's abilities to seek solutions to instructional problems by working with other teachers in productive collegial relationships. This strategy could be called colleague training.

Colleague Training

Teachers, like all professionals, need training to develop their collegial abilities. To understand what this training might consist of, it is necessary to consider the process by which teachers would interact if they want to seriously pursue solutions to instructional problems.

Consider the following conversation between two teachers sitting in the faculty lounge or standing on the playground.

Mr. Jones: You know, I'm having a real problem in my class leading discussions.

Ms. Smith (who wants to be helpful): Have you tried sitting them in a circle?

Mr. Jones: Yea, that's not the problem. I think they lack order.

Ms. Smith: Well, eighth graders are pretty squirrelly. You know, you have to be firm with them.

Mr. Jones: I'm as firm as I can be and I do want them to feel free to express their ideas.

Ms. Smith: Yea, well, freedom might be good but you have to have order. I used to have the same problem. You know, working in learning centers is really demanding and helps in getting a needed routine.

Mr. Jones: Have you started your centers yet?

Ms. Smith: Yea, last week. I'm trying something different this time. It's a new way to . . .

This conversation although intended as helpful, is cursory, lacks focus and is likely of little utility in helping Mr. Jones with his problem. First, although Mr. Jones is to be lauded for revealing a professional difficulty to another, and has been willing to share his problems and seek a colleague's help, Mr. Jones has not defined his problem in terms specific enough to allow productive work toward a solution. In point of fact, if he were pushed to define it, he would say that the problem is not so much with general discussions but with the specific calling-out behavior of one pupil, Eddie White. Eddie is bright but insists on monopolizing the discussion. Mr. Jones believes that Eddie's shouting-out behavior inhibits other participation and he would like to train Eddie to raise his hand and wait for recognition but he has not been successful.

Second, without having a clear understanding of Mr. Jones' problem, Ms. Smith has nonetheless offered a solution to it—sitting in a circle. This premature suggestion, however sincere, is of no help to Mr. Jones who has already tried that strategy and dismissed it. Ms. Smith makes another suggestion—firmness. Because of its vagueness, Mr. Jones struggles to make this "solution" fit his problem. Unsuccessful, he uses Ms. Smith's next comment to turn the conversation to another subject. He is no closer to a solution and more convinced that he pursue it alone.

The perception here is that conversations such as this are common. The professional preparation of many teachers has not equipped them to engage in fruitful and substantive interaction in pursuit of solutions to instructional problems. To help teachers establish more productive collegial relationships, components of a training program are outlined below. A colleague training program should attend to at least seven clusters of skills needed for successful collegial interaction in education:

1. *Interpersonal Communications.* Colleagues must communicate clearly and, further, must sense miscommunication quickly and act to clear it up. Specific communication skills such as asking clarifying questions, paraphrasing, checking perceptions, and active listening can aid in improving interpersonal communications and can be mastered with

appropriate practice. In the dialogue above, Mr. Jones' statement that his pupils "lack order" is quite vague and could lead to many different interpretations about his concern. Yet, instead of pausing to verify his meaning by using a clarifying question, e.g., "What do you mean by lack of order?", Ms. Smith proceeded with the conversation, adding another idea and risking loss of the message Mr. Jones intended to communicate.

2. *Low-Inference Descriptive Language.* Unlike most professionals, teachers do not share a precise and common technical vocabulary. All carpenters know what a dove-tailed joint is. Teachers disagree about the meaning of such basic terms as intelligence, handicapped, participation, mastery, individualization, and acceptable behavior. In the absence of a common vocabulary, clear communication requires colleagues to make use of a style of language which is low-inferential and descriptive. The low-inference language style requires colleagues to avoid words as often as possible which might be interpreted in a variety of ways, e.g., "the pupils were bored" or "the teacher is enthusiastic." Different observers, watching the same pupils or teacher might infer different qualities or mental states. For some, these pupils might instead be seen as "distractable", or the teacher might be perceived as "theatrical." Low-inference observations, rather, would note that "all but four of the pupils were not engaged in the learning task" or that "the teacher frequently walked through the aisles of the classroom."

In addition to its low-inference characteristic, the language style called for is also descriptive. Descriptive language is contrasted with judgmental language. Use of descriptive language in this scheme prohibits colleagues from judging one another. A teacher who is seeking a solution to a problem may be seen to be engaged in the process of formative evaluation, and any evaluation procedure involves two operations, description and judgment. Colleagues may legitimately use one another to aid in describing the circumstances surrounding a problem. Colleagues may help the teacher understand *what* she or her pupils are doing. Only she may judge what this means. Hence, the language used by colleagues should be as richly descriptive and accurate as possible but should not contain expressions of judgment. In the above dialogue, Ms. Smith's statement of her preference for order over freedom of expression in classrooms served to cut short Mr. Jones' consideration of what, for him, was a weighty problem.

3. *Problem Definition.* Successful solution of any problem depends, first of all, on an adequate definition of the problem. Colleagues should be skillful at defining accurately what the problem in the teacher's classroom

is. Mr. Jones' initial statement about having a problem leading discussions was not an accurate problem definition. In reality, he wanted to know how the behavior of a specific pupil, Eddie White, could be changed. Without a good problem definition, Ms. Smith's intitial suggestions, barring pure chance, were doomed to be less than helpful.

Talking with a colleague can help define a problem which is vaguely felt or understood. Use of interpersonal communication skills and low-inference descriptive language can assist in such a discussion. But additionally, colleagues must have practice in problem definition if they are to successfully interact toward productive solutions.

4. *Observation Techniques*. A major area of assistance which a colleague can offer another teacher is providing him or her with additional information about teaching and learning behaviors in her classroom. Teachers, like all humans, perceive selectively. At any point in time a teacher who is engaging his or her students in a learning experience is only partially aware of that which is occurring in the classroom. After years of experience, good teachers develop what some call "teacher's eyes." They are able to see much in the normal course of the class that would pass by the casual observer or even the beginning teacher. Yet even the most experienced teacher, while thinking about the material to be learned, *and* while trying to respond to needs which arise, *and* while trying to remember to compliment Edward if he volunteers an answer, will find it close to impossible to carefully watch any five particular students in order to determine how much time they spend on task during any 30-minute activity period. Yet, for these five pupils, their actual time on task might be the key to their mastery of the material.

Not only do teachers have difficulties in observing with some precision the learning behaviors of their students, many times they are not aware of some of their own teaching behaviors. We have all experienced the teacher who answers his or her own questions and, in so doing, conditions the students not to think about or volunteer answers. We have seen teachers who repeat all students' comments thereby demonstrating in a continuing manner that it is not important to listen to fellow class members but only to the teacher. We have known the teacher who says that she wants to engage the class in a free-flowing discussion in which students react spontaneously to one another's ideas and yet who feels compelled to comment on each student's statement before another student is allowed to talk. Teachers who continually offer compliments to students whenever they do anything appropriate may be unaware of this compulsive rewarding behavior and of the unintended effects of such actions.

A colleague who is not involved in the teaching, however, can be of considerable help in observing and recording important classroom behaviors that may have previously gone unnoticed by the teacher. Systematic observation in classrooms which yields specific and understandable information related to the reality of the classroom is becoming an increasingly important tool in the improvement of instruction. Techniques of systematic observation have been developed in recent years which allow observers to record specific information about such things as student question-answering behavior, discussion participation patterns, student-to-student and student-to-teacher interaction, teacher questioning techniques, teacher verbal and nonverbal rewards, student on-task behavior and a host of other teaching/learning actions that are related to the quality of the classroom learning experiences. Unlike more general and more impressionistic observation, the information derived from the use of such systematic observation techniques has a specificity which allows teachers to *focus* on particular classroom occurrences and initiate deliberate change in an effort toward improvement. If the teacher is told by an observer that student participation in a recitation session "didn't seem to be enthusiastic," the teacher has been given little information which will help make the discussion "more enthusiastic." On the other hand, if a colleague points out that, during the thirty-five minute class the teacher called on students who *volunteered* answers only nine times and if the point is further made that of those nine times only twice did the teacher accept and use the ideas the students had offered in her next statements, such information might enable the teacher to make some deliberate changes in his or her teaching.

The use of such systematic observation techniques by colleagues should offer at least three advantages. First, and most obvious, systematic observation can increase both the amount and quality of information available concerning specific teaching/learning behaviors in the teacher's classroom. Access to such information enhances the teacher's ability to make decisions intended to bring about improvement in learning. If Mr. Jones' problems had been defined more specifically, it would have been possible to observe the three important behaviors about which he was concerned by devising a simple observation scheme. The following simple notation could be used for example:

If Eddie White shouts out, record   X
If Eddie raises his hand, record   +
If Mr. Jones calls on Eddie, record   0

Such an observation of his discussion that morning would have yielded the following data:

- + - - - + + X + + + X + X X X X

Knowing that Eddie did raise his hand early in the lesson, that he was not called on during the middle and that his shouting-out behavior was concentrated toward the end of the lesson could well have helped Mr. Jones change Eddie's shouting-out behavior.

Second, information derived from observation of classroom behavior allows the testing of decisions intended to improve learning. If it is suspected that a change in teaching behavior, classroom organization or curriculum will bring about desired improvement, such hypotheses can be tested by initiating the change and observing classroom behavior to determine its effects. It was noted by a colleague observer, for example, that Lynn Higgens, a student about whom a teacher was concerned, devoted only about five minutes of her twenty minute practice time to actually working math problems. Lynn's past test performance in math had been quite poor. The teacher suspected that, for Lynn, a particular programmed text which provided small, incremental steps and immediate feedback in a humorous style might catch her attention and increase her on-task time. After Lynn was started on the text the observer recorded a 30% to 50% increase in on-task time for Lynn. Her scores on the next test showed improvement in a similar direction.

Third, increased awareness of teaching-learning behaviors provided by systematic observation may encourage helpful change in the teacher's behavior. A teacher is more likely to make meaningful changes in her teaching performance when she perceives the need to change. Many times a difference exists between the reality of the classroom as reflected in the observation record and the teacher's perception of reality, formed and filtered as it is by selective and subjective interpretations. When information derived from systematic observation provides the teacher with a conflicting perception of reality, the teacher is confronted with a discrepancy. He or she believed certain things were occurring in the classroom; observation reveals different occurrences. Such discrepancies tend to create dissonance in the teacher and usually a need to resolve or reduce this. A basic strategy to reduce such dissonance will be to initiate changes. Mr. Atkinson was concerned that his students did not generally answer questions during class discussions as he desired. His perception was that after he asked a question, there was typically a long period of silence indicating that the students either didn't know the answer or were unwilling to volunteer it. Systematic observation revealed, however, that not once in the 40-minute class did Mr. Atkinson allow silence after his questions to last more than two seconds. Instead, he followed each question he asked almost immediately with a comment, a restatement of, or an answer to the question. When presented with this information, Mr. Atkinson realized that the "long periods of silence" which he had assumed did not, in fact, exist. Faced with a discrepancy between what he had thought was occurring in his classroom and what was revealed to be occurring by systematic observation, Mr. Atkinson realized that he must modify his verbal behavior immediately following questions, allowing more time for his students to think and respond.

5. *Data Analysis.* While the information derived from systematic observation of classrooms may have rich potential for identifying avenues of improvement, such potential may not be apparent at first glance. Typically, this information is in the form of rapidly written notes, symbols, check marks and shorthand recordings. In order to help a teacher use this information to advantage, a colleague may conduct a data analysis aimed at detecting both patterns of behavior that persist over time and critical incidents that seem to signal changes in behavior.

Recall Ms. Smith's observation of Mr. Jones and Eddie White. In that observational data three patterns of behavior and two critical incidents occur. Early in the lesson Mr. Jones called on Eddie's raised hand many times (pattern #1). A third of the way through the lesson Mr. Jones realized that Eddie's participation was out of proportion to the other pupils and decided to stop calling on him (critical incident #1), though Eddie continued to raise his hand (pattern #2). At one point in the latter part of the lesson (critical incident #2), Eddie perceived that he was no longer being allowed to participate and therefore decided to shout out. He continued that behavior through the remainder of the class (pattern #3). Identifying patterns and incidents can help Mr. Jones speculate about how to pursue a solution to his problem with Eddie.

6. *Feedback of Observational Data.* After observation of the class the colleague will want to make the results available to the teacher. The manner in which this feedback is performed is extremely important. Feedback can be a very threatening experience. Deliberate, focused, data-based feedback differs greatly from the general feedback to which many teachers are accustomed. Because this type of feedback can have a profound impact on a teacher's self-perceptions and behavior, the collegial relationship must be characterized by an atmosphere of trust and a tempo which will allow the teacher freedom to explore the data. Feedback which

is too rapid or too direct can damage the relationship and can render any constructive results impossible.

The colleague's basic function during feedback is to facilitate the teacher's acceptance and understanding of the observational data. The two colleagues *work together*, looking for patterns and critical incidents and developing alternatives for change. It is important to recall that ultimately the target for improvement is target pupil behavior.

Colleagues must be skillful in identifying the behaviors of teachers that appear to be related to desired pupil behavior. Probably no teaching behavior is appropriate in all circumstances. One teaching behavior may produce desirable effects on pupils under certain conditions, but under other conditions the same behavior may have an adverse effect. To make the problem more complex, a particular teaching behavior may have desirable effects on some pupils and undesirable effects on others. For example, asking a particular type of analytic question may stimulate some pupils to be more reflective and probing but it may cause others to feel threatened because of past experiences with similar questions and lead to "tuning out" the teacher.

Because of the complexities of the teaching/learning encounter, colleagues must rely heavily on the insights acquired in their histories of teaching experience. Hopefully, combining these experiences will assist the teacher in making reasoned and accurate judgments about the appropriateness of teaching behaviors which are observed. In the example provided earlier, Mr. Jones decided to change his pattern of calling on Eddie, after examining the data collected in his class with the help of Ms. Smith. He recognized Eddie less often during the early portion of the lesson but continued calling on him intermittently as the lesson progressed. Mr. Jones and Ms. Smith agreed that he could establish such a pattern.

Attention to a process. In addition to these seven skill clusters, a training program intended to promote collegial relationships should attend to a process by which the skills can be focused on staff development and through which the colleagues can work toward improvement of instruction. That process involves a series of steps that can be followed by colleagues as they interact to solve problems. These steps include:

1. Identification and definition of an instructional problem. In this step the colleagues use a variety of communication and language skills to identify an area of concern held by one member which needs improvement, and define in low-inference descriptive terms the target pupil behaviors that require change and possible teacher affecting behaviors that could bring about that change.

2. Develop an observation instrument. Working together, the colleagues either select an observational instrument that fits their particular area of concern or create one if a ready-made instrument is not available. It is critical that the instrument created or selected focus on those particular behaviors identified in Step #1.

3. Classroom observation. While one colleague teaches a lesson, the other(s) uses the adopted instrument to observe the class, gathering data relative to the area of concern.

4. Data analysis and feedback. The colleagues examine the data, identifying patterns, critical incidents and strategies for change.

5. Implementation and verification. The teacher implements the identified strategies while her colleagues assist in determining the adequacy of the implementaion and the results obtained on the pupil target behavior.

Taken together, these steps encourage teachers to adopt a deliberate, hypothesis-testing stance toward improvement of instruction. Problems are identified. Solutions are hypothesized and tested. Results are verified and alternative approaches generated. Yet, though the process is direct and purposeful, it is founded upon and respects the integrity of the individual teacher. Changes are not imposed from without but, instead, are adopted as their appropriateness emerges from the teacher's needs and from his growing awareness. The teacher is thus able to integrate his or her own style, educational goals, and previous experience into a process of change, an *integration* that is crucial to the permanence of that change.

Attention to building relationships. In addition to the acquisition of a set of skills and to understanding a process by which colleagues can pursue solutions to problems, a colleague training program should provide multiple opportunities to experience collegial relationships.

It is important to consider the nature of a collegial relationship. In terms of institutional authority, colleagues must perceive themselves as equals. No member of a colleague group should carry institutional power which could be used to influence or coerce the other into a course of action which they do not choose. Yet, colleagues are not equal in all ways. Most importantly, they vary in terms of their abilities. Within a collegial relationship each member is capable of performing different functions. Differences in capability might reflect a difference in expertise, as in the case of the medical radiologist who, by virtue of training and experience, can better read x-ray negatives than can his colleague the internist. On the other hand, differences in capability can reflect a difference in technique or style as when two ballet dancers take time to watch each other practice and offer critical suggestions. One dancer has the capability of helping the other by virtue of his or her opportunity to stand back and watch, something the performing dancer cannot do for himself.

When teachers engage in a collegial relationship, each member brings to that relationship unique capabilities, both of expertise and of opportunity. First, a colleague can offer access to a second set of experiences gained over a teaching career. The expertise derived from these experiences, though not necessarily better than that of the others in the colleague group, will, in all likelihood, be different. Access to a different set of experiences as well as a different expertise can be of considerable utility as a teacher seeks solutions to problems.

Additionally, a colleague is helpful in systematically pursuing solutions. Having to explain the problem to a colleague forces a teacher to be explicit, to define the problem in unambiguous terms understandable to another person. This process of explicit problem definition is often avoided by people working alone but is required by colleagues working together. Further, it is absolutely necessary for the successful pursuit of solutions.

Thus, by providing some different expertise, some additional experience, by providing guidance in problem definition and in the process of seeking solutions, and by providing information about the teaching and learning that occurs in the classroom, a colleague can offer a teacher much that is useful in the improvement of instruction. It should be emphasized that the teacher brings his unique capabilities as well to such a collegial relationship. His or her own perception of a problem or area that needs improvement, solution to the problem, understanding of particular students and their histories and knowledge of the classroom environment are incorporated as well in the process. Further, he or she brings a personal need and professional openness to make decisions about possible courses of action in his or her classroom without having prescriptions forced from without. The relationship between teaching colleagues, then, should be characterized by mutual work towards solutions. The colleagues work together, one offering interaction, experience, and information gained from classroom observation, the other insights into their own behavior and classroom.

Summary

This paper has suggested that within school faculties there is the potential for implementing significant change in teaching/learning behaviors. Much of that potential is not shared. Colleague interaction has been thwarted by time and tradition, by structures in schools, and by lack of training for teachers. If teachers interacted as professional colleagues, offering in in structured ways their capabilities to one another for use in identifying problems and implementing solutions, a truly dynamic staff development program could accrue. Such a program would focus on the perceived needs of individual teachers, would recognize and encourage the power of teachers to improve their instruction, and would employ a systematic strategy for developing and testing strategies for improvement. This strategy would, above all, cast the teacher in the central role of staff development as a source of energy, direction, and motivation.

BIBLIOGRAPHY

Blumberg, A. *Supervisors and teachers: A private cold war.* Berkeley, Calif.: McCutchan, 1974.

Boyan, N. J., & Copeland, W. D. *The instructional supervision training program.* Columbus, Ohio: Charles E. Merrill, 1978.

Cogan, M. *Clinical supervision.* Boston, Mass.: Houghton Mifflin, 1973.

Croft, J. C. The principal as supervisor: Some descriptive findings and important questions. *Educational Administration Abstracts, 4,* Spring 1969, 71.

Eaker, R. E. *An analysis of the clinical supervisory process as perceived by selected teachers and administrators.* Unpublished doctoral dissertation, The University of Tennessee, 1972.

Garman, N. *A study of clinical supervision as a resource for college teachers of English.* Unpublished doctoral dissertation, University of Pittsburgh, 1973.

Goldhammer, R. *Clinical supervision: Special methods for the supervision of teachers.* New York: Holt, Rinehart & Winston, 1969.

Goldstein, W. An enlightened approach to the supervisor of teachers. *The Clearinghouse, 46,* March 1972, 392.

Krajewski, R. Clinical supervision: To facilitate teacher self-improvement. *Journal of Research and Development in Education, 9,* Winter 1976, 58.

Lortie, D. *School teacher.* Chicago, Ill.: University of Chicago Press, 1975.

Osborne, G. S., & Hurlbult, A. S. Credibility gap in supervision. *Schools and Society, 99,* Nov. 1971, 415.

Paulin, P. *Teacher perception of autonomy and resistance to evalution.* Unpublished doctoral dissertation, University of California, Santa Barbara, 1980.

Reavis, C. A test of the clinical observation model. *Journal of Educational Research, 70,* July-Aug. 1977, 311.

Shuma, K. *Changes effectuated by a clinical supervisory relationship which emphasizes a helping relationship and a conference format made congruent with the establishment and maintenance of this relationship.* Unpublished doctoral dissertation, University of Pittsburgh, 1971.

Skarak, N. D. *The application of immediate secondary reinforcement to classroom teaching observations in clinical supervision.* Unpublished doctoral dissertation, University of Pittsburgh, 1973.

Young, J. M., & Heichberger, R. L. Teachers' perceptions of an effective school supervision and evaluation program. *Education*, *96*, Fall 1975, 10.

Chapter 12:

Organizational Development and Public Law 94-142 in Jefferson Elementary School

Charles W. Case

This chapter offers a scenario of an organizational development approach to school-focused inservice education. The total staff at an elementary school is the focal point for change. Better meeting the needs of exceptional students is the primary goal. Organizational development and a school-focused teacher educator provide the process.

The chapter provides an overview of the Jefferson Elementary School.

Background

Jefferson Elementary School is one of eighteen elementary schools in Riverside School District. In addition, the district has four middle schools and two high schools. The eighteen elementary schools are organized into four clusters, with each cluster feeding into one of the middle schools and one of the high schools. Jefferson School has 450 students; grades K-6; twenty-two teachers; and a principal, George Farris.

The city of Riverside has a population of about 60,000 people. The economic base of the city consists of about five manufacturing firms, each employing between 1,000 and 3,000 persons, numerous small businesses, and a state university with about 10,000 students and 1,500 employees. While the economic base of the city is fairly stable, it does shift upward and downward in line with the overall national economy at any particular moment. The members of the community are generally hardworking and largely conservative.

The initial response of the school district to P.L. 94-142, The Education of All Handicapped Children Act, could be described as a "literal response," that is, the district has done basically only that which is necessary to comply with the law. Students are identified and diagnosed (though it is common for a four- or five-month delay between identification and diagnosis), staffing occurs, and an individual education plan (IEP) is prepared. Many children are still in special classrooms. Many of the children with special needs who are placed in regular classrooms (mainstreamed) are viewed as slow learners and, therefore, engage in the regular curriculum at a slower pace and receive some extra assistance from a specialist, when one is available. In private, many teachers express anger and frustration at having to serve "those kids." Some teachers have suggested to parents that their "normal or about normal" kids are being robbed of the teacher's time. Occasionally, some parents have expressed the sentiment, "Once again the average kid is being shafted for the benefit of the poor and dumb kids."

Allison Burke has been a teacher at Jefferson School for ten years. Her undergraduate preparation was as an elementary teacher and she has taught fourth and fifth grades for five years in Jefferson. She recently took a leave-of-absence for a year and completed a Master's Degree in learning disabilities. She returned to Jefferson School to teach third and fourth grades, especially the low achievement students. During the past year, Allison has also been taking additional courses and workshops in the areas of organizational development and change processes.

Allison has had many discussions with her principal, George Farris, regarding the spirit and intent of P.L. 94-142 and her perception is that the Riverside Schools are only in minimal compliance; they are meeting the "letter of the law." To a great extent George agrees with her, but he is not sure how to change the attitudes and practices of the teachers at Jefferson. Two or three speakers from the university have been brought in to provide information on days set aside for inservice education (three one-half days per year). His impression is that one presentation was entertaining, one chided, and one was a "yawner." Needless to say, little resulted from these one-time experiences. The school district has also provided some supplemental money for additional curriculum materials. However, again, not much has resulted.

A Proposal for Change

As a result of her recent work with organizational development theory and processes, Allison suggests that she may have some of the organizational and communication skills necessary to make such an approach work if the district is able to provide some funds for an external consultant to assist her and if she can spend half of her time for the coming year implementing such an organizational approach.

Such a plan will require agreement by and the willingness of most of the teachers to work both in groups and individually to analyze their present situation and to determine the goals and procedures to make any necessary changes.

George suggests to Allison that they contact Professor Bert Johnson at the local university to work with them in developing a proposal to submit to the teachers, central administration, and the school board. Professor Johnson's area of interest and expertise is organizational development, particularly educational organizations. Bert accepts the opportunity to work with George and Allison and requests permission to involve a graduate student, Sue O'Neil, since she has been looking for an opportunity to receive some direct experience in organizational development. Bert and Sue are both interested in the organizational implications of P.L. 94-142. All are in agreement that any plan is subject to the approval of the teachers, central administration, and the school board.

After three meetings of this new team, a proposal is prepared. In brief, the proposal contains objectives to conduct a preliminary analysis of the school as it now operates with regard to mainstreaming. In the first phase of the proposed project, the team (Allison, George, Bert, and Sue) will construct and implement a structured interview to assess attitudes, knowledge, procedures, problems, available resources (human and material), and goals. Some of the information will be derived from examining existing documents, such as budgets, policies, procedures, achievement information, and the like. The interview data and other information collected will be classified according to the following categories derived from viewing the school district as a "macro system" in organizational development terms:

1. Environment
    a. legal mandates, existing and emerging,
    b. community attitudes and norms about handicapped,
    c. boundaries between the school system and other relevant systems (such as social agencies),
    d. internal and external expectations for the schools,
    e. available resources and services from the community,
    f. major constraints from the environment.
2. Inputs into the School (System)
    a. goals/purposes (degree of clarity and consensus),
    b. expectations (consensus, conflict),

c. resources.
3. Internal Processes (within Schools)
   a. type of organizational structure,
   b. types of communications patterns (Who communicates what to whom, when, and why? Where do individuals get information and what form?),
   c. types of decision-making patterns,
   d. formal and informal role structure and expectations within the school and the district organization,
   e. permeability of organizational boundaries within the school, and district organization, among schools, and among roles.
4. Outputs from the School (System)
   a. goal achievement and discrepancies with stated goals and expectations,
   b. state and morale and organizational climate,
   c. integration between individual needs (staff) and organizational needs,
   d. means of evaluation of organizational outputs,
   e. means for identification of unmet needs.
5. Feedback to School (System)
   a. formal means,
   b. informal means,
   c. use or non-use of feedback.

During the second phase of the project, their plan is to summarize the information and present it to the teachers in a one-day work session. The goals of this workshop will be to achieve consensus on:

1. major and minor problems,
2. potential causes of the problems,
3. strengths of the school,
4. weaknesses of the school.

The third phase of the project will consist of a one- or two-day work session with the Jefferson teachers where they can step back and dream together about what the school would be like if it were mainstreaming handicapped students in the best possible fashion. The project team will coordinate the various teacher groups and subgroups in:

1. Preparing scenarios on a desired future state of school regarding P.L. 94-142,
2. Comparing these scenarios with information agreed to in phase two, to determine:
   a. areas of consensus,
   b. system constraints,

c. system facilitators,
3. Describing discrepancies between where the district is and where it wants to be,
4. Defining areas of consensus on goals for the system,
5. Developing and assessing alternative strategies for achieving goals,
6. Selecting strategies to be used.

The fourth phase of the project will be designed to achieve consensus among the staff of the school on specific change proposals. These proposals will be developed by both individuals and small groups and submitted to the total staff for consensus. Specific proposals will address:

1. Goals and strategies,
2. Changes needed in
   (a) communications system,
   (b) decision-making system,
   (c) roles and interrelationships among roles,
   (d) task interaction patterns, and
   (e) linkages with external systems.

The fifth phase of the project will be the writing and implementation of individual and group learning contracts intended to promote change in individuals both in instructional behavior and organizational behavior. The team, together with individuals and subgroups, will develop these learning contracts based on agreements in phase four.

The plan is that the entire process will be continuously monitored and adjusted when necessary. The final evaluation will reflect not only specific successes, but failures and unanticipated outcomes of the project.

The major cost for phases one through four center on the needed released-time for the Jefferson School staff and the preparation and duplication of print materials. The projected costs for phase five will be determined just prior to the implementation of that phase. It is anticipated that phases one through four and the designs for phase five can occur within one school year. Phase five will take one to two years to "complete."

Implementing the Proposal

The team took the proposal to the superintendent and assistant superintendent for discussion. Their initial reactions were that the process was too long and costly and the outcomes uncertain. How could they make such a major investment in just one school? After three lengthy meetings, the team finally secured agreement from the central administration. The problem had to be addressed, since other inservice education approaches to that point in time had been largely unsuccessful. The argument prevailed that significant educational and organizational change often takes three to five years. It was underscored that members of an organization (teachers) must have significant participation and self-determination in any major change processes. The superintendent and assistant superintendent were convinced and agreed to support the proposal before the school board if the team could secure support and consensus among the Jefferson staff.

The team then met with the Jefferson staff. A wide range of reactions was elicited: "We are doing what is necessary for handicapped kids already." "Congress made the law, let them try to teach these kids." "It's about time we had some say." "Damn it, let's try it; nothing else is working." "What's the university getting out of this?" The team took time to deal with every question directly and in a non-defensive, sensitive fashion as possible. Eventually, about one-half of the staff indicated support, one-quarter agreed it was worth a try, and one-quarter took the position that they would neither actively support nor block the project.

The superintendent submitted the proposal to the school board for approval. The project team was invited to be in attendance. Most of the concerns expressed previously were reiterated by various members of the seven-person board. In addition, one member of the board suggested that such a project should be supported through some federal grant. The project team again responded to all questions and concerns. Eventually the board approved phases one through four for the coming school year with the proviso that before phase five was approved, it would require a specific proposal at the appropriate time. They also directed a request for additional inservice education days above the normal number of days allotted annually be submitted for exception to the Department of Public Instruction. The proposal passed on a five to two vote.

The team members agreed they would meet periodically during the summer to prepare phase one for implementation in September. During the summer a variety of school documents were analyzed and the structured interview questions were prepared.

In September, at the opening orientation session, George and Allison reviewed the purpose of the project and the processes to be followed. It was announced that all staff members would be individually interviewed during September and the summary report presented at a work session in early October.

The major findings of the summary report from phase one included:

The processes of student identification, diagnosis, IEP preparation and implementation, evaluation, and follow-up relative to P.L. 94-142 were unsystematic. For example, it was apparent that some students who needed particular services were not receiving them, some students were receiving inappropriate services, and many children who did receive specialized services did not receive periodic follow-up evaluations. It was also clear in many instances that the communication between teachers and specialists and among teachers with regard to individual students was not adequate. Similarly, staffing conferences were impeded by inadequate or a lack of communication.

It was determined that there was no clarity on the purposes and goals of mainstreaming among the staff at Jefferson School. In some instances there was little commitment to the concept. Similarly, there was little agreement on appropriate methods to individualize instruction generally. Probing during the interviews indicated that many staff members saw themselves as limited in their ability to individualize instruction. There also appeared to be little understanding by the teachers of the relationship among different student learning styles and possible curriculum and instructional alternatives.

It was also apparent that teachers, administrators, and specialists were unclear about one another's role and how to best work together in a complementary fashion.

Each of these major concerns was broken down further, but these details will not be discussed here. To summarize, it was clear that both within the school and the environment of the school (school system and community) the purposes, goals, and objectives of P.L. 94-142 were not clear. This resulted in considerable frustration, anxiety, and at times inadequate service to students. Furthermore, it was clear that the school as an organization generally had not changed in response to new demands. Mainstreaming, for example, requires new patterns of interaction and more responsibility for student progress shared among teachers, administrators, specialists, and parents. The school, however, was structured basically around the concept of a single teacher responsible for a single class.

Both formal and informal communications were unsystematic and ineffective. Not only did teachers and others not know how to use one another's expertise, they also did not provide one another with needed information in useful and timely ways.

This summary and specific backup information acquired through the interviews and the analysis of documents were presented at the staff work session in early October.

After lengthy discussion and some confrontation, the focus of the October meeting shifted to some of the general *causes* of the problems enumerated in the summary paper. Most of the staff believed they had been trained to instruct as individuals, responsible basically for the education of the 20-25 students under their tutelage. They acknowledged they knew little about how organizations could affect the interactions and performances of its members. They had very little experience as members of a team, where the expertise and contributions of different persons are needed in order for a task to be accomplished or a goal to be achieved. Some staff members also admitted they knew very little about various handicapping conditions or how to provide instruction to meet the needs of different handicapped learners.

As the discussions progressed, it became clearer to the group that there were many different perceptions with regard to one another's roles and responsibilities. More specifically, there was confusion over who was supposed to communicate what to whom and when, during the vaguely defined process of identification, referral, diagnosis, and educational planning and programming. At times discussions would degenerate into blaming or scapegoating, or general expressions of futility. At such times Bert Johnson would move into the fray as a process facilitator in an effort to increase and improve interpersonal communications.

It had been agreed to prior to the work session that Allison Burke would present the summary report and lead the discussion. George Farris agreed to be a non-defensive but active participant in the discussions and answer questions directed specifically to the administration. Bert Johnson would serve as a process facilitator and share insights and information as appropriate. Sue O'Neil would serve as an observer and recorder for the discussions as requested.

In the latter part of the work session the total faculty broke into small groups to determine the strengths and weaknesses of Jefferson School and its staff. (The weaknesses identified were similar to those previously discussed but with further elaboration.) The strengths identified included generally good communication and rapport between teachers and students, and teachers and parents. There was a great deal of caring by the teachers for the students. Sixty-five percent of the students consistently, over the many years, scored at grade level or above on all standardized tests. Generally, the feelings about all levels of the district administration were positive.

The project team indicated that they would summarize the information generated during the work session and distribute it to the staff within a week. The project team also agreed to seek answers to questions that had been raised but unanswered during the discussions. One such question was a request that exemplary schools in mainstreaming be identified and the faculty have the opportunity to interact with some staff members of those schools. (This opportunity was arranged at a later date by the project team.)

In preparation for the next session, the staff was asked to envision an ideal elementary school relative to mainstreaming. At the request of some teachers, the project staff agreed to place in the teachers' room, copies of articles on a variety of handicapping conditions, organizational communications, and individualizing instruction. The teachers were encouraged to make similar requests for materials at any time to Sue O'Neil. Allison Burke indicated that she had identified common concerns among the small groups and she would arrange for a discussion of these common concerns. She would also work with Sue to identify resources or resource persons who could respond to the concerns. As the meeting ended, one veteran teacher, who had been silent throughout the session, commented to the principal, "Just maybe, at last, we'll have an opportunity to work together like real professionals!" However, another teacher commented, "How will any of this help me on Monday morning?"

At the next session the staff reviewed the summaries of the previous session and reflected on events and activities in the school since that time. The school staff was generally anxious to tackle the next task. A number of teachers had prepared written descriptions of what they saw the ideal school to be; others presented verbal descriptions. A few wanted to know what all this had to do with the "real world." Subgroups worked to cull out a list of the common denominators among the scenarios.

The common denominators were presented to the total group for discussion, modification, and consensus. Following this, new subgroups were formed to examine the common desired characteristics. Constraints and facilitators in the school, district, and community relevant to the desired ideal were identified. Members of the project team worked with the groups to discuss further their perceptions and achieve as much clarity as possible.

The project team then presented additional data and information about the school based on examinations of policies, procedures, student progress, and the like. The staff was asked to add this information to the data they had generated in previous sessions and, in small groups, to describe the school as they perceived it. Having done this, they were asked to describe the discrepancies between where they perceived the school to be and where they wanted it to be. This process took place in three subgroups led by George, Allison, and Sue. Bert sat in as an observer with three groups and later provided the three group leaders with private, individual feedback on their behavior. Later in the session he shared his observations of the communications with the total group and made a series of suggestions.

Following an evening of socializing together, the school staff reconvened to review the work to date. Sue provided printed summaries of the information generated by the group. Bert asked the group to clarify further some of the perceptions shared earlier.

New subgroups were formed and asked to define major change goals for the school that would, over time, take the school from where it was to where the staff desired it to be. After lengthy discussion in both subgroups and the total group, some of the major goals agreed upon were to:

1. Develop policies and objectives for services to handicapped learners through a collaborative decision-making process, involving teachers, administrators, specialists (from school and from community), representative parents, and a sub-committee of the board of education.
2. Identify resources and resource persons in the district and community.
3. Redefine the process of identification, referral, diagnosis, educational planning and programming, evaluation, and follow-up.
4. Develop a communications system to insure the transmittal of information to appropriate persons in a timely fashion.
5. Develop a more systematic diagnostic process.
6. Define roles, functions, communications channels and patterns of coordination to maximize the delivery of services to handicapped learners.
7. Provide continuous inservice education programming based on staff needs and agreed-upon school goals.
8. Provide additional training to the staff on a variety of means and techniques to individualized instruction.

Ninety percent or more of the staff agreed to each of the foregoing goals.

The project team and staff next spent many hours of detailed planning and analysis to generate and assess a variety of alternative means through which these might be accomplished. Bert continued to lead the team in the development of their own skills.

During this phase of the process, the expertise of a variety of additional persons from other human service agencies was also utilized. One unanticipated outcome of this activity was the increased use of available services in the community such as mental health and social services agencies as well as judiciary and the university services.

A few months later the project team and staff expressed the need for a unifying structure to support various changes that were occurring or proposed. After much examination and additional assistance from the university, it was decided to adapt the Problem-Oriented Medical Record System (which is used by many health professionals) to their own situation. The system greatly clarifies the process and procedures for identification, referral, diagnosis and educational planning. At the same time it provides an efficient and effective recording system to measure the progress of individual students. It also allows periodic evaluation of the overall system.

The school staff flowed into the final phases of the originally designed project, *without* having to seek additional support and approval from the school board. Allison Burke is now a full-time school-focused staff development coordinator serving all four elementary schools in her cluster. Two of the other three elementary school clusters have now trained and employed similar persons. The middle schools have requested that this approach be extended to them. The high schools still do not perceive a need for such services. Mainstreaming has been greatly facilitated in the elementary schools. Inservice education related to individualizing instruction now occurs in a variety of ways: formal instruction, one-on-one consultation, individual and small group learning contracts. Examples can be found of teachers teaching teachers and ongoing teams comprised of teachers, professors, and students from the university. Seven years later the changes introduced in the first organizational development scheme are still visible. Greater student progress is evident. Professional interaction is greatly intensified. Some staff members are suggesting that it is time to repeat the process and take the next step in organizational development.

Chapter 13:

Inservice for Team Teaching to Promote Professional Growth through Team Teaching

Gerald D. McDermot
with
Kenneth R. Howey

Teaming: A Highly Interpersonal Endeavor

   Those of us that have been involved with team teaching and its implementation, for a number of years, have all likely developed some unique perspectives. I, just as many other building administrators, have experienced many different and varied learning activities to develop my own leadership skills to assist teachers with teaming. Likewise, there are different concepts of and approaches to team teaching. If there is one thing I have found during fifteen years of developing team teaching concepts, it is that every school has, to some degree, its own "personality." This personality is a result of the students we serve, the parents we represent, and the staff we work with to achieve specific goals. Thus, the processes used to develop specific components of team teaching may be similar, but the end results are invariably different. I believe the "human element" is the major factor of how teams evolve differently. "Human element" can be defined in many ways, but my definition for this term is: those behaviors, both work and social, that govern an individual's actions in a given situation and which affect both personal relationships and task achievement.
   This human element is obviously critical to achieving effective teaming. Whatever team teaching model is decided upon, developing staff unity or cohesiveness is of the greatest importance. Both certified and uncertified staff members must have an understanding of his or her own and others' work behavior patterns and roles. Having this understanding in turn greatly facilitates interpersonal relationships. An important point

to be made here is that noncertified staff *should* be included in many of the staff development activities. Secretaries, aides and custodial personnel are an integral part of the school as an organization and as a social system and they should be knowledgeable not only of the primary goals of the program but of the work behaviors each member of the organization employs to meet these goals.

A Developmental Process

Staff development activities for teaming have two major concerns. The activities should help develop staff unity and cohesiveness and also help eliminate personal concerns and anxieties. As members of organizations, those in a school building proceed through stages of development in working together and as greater staff unity is achieved and personal concerns are alleviated, individuals and teams can make the transition from what I refer to as *convergent* staff training to *divergent* exploration. Convergent staff development tends to focus on those processes and elements that are necessary in making a team teaching model functional. Divergent exploration includes more self-directed inservice activities aimed at individuals and teams in order to analyze and promote aspects of individual realms of responsibility. It is at this second level of training that individuals and teams can develop a format which helps each of them make needed modifications to enhance instruction in their spheres of influence.

The following, then, are critical elements in developing a functional team teaching program in a school: 1) provision for *administrative* training is usually needed to assist the team in developing the skills and attitudes of working together, 2) constant attention to the *human* element of the teaming operation is necessary in order to provide staff development that enhances both the understanding of work behaviors and interpersonal relationship skills, 3) attention to the roles and needs of all persons in a school, both certified and noncertified, is needed, and 4) attention to the organization is needed in order to assist personnel to make a transition from convergent staff and development to divergent exploration.

A Systematic Scheme

Jumping on the "band wagon" has often been a problem for school administrators. There aren't many administrators that would admit to going into an innovative project rather blindly, but it does happen. It is a situation that parallels that of the novice duck hunter. Many times a flock of ducks are at the appropriate range and the hunter fires into the middle of the flock, *hoping* that just one of the pellets may hit a target. Given the many problems and agendas an administrator faces, this rather random approach to staff development can occur. However, the administrator who understands his capabilities, where he or she is going, how he or she is going to utilize personnel and time and why, and who has the ability to evaluate program and personnel performance is in a leadership position. A systematic scheme of development is essential for effective teaming to occur.

Ideally, the building leader understands and comprehends all aspects of the desired team teaching model and perhaps will even have training experience in the various roles of the teaming model. It may take two to three years of administrative training, however, for the leader to understand and make a commitment to the implementation of an effective team teaching organization. During this administrative training, other key staff members should be involved as well. In this way, when actual implementation is begun there will be a core of knowledgeable people available to decide courses of action and develop a program for the division of labor. The more key people involved at the beginning stages of implementation the greater the chance for later success. These individuals will have also a greater commitment to get the job done, regardless of the considerable effort and time needed to achieve success. It is extremely important that the core of people responsible for the initial implementation identify realistic first steps and place them on a realistic time table for accomplishment. We have found that two (2) major outcomes a year is enough for most staffs to handle. We are talking about an over-all time frame of anywhere from five to seven years to implement the concept fully.

In this systematic and longer range planning process, consideration is given to several key elements:
1) setting key objectives to be achieved,
2) identification of personnel who have primary responsibility for meeting the objectives,
3) identification of tasks that have to be completed,
4) setting up a monitoring system, and
5) identification of the possible obstacles to be encountered along the way and potential strategies for resolving these problems.

Staff development usually starts at the information level, moves to interpretation and activities, then finally makes the transition to the application level. At each of these three levels the foundation for success is created and a great deal of structure is needed at each of these levels. By structure I mean *well-defined* inservice sessions with both considerable *nurturing* and *monitoring* by those responsible for this.

Assessing Work Behavior Patterns

As stated previously, the "human element" is a critical factor that every building leader must attend to as the organization moves towards better goal achievement, proper utilization of personnel, and quality use of the physical facility and time. The work behaviors of individuals can obviously either be a negative or a positive force in organizational growth towards these ends.

The primary needs of all members of the organization can be identified. The work environment must foster an atmosphere that highlights the personal worth of the individual and provides security. Inservice activities that enhance the understanding of one's own work behaviors and those of others build towards this. This increased understanding of work behavior patterns enables the development of better working relationships and better communication between individuals and teams.

One instrument we use to help provide these understandings is the Personal Profile System (Geier, 1977). The Personal Profile System among other things helps provide answers to the following questions:

1. What is my individual style of interacting with people?
2. How do I tend to go about getting things done?
3. In what type of situation do I tend to lead most effectively?
4. How will I tend to react when faced with strong opposition?
5. How do/will I conduct myself as a member of the group?
6. Am I more comfortable when dealing with a problem of a technical or a human nature?
7. In carrying out leadership responsibilities, how aware am I of what motivates and satisfies people?
8. What additional skills might I need to be even more effective than I am at the present?

This inventory provides each staff member with an understanding of four of his or her major work behavior patterns and their value to the organization. These patterns provide insights into how each individual functions and performs tasks. They help identify the strengths of each individual, and also point out that an over-extension of a strength can be self-destructive. The division of labor concept and the development of complementary strengths obviously is a key to effective teaming. Blending of work behaviors of team members to achieve cohesiveness becomes easier when individuals *understand* and *accept* different behaviors in their colleagues. One person's strength is often another person's weakness. As members work on a task in a united effort one staff member may provide a model for others to strengthen a specific behavior. Inservice occurs continually in this way.

Shortly after this assessment of individual patterns in a group situation, I meet with individual teams to analyze the data in terms of what this information means to developing a team concept. I focus on the strengths of each individual and how we can best utilize that person's strengths in the group. This integration of each individual into a collaborative work structure provides a better understanding of just who is going to do what and also clarifies the personal worth of each individual.

Individual conferences are also scheduled in the hope of gaining better insight into each person's work behaviors, what is required of the total team, and the interpersonal concerns likely to evolve from this mix of personal and professional characteristics. It is in this situation that discussions may focus on an individual's concern for further development and how this might be accomplished.

Non-certified staff are included in this process. They are important people and I want them and everyone else to realize the contributions they make, how they complement the efforts of others, and what they can share. One obvious example: if the custodian is not aware of the structure and the goals of the kindergarten program and how the kindergarten teacher functions in providing an education for five-year-olds, he or she may view the situation as merely calling for more work. Reciprocally, it is just as important for the kindergarten teacher to understand the role and work behaviors of the custodian, and how the custodian can be helpful to the total educational program. It is important to appreciate the value of the role and the person's worth to the organization. Occasional blending of roles and respect for one another as human beings promote growth and achievement by all within the school organization.

As the team members gain the needed knowledge to understand and apply the concepts of team teaching they are ready to move to newer horizons of organizational effectiveness. Individuals at this level also call the administrator to use leadership skills appropriate to this level of performance. When a team or the total school organization is at that level referred to as "divergent exploration," the administrator assumes more the role of a resource person. At the divergent exploration level the team also frequently engages in problem solving as a form of inservice. One tool I use in problem-solving is the force field analysis. Here we identify those forces, both negative and positive, that influence conditions we wish to alter. The process provides a relatively rigorous analysis of a problem and demands specific formulation of a plan of strategies. The plan generally includes: 1) specific objectives to be achieved, 2) personnel who have both a direct and indirect impact on achievement, 3) specific strategies to be utilized, 4) a tentative time line for achievement, 5) likely future obstacles, and 6) a division of labor amongst team members.

At weekly team leader meetings, the resources needed to assist the team in achieving its objectives are discussed. Needed resources might include consultants, specific courses or involvement in workshops and seminars. Whatever, a specific plan of action to assist individuals in acquiring more knowledge and information related to his concern or area of interest is evolved.

As each staff member grows in relation to a problem area he or she is investigating, he or she brings back a knowledge that can be shared with other team members. This is a continuing form of staff development. He or she continues to develop new areas of "expertise." Not only can this expertise be used internally, but often shared with other teams, schools, and even school districts.

The league concept, where a number of schools involved with team teaching share information and provide resources to one another, has been a most helpful arrangement. Each of our league administrative committees has representatives of each of the roles found in a team teaching scheme, plus a representative from an institution of higher education. The university personnel help by identifying additional resources, making available research data, and assisting in developing research projects with the practicing professionals.

Summary

As one can readily see, then, once the necessary staff development to ensure effective teaming is in place, considerable opportunities for continuing professional growth, or what I refer to as divergent forms of development, are promoted. Not only sharing of a variety of types but modeling for one another can occur in a natural and continuing manner among team members. In addition, various forms of collaborative planning and problem-solving are also facilitated and these too can appropriately be viewed as forms of staff development. The following are just some of the job-embedded inservice activities which are enhanced by a team teaching arrangement:

1. systematic description of and feedback about specific facets of a teacher's instructional behavior;

2. joint "case studies" of specific students where multiple perspectives of what might contribute to a problem situation are generated;
3. demonstration of specific teaching techniques;
4. collective review and revision of existing curriculum materials;
5. joint development of instructional tools and aids;
6. systematic scrutiny of planning and assessment procedures;
7. increased flexibility through different forms of student grouping to release different teachers on the team to engage in self-directed activities during the course of the instructional day;
8. increased opportunities to experiment with different roles and assume modified responsibilities, e.g., materials developer, community liaison, diagnostician of student needs, small group facilitator, documentor/evaluator of classroom interaction, technological support;
9. increased opportunities, because of the numbers of teachers working closely together, to examine facets of organizational functioning, i.e., time, space, communications, work norms;
10. opportunities to assume a number of leadership roles from time to time, including staff developer;
11. periodic dialogue about and clarification of assumptions about the nature of teaching and learning;
12. shared reactions to common readings of critical interest among team members;
13. opportunities to plan and work together in experimental projects and action research (comparing and contrasting two different approaches, for example);
14. occasional opportunity for the principal to assume a team member's responsibility in order that the team member can assume a "mini" internship in a basically different context;
15. planned and periodic opportunities for joint reflection about present practice and future potentials.

It is obvious that many teams do not begin to realize their potential for growth opportunities through teaming. This is partly attributable to the fact that in many situations they have not seriously considered how the above type of activities could be facilitated in some type of coherent plan for staff development. The team is not viewed as a vehicle for further growth. This gets to the more fundamental problem. Too many teams are too consumed with operating effectively as an instructional unit for their students to consider their other needs.

It was emphasized repeatedly in the first portion of this paper that a very well delineated, developmental plan is needed to first develop a team that can operate effectively. A reasonable division of labor and differentiation of responsibilities is essential. The team must be able to generate diverse instructional approaches which at various times will allow different team members to meet and work on different tasks while others are teaching. Time for planning and inservice is critical and the team arrangement must be viewed as a scheme to generate time for more diverse activities, not close them off. Specific skills in interpersonal communication and joint curriculum planning will have to be developed over time and in the specific work situation. The principal's role in this process is a critical one. Effective staff development is greatly enhanced through a positive interpersonal climate and the appropriate and creative mix of personnel we refer to most commonly as teaming. Too often, like the novice duck hunter, the principal aims blindly at improvement. He or she is in the ideal leadership position to create the climate and conditions for staff development to occur rather naturally and divergently to accommodate the variety of needs and interests on a school faculty.

Bibliography

Geier, J. G. *The personal profile system.* Performax Systems International, 1977 revised 1978.

Chapter 14:

School-focused Inservice Education: An All-school Approach

Clifford D. Sibley

Goal Setting

Several prerequisites must be met before effective goal setting for a school can occur. Those who set goals for the school must understand the purpose for goal setting and what their responsibility is in this process. The relationship among goal setting, inservice education, and the appraisal process must also be understood by all participants. Also, the principal and staff should be familiar with the technical aspects of goal setting. This latter skill may require the district to provide inservice training for principals and staff.

The goal setting process should be done within a specific framework. For example, what are the expectations held by the district for teachers? These expectations help define the framework for goal setting. One role of the principal is to assist individual teachers in assessing their knowledge and skills in relation to these expectations.

Just as the principal plays an important role with individual teachers in the setting of goals, an equally important role is that of facilitating staff agreement in the development of building-wide goals. Here, the principal works with the entire staff to assess total building needs. Several instructional goals are then developed and discussed, and a selection is made. Realistic priorities are set for both individuals and the entire faculty. How one might measure the extent to which different goals are achieved is considered. Principal observation is one realistic means of assessment.

Successful goal setting is based upon several principles which an effective building administrator should follow:

1. Goals must be *important to the person* setting them and *realistic*, both as to the setting, and the ability of this person to attain them.
2. Goals must relate to both the *personal* and *professional* needs of the individual setting them.
3. The individual attempting to achieve a goal needs to *receive information regarding progress* toward achievement of the goal.
4. Goals must have the continuing *involvement of the teacher* in their development and selection.
5. Goals should have as a primary purpose *improving teacher skills* and the instructional program *rather than* being used for *evaluating* the performance of the teacher.
6. Goal setting should be an *ongoing process* not a process used only as difficulties arise.

Once building-wide and individual goals have been reached, attention can be given to planning inservice that supports the achievement of these goals.

Inservice Planning

After analyzing both individual and building goals and objectives in *cooperation* with teachers, *options* for inservice activities may be considered. Once realistic options have been identified and agreed upon, the principal can spearhead the process of matching these options to the resources available within the building and district. Dates, times, and locations (both within and outside the building) are set. A communication system for keeping everyone informed is arranged. This communication plan calls for reporting evaluation of the inservice activities back to all of the participants. This includes evaluation of my role as a principal. I approve inservice with the view that teachers are intelligent and capable people. Inservice education is a means for them to maintain, improve, and gain new knowledge and skills in a rapidly changing society. Inservice cannot be seen as remedial. The learner for whom the program is offered should be a partner in determining the need for the program, planning the program, and evaluating it. Inservice programs should be rewarding rather than penalizing to a staff member. When possible, activities should be offered during regular working hours at convenient locations with little or no cost.

Once individual and building goals have been set and a school-focused inservice program has been designed to facilitate their achievement, the principal must then relate these activities to the broader process of staff appraisal.

Staff Appraisal

The school district should clearly communicate to all teachers the purpose and procedures of staff appraisal. The position taken here is that a productive appraisal process is one that operates from participants' *strengths* rather than from their weaknesses. This process focuses upon the *improvement* of a staff member's skills rather than the evaluation of a staff member's performance. A collegial, trusting atmosphere is needed between the principal and staff. Each of us has responsibilities for promoting the growth that will contribute to an improved instructional program.

I meet with each individual to discuss this appraisal process. Observations by the principal are critical and time must be found to be in the classrooms on a regular basis. Frequently observations will focus upon specific activities being undertaken by the staff member to achieve either individual or building goals. Visitations are always followed up with a face-to-face discussion in order that suggestions for continuation or change and planning for other activities may be pursued.

In addition to visitations, a principal can facilitate the teacher's inservice program in several other ways as well. This may include arranging for the teacher to visit elsewhere in the school or in another school; securing a consultant or other specialist to observe or meet with the teacher to discuss techniques and strategies; helping the teacher himself or herself design and conduct an informal analysis of what they are working on; or arranging for a teacher to attend a desired workshop, seminar, or conference. Periodic times must be set aside for the principal and teacher to meet to review progress toward goals. Agreement is reached on whether to discontinue the goals, continue as is, or continue with modification. My role as a helper in this process is also discussed.

As stated earlier, the climate for learning in the building is greatly affected by the role of the principal in this goal-setting, staff development, and appraisal process.

Building Climate

Underlying an effective instructional program is a climate conducive for learning. How many times have you heard comparison made between schools? These comparisons are usually not made on the tangible aspects of schools such as the size of the library or the types of resources available. They are more likely to be made about the intangibles of schools—"the teachers are really helpful," "the principal will talk with you," "the children like the school," are typical comments. These types of comparisons reveal the general climate for learning in the school. The principal's role is paramount in fostering and maintaining an effective learning climate in a school. I believe the quality of the interaction between the teacher and student parallels that between principal and teacher.

A primary role for the principal is to facilitate the involvement of everyone affected and insure that all faculty members view themselves as learners and models for one another, students, and parents. The principal must use every opportunity to give recognition and support to staff and students.

The role of the principal described to this point is analagous to the craftsmanship of a mechanic. The mechanic recognizes the interaction of each of the various systems in a car and blends the systems together until the car is finely tuned. The mechanic does this through involvement with the car's owners and later relates (the car's problems) to the owners, how they were repaired, and how they can be avoided in the future. An effective principal blends together the efforts of a district and building to provide a sound educational program. Hopefully, such efforts can be as finely tuned as the engine of a car. Unlike the mechanic, however, the principal's responsibility occurs primarily in the human dimension. Consequently, more time and greater effort is required to maintain the fine tuning. An example of the principal's role in "fine tuning" a school over a one-year period is given in the following section.

Tying It Together

Goal Setting

As stated at the outset, goal setting is the first process undertaken in finely tuning a building's total program. In my own situation the goal setting process begins in February and is usually not completed until early to mid-March. The goals arrived at are ones which will be focused on beginning in August and continuing until July of the following summer. For our situation we conduct an assessment of what the staff is achieving in all areas of instruction, student management, and home-school relations. We look at where we are relative to what the staff would like to be achieving. This is a process of give-and-take and is either formal or informal as needed. Again, the key is providing for the involvement of everyone affected. Clear, concise statements of existing conditions and summaries of options, points of view, and positions agreed upon are distributed to everyone affected. Providing immediate information to all involved helps to keep the process moving smoothly and is a major time commitment for the principal. Through a process of give-and-take, concensus is reached regarding what priorities will be set to strengthen identified areas of concern. This concensus is partially gained through matching choices to the actual resources available so that impractical choices are eliminated. The staff is divided into teams which can discuss and pare down the choices.

Goals set or mandated by the central office of a district are also dealt with at this time. When possible, a meshing of goals determined at the building level with goals identified at the district level is attempted. Obviously this matching contributes to an efficient use of time, money, and other resources.

After building goals are set, I begin the process of working with teachers to set individual goals. This often takes from early March until late April. The goals are included in a comprehensive inservice plan which allows those who desire to undertake summer inservice activities, whether this be teaching, attending summer school, travel, conducting research, or preparing materials.

Often I divide the teachers into two groups. One group consists of teachers who will be in the district's formal appraisal process the following school year. This usually is about one-third of the teachers. I usually begin the process of individual goal setting by meeting separately with each of these groups of teachers. This meeting focuses upon the primary purposes of goal setting (both personal growth and improvement of the instructional program); the limits within which the goals may be set, such as cost considerations, district concerns, and the number of goals that an individual can reasonably work toward (usually one to three). We examine how individual goals may relate to building and/or district goals and finally the role of both the teacher and myself in seeing that the goal can be accomplished is discussed.

After meeting with both groups of teachers, I follow up individually with teachers. The only difference in follow-up between the two groups of teachers appears whenever budget and time constraints require further priorities to be set. If this happens, teachers in the district's formal appraisal process are more likely to be given more attention in their inservice activities and support in the efforts they undertake to achieve their goals.

As individual goals are agreed upon between the teacher and the principal, they are *written* down. This requires stating the goals and listing the inservice objectives and specific activities the teacher will undertake towards meeting these goals. The written plan also includes times and/or timelines set for the activities, resources needed to undertake the activities (people, materials, and money), and a method of evaluation. The teacher and I each keep a copy for reference throughout the coming year.

Staff Appraisal

A teacher's individual goals, and whatever inservice activities are designed to help the teacher accomplish those goals, serve as the focus of the appraisal process. Appraisal is concerned with improving teaching knowledge, skills, and attitudes with the ultimate aim of improved instruction for students.

Early in the school year, usually during the first two or three weeks, I meet briefly with each teacher who is on the district's formal appraisal schedule. Any summer activities related to individual goals are reviewed and evaluated. Plans for inservice activities for the coming year are also reviewed and possible changes considered. Both of us reaffirm our responsibilities. During visits to the classroom, I may take part in activities, assist with activities as requested by the teacher or simply observe. Whatever is done, I focus upon the specific areas which the teacher has identified for improvement. Following each classroom observation we meet to mutually discuss the observation/visitation and how the teacher is progressing toward achievement of his or her individual goals. These meetings provide an opportunity to modify activities, if necessary, and to evaluate the success of completed efforts. In later winter, prior to new goal settings, we evaluate all inservice activities to this point in time and agree upon whether the individual goals have been accomplished or are still in progress. Those which are still in progress may be continued, modified or discontinued on the basis of these discussions. A formal report is made at this time to fulfill the district's appraisal requirement.

Building Climate

The more consistent and purposeful the principal's leadership is in facilitating effective staff involvement in general goal setting, inservice education, and staff appraisal, the more consistent and purposeful the building's climate for learning is likely to be. I believe the example set by the principal in working closely with teachers to articulate the building's efforts to provide a sound instructional program, carries over to the classroom. Hopefully, through their participation in this building-wide process, teachers gain a clearer sense of purpose as well as a more positive view of themselves as intelligent, capable individuals. The climate for learning is further enhanced when the principal provides the necessary leadership to inform parents and others in the school community of these plans. I do this through a listing of goals in the building's *Handbook* given out at the beginning of the school year. As inservice activities are completed, reports to parents and others help keep communication open and everyone informed of efforts to provide a sound instructional program. A final report outlining building goals and their level of accomplishment is distributed as a *Report to the School Community* at the beginning of the new school year. The *Report* contains a listing of goals, objectives, inservice activities, and the level of goal accomplishment.

Summary

This chapter attempted to illustrate how inservice can be accomplished at the building level and to define the role of the principal in this process. In conclusion, inservice programs will likely be more successful if the principal assumes a central but not dominant role in the process. He or she is in the ideal position to interrelate district, school, and individual goals. This is both a time-consuming and highly participatory process. It is also a most critical one. The primary scheme outlined in this chapter calls for the principal to assume a leadership role in relating inservice to priority goals in the instructional program, in a positive way, to the formal appraisal process, and to use this as a means of attaining a desired school climate.

Bibliography

Bishop, L. J. *Staff development and instructional improvement.* Boston: Allyn & Bacon, Inc., 1976. Pp.334.

Edelfelt, R. A. Inservice: The big picture. *Noteworthy*, I (Fall 1979), 7-9.

Edelfelt, R. A., & Johnson, M. (Eds.). *Rethinking in-service education.* Washington, D.c.: National Education Association, 1975. Pp. 93.

Klopf, G. J. *The principal and staff development in the schools.* New York: Bank Street College of Education, 1979. Pp 94.

Krajewski, R., & Anderson, R. H. Goldhammer's clinical supervision a decade later. *Educational Leadership*, XXXVII (February 1980), 420-423.

McGreal, T. Helping teachers set goals. *Educational Leadership*, XXXVII (February 1980), 414-419.

Nicholson, A. M., & Joyce, B. R., et al. *ISTE Report III: The literature on inservice teacher education: An analytical review.*Syracuse, NY: The National Dissemination Center, 1977. Pp. 99.

Wood, F. H., & Thompson, S. R. Guidelines for better staff development. *Educational Leadership*, XXXVII (February 1980), 374-377.

Chapter 15:

Interactive Research and Development as a Form of Professional Growth

William J. Tikunoff
Beatrice A. Ward
Gary A. Griffin

Interactive Research and Development on Teaching (IR&DT) was proposed in 1975 by Ward and Tikunoff as an alternative educational research and development (r and d) strategy. The basis for this recommendation built from demonstrated inadequacies of the characteristics and outcomes of the commonly-used linear r and d strategy. These include conduct of reseach on teaching by persons knowledgeable about but usually not involved in the process of classroom instruction, and development of products incorporating this research by persons who also are not engaged as classroom teachers. This, in turn, frequently results in answers to questions teachers are not asking or solutions to problems they consider to be less than critical. In addition, when important and needed outcomes are obtained, findings usually are presented in language that is largely unfamiliar and uninterpretable at the classroom level. Further, in a linear r and d approach the teacher is viewed as a "consumer" and "adopter" of r and d outcomes rather than as a participant in the process of school improvement. Finally, in a linear approach, because each step in the r and d process is discrete and separated from the others, the time required from research to classroom application, if and when it occurs, often is 5-10 years.

Subsequent to the 1975 proposal, the National Institute of Education, Division of Teaching, funded an investigation of IR&DT in order:

- *to investigate and understand the process of implementing IR&DT in order to identify and describe the requirements and characteristics for "successful" use of the strategy,*
- *to determine whether the r and d outcomes that result from an IR&DT approach provide important and useful new information, procedures, and processes to the field of education while successfully achieving (maintaining) commonly accepted r and d standards, and*
- *to determine what changes, if any, in persons and institutions might result from participation in IR&DT.*

The following discussion provides a summary of the outcomes of the IR&DT Study. A complete report is available: Tikunoff, W. J., Ward, B. A., and Griffin, G. A. *Interactive Research and Development on Teaching Study.* Far West Laboratory for Educational Research and Development, 1979, Report No. IR&DT 79-11.

Essential Features of IR&DT

The title, Interactive Research and Development, was selected purposely to give prominence to the undergirding principles of the strategy. IR&DT places teachers, researchers, and trainer/developers together *as a team*, beginning with the initiation of the r and d process to inquire into the questions, problems, and concerns of *classroom teachers.* An IR&DT team is charged with conducting research and *concurrently* attending to the development of training based *both* on their research findings and the research *methods* and *procedures* employed in their study. Decisions are made *collaboratively.* For IR&DT, this means that each member of the team has *parity* and shares *equal responsibility* for the team's decisions and actions, from identification of the question/problem through completion of all resultant r and d activities.

In all, six major features must be present for an r and d effort to be judged *interactive.* While certain of the features may exist in a more or less ideal form, *all* must be manifest in some way. They include: (1) r and d team composition, (2) the nature of collaboration, (3) problem-solving focus, (4) conducting concurrent r and d, (5) maintaining the integrity of the classroom, and (6) recognition of the strategy as an intervention as well as an r and d process.

Team Composition

Minimally, the team must be composed of a *teacher*—that practitioner who is responsible for the day-to-day conduct of the schooling process; a *researcher*—that practitioner whose major day-to-day responsibilities are to inquire systematically into the teaching and learning process in order to ask questions, gain new knowledge, and/or resolve problems; a *trainer/developer*—that practitioner who is responsible for designing and providing preservice training of teachers, professional development opportunities for teachers-in-service, and/or technical assistance at the classroom level.

Collaboration

Teachers, researchers, and trainer/developers are each assumed to bring unique contributions to conducting r and d on teaching. Thus, within IR&DT, collaboration means teachers, researchers, and trainer/developers *working with parity* and *assuming equal responsibility* to identify, inquire into, and resolve the problems/concerns of classroom teachers. Such collaboration recognizes and utilizes the unique insights and skills provided by each participant while, at the same time, demanding that no set of capabilities is assigned a superior status. It assumes a *work with* rather than a *work on* posture—the latter more frequently being the *modus operandi* when teachers are asked to join reseachers or trainer/developers in a linear r and d endeavor. Parity is granted when team members agree to participate in IR&DT. Equal sharing of responsibility is achieved only when each team member *assumes* his or her share based on his or her unique abilities and insights.

The *interactiveness* of an IR&DT effort, then, is determined in part by the degree to which IR&DT team members, regardless of professional role, are able to command the attention of the team at each step of an r and d process (parity), and the extent to which team members offer successfully their unique perspectives, knowledge, and skill and engage collaboratively in the accomplishment of the various tasks undertaken by the team (assuming equal responsibility).

Problem-solving Focus

IR&DT focuses on solving classroom problems which practicing classroom teachers perceive to be important. Thus, while in IR&DT, the problems must emerge from the mutual concerns and inquiries of the team; above all, they must attend to teachers' problems.

Concurrent R and D

While an IR&DT team is to produce a piece of research,—i.e., identify a problem, select an appropriate research methodology, select and/or develop and employ appropriate data collection and analysis procedures, and interpret and report findings—inclusion of a trainer/developer on the team introduces the capability of *concurrently* attending to the development of training procedures and processes that grow out of the IR&DT research effort.

By attending to development concerns from the beginning of an r and d effort in addition to applying research findings in a training program, it is possible to employ as training foci the procedures utilized to identify the problem under investigation as well as the procedures used for data collection and analysis procedures from the research. Since training programs can be developed that build others' capabilities to inquire within their own classrooms into the same aspects of teaching and learning as are being studied concurrently by the IR&DT team, development need not await completion of the entire research process. As a result, at the same time the research findings are being reported, training strategies may already be developed that utilize the techniques devised to study and resolve both the specified problem and the research findings.

Maintaining Integrity of the Classroom

It is only natural for the IR&DT strategy to be sensitive both to the complexity of the classroom setting and to the extent to which r and d may interfere with this setting. Inclusion of at least one teacher (and more likely two or more teachers) on an IR&DT team should highlight these sensitivities and cause the researcher and trainer/developer to select and use data sources, data collection procedures, training procedures, etc., that do not intrude upon the naturalness of the everyday settings in which teaching and learning occur.

Intervention Strategy

IR&DT, while leaving the teacher, researcher, and trainer/developer roles as intact as possible, proposes certain alterations in the conventional functions of those individuals. For example, through involvement in all types of research and development decision-making, teachers may acquire new mind sets geared toward inquiry into their own ongoing teaching-learning concerns, thus gaining practical experience with r and d tools that can be used to investigate and resolve these concerns. The researcher, through involvement with teachers, may identify new research procedures and methods, become aware of critical research issues he or she had not considered previously, and gain credibility with teachers in general. The trainer/developer may acquire new skill and insights into building staff development agendas that emerge from teachers' concerns.

Institutional settings—e.g., the classroom, the school, the school district, the institution of higher education—also may be required to change in order to accommodate the mutual and individual interests and concerns of the participants and the modifications in teaching, learning, and teacher training that may result.

Assumptions Underlying IR&DT

Four major assumptions form the foundation for the IR&DT strategy. These build from the knowledge gleaned from the experiences of those involved in educational r and d, both recently and over the past several decades. They are:

- Participative r and d strategies which include teachers are needed.
- IR&DT will contribute to educational knowledge and theory building.
- The results of IR&DT will be generalizable, particularly at a logical-situational level.
- Participants' unique skills and perspectives will contribute to the success of IR&DT.

Participants in IR&DT Implementation

For purposes of the IR&DT Study, the strategy was implemented at two sites—one in an urban setting in California, the other in a rural setting in Vermont. The settings were selected purposely in order to observe IR&DT implementation under diverse circumstances.

California Site

The California site was located in the San Diego Unified School District, San Diego, California, the ninth largest municipality in the United States. This is a large, urban public school system which served 118,697 students in the 1977-78 school year. The California IR&DT team included four teachers, one researcher, and one trainer/developer, all on the school district staff. Three teachers (at kindergarten, 1st, and 2nd grades) taught in an elementary school in a lower socio-economic neighborhood. In 1977-78 the student enrollment in the school was approximately 400 with 75 percent Black, 20 percent Hispanic, 3 percent Asian American, and 2 percent White students. Eighty-five percent of the students were eligible for free lunch and an additional 13 percent qualified for reduced-price lunch. The fourth teacher taught a combination 3rd-4th grade class in another elementary school in the district. This school served 1200 students, 77 percent of whom were White, 11 percent Hispanic, 9 percent Asian American, and 3 percent Black. Both schools included innovative programs—the first, Follow Through, the California School Improvement Program, and ESEA Title I and other categorical aid efforts; the second conducted a special district-wide program for gifted students. The researcher on the California team was on the district's research and evaluation staff. He had taught high school mathematics and had served as a resource teacher for the district prior to becoming a program evaluator. The trainer-developer was employed as a curriculum resource teacher in the school district. Prior to undertaking this assignment, he had taught sixth grade for 11 years. Two teachers and the trainer-developer had completed Masters' degrees. The researcher completed his doctorate while involved with IR&DT.

Vermont Site

The Vermont site included two cooperating institutions—the College of Education and Social Services, University of Vermont and the Underhill Independent School District.

In 1977-78, the college—located in Burlington, Vermont, a city of some 40,000 people—served approximately 1,000 students of whom some 120 were enrolled in the preservice elementary teaching program.

The school district is part of a supervisory union school district which is a loosely connected federation of seven small independent districts, each with its own board of education but served by one superintendent and his staff. The Underhill Independent District includes only one school, an elementary school serving grades kindergarten through four. In 1977-78, the school enrolled 130 students, most of whom were white. The faculty was comprised of five teachers including the teacher/principal.

The Vermont IR&DT team included three teachers who taught in the Underhill School at kindergarten, grade 1, and grade 3, one researcher, and two trainer/developers, one who worked with the team for the first two months of IR&DT implementation and one who was on the team from the middle of the third month of implementation through the completion of the process.

The researcher and both trainer/developers were on the faculty of the College of Education and Social Services. The researcher had had two years teaching experience. Both trainer/developers had taught school, the second having had more teaching experience than the first. The researcher had completed a doctoral degree; the trainer/developers both had Masters' degrees (the second was involved in doctoral studies while participating in the IR&DT effort). None of the teachers had advanced degrees.

Underhill School had not been involved previously in innovative educational programs or projects. The College had planned and implemented several innovative preservice teacher training programs, one of which had won national recognition.

R and D at Each Site

The question upon which the California IR&DT team focused its research was:

> What are the strategies and techniques which classroom teachers use to cope with distractions to classroom instruction and how effective are these techniques?

Inasmuch as the school district was devoting attention to the importance of students' "time-on-task" (i.e., the amount of time students are engaged in meaningful learning activities), this question was considered to be particularly appropriate and timely by teachers and others in the district.

The purpose of the research study, then, was to examine the techniques classroom teachers used to cope with distractions to classroom instruction and to determine how effective these techniques were with respect to: (1) minimizing instructional time lost due to distractions, (2) dealing with distractions at a level which has a minimal disruptive effect upon the flow of instruction, and (3) eliminating distractions. Classroom distractions were defined as those events which take teachers and/or their students off the intended instructional tasks. Coping techniques were defined as mechanisms, verbal or nonverbal, used by the teachers to eliminate a distraction.

Concurrent with conducting their inquiry, the team designed a training program for other teachers. This featured several components from the research methodology, particularly the data collection techniques developed by the team to inquire into their question. In addition, the training design included information about classroom distractions and coping techniques obtained through the team's research study and engaged participants in inquiring systematically into their own classrooms for evidence of these.

Research was conducted in the winter and spring of 1978 in eight classrooms (those of the four teachers on the IR&DT team and four additional teachers matched by grade level). The data set included quantitative coding of occurrences of distractions and coping strategies, narrative descriptions of teacher-student interactions, and other relevant context information for each classroom. Two observers collected the data simultaneously, one recording quantitative data and the other developing the narrative description. Data were analyzed in the spring and early summer. Data interpretation and report writing took place over the summer. The training design was completed and reviewed by the National Advisory Panel in late spring and the training was conducted in the fall of 1978.

Four major reports summarize the California IR&DT team's r and d outcomes: *Evolution of the Study,* which describes the process the team went through in conducting its r and d; *Formal Research Report,* which summarizes the conduct of the research and presents findings and interpretations across the eight classrooms; *Four Teacher Case Studies,* each of which describes the context of two paired classrooms based on grade level taught, as per the matched sample noted above; and each of which presents findings for each pair of teachers as well as the teachers' insights about their teaching that resulted from participatiing in the research; and *Formal Training Report,* which describes the training program designed and conducted for other teachers, and presents results of the training.

The question upon which the Vermont IR&DT team focused its research was:

> Are there relationships between the mood of the teacher and the teacher's classroom supportive instructional behavior? If so, what is the nature of these relationships?

Mood was defined as a state, not a trait. The instructional behaviors selected by the team to be studied for their possible connection with mood were called supportive instructional behaviors (SIBs). A set of such behaviors was selected from existing research on teaching literature. The SIBs included acceptance, attending, conviviality, cooperation, engagement, monitoring, pacing, promoting self-sufficiency, and optimism.

Concurrent with conducting their research, the team designed a training program for other teachers. This featured topics outside their research as well as data collection strategies developed by the team to inquire into their question.

Research was conducted in late Spring 1978 in nine classrooms (none of the teachers was on the IR&DT team). The data set included narrative descriptions of what occurred in each classroom during the reading lesson and each teacher's most difficult time of the day, teacher ratings of a mood adjective checklist (obtained prior to each observation), and observer-teacher interviews. Data were analyzed and interpreted late in the summer. Reports were written in early fall. The training design was completed and submitted for review by the National Advisory Panel in early summer and training was conducted in the fall. Three major reports summarize the Vermont IR&DT team's r and d outcomes: a *Formal Research Report,* which summarizes conduct of the research and presents findings, interpretations, and conclusions across the nine classrooms; *Nine Case Studies* for the teachers who served as research subjects, each of which describes the context of the teacher's classroom and discusses findings for that particular teacher; and a *Formal Training Report* which describes the training program designed and conducted for other teachers and presents results of the training.

IR&DT Implementation

The implementation of IR&DT at the California and Vermont sites was studied from the beginning of the team orientation session held at each site in August 1977 through completion of the final research and training reports in November 1978. The primary data source was audiotape recordings of all team meetings. Eighty-five hours of formal team meeting time were monitored for each site. This represented more than two-thirds of the total formal meeting time for the California team and approximately half the formal meeting time for the Vermont team. What topics were discussed and who was involved in the discussions in what ways, was analyzed and summarized. In addition, interviews, on-site observations, and questionnaires were used to obtain information regarding the extent to which team members carried out the hypothesized roles and responsibilities and achieved parity in decision-making as well as to monitor the degree to which IR&DT was related to changes in people and institutions.

Using the six essential features of IR&DT as a basis for describing the degree to which a "desired" level of implementation was achieved, the following discussion summarizes the findings.

Team Composition

Based on the role contributions hypothesized as being necessary for a successful IR&DT team, the teachers in both California and Vermont demonstrated the knowledge and skill related to teaching that were considered important. However, based on implementation findings, the California teachers were more aware of and sensitive to the *complexity* of the classroom environment than were their Vermont counterparts. To some extent, this difference may be explained by the institutional contexts in which the teachers worked. The California teachers had experienced the benefits and frustrations of working in a large, urban, multidimensional school system with a long and sustained history of professional development activities, special school improvement projects, and other opportunities to extend and deepen their understanding of classroom practice. The Vermont teachers were members of a significantly less complex school system which included only one school, provided few inservice opportunities, and isolated the teachers from other professionals. Further, it will be recalled that the three Vermont IR&DT teachers comprised three-fifths of the entire faculty of the school in which they taught. Nonetheless, both groups of teachers demonstrated awareness of and sensitivity to the problems that could arise when classrooms were entered for the purpose of conducting research on teaching, and used these insights artfully during the course of IR&DT implementation.

The California researcher was found to align more closely with the hypothesized need to be knowledgeable about and skillful in approaching the conduct of educational research in a broad and multidimensional manner than was the Vermont researcher. One explanation for this finding may reside in the fact that the California researcher completed his doctoral dissertation during the course of IR&DT implementation whereas the Vermont researcher had completed his graduate work some time prior to his participation in the project. Also, the California researcher, by virtue of his position in the school system, was regularly engaged in studying the complexities of teaching and learning whereas the Vermont researcher had been more immediately involved in the formulation and demonstration of a model teacher education program. Both researchers demonstrated the desired combination of (a) willingness to move beyond already-known research paradigms and technologies and (b) effectiveness in sharing their acquired knowledge and skill with other team members.

The trainer/developer on an IR&DT team is expected to demonstrate knowledge and skill in the application of research outcomes and methods to training programs and to be aware of ways to deliver training processes and products to potential client groups efficiently and effectively.

The original Vermont trainer/developer was observed by Far West Laboratory staff and by team member colleagues as being confused about his role on the team, persistently lacking in focus for his work on IR&DT, and, to a degree, in a position of rivalry with the team's researcher. The trainer/developer who replaced the original person can be characterized as task-oriented, supportive of colleagues, and persistent. Subsequent discussion of the trainer/developer role contributions includes only the second Vermont trainer/developer who remained with the team until the completion of IR&DT implementation.

Both the California and Vermont trainer/developers demonstrated the positive contributions to IR&DT that were specified for the role, although different vantage points and different emphases were exhibited by each. The California trainer/developer had taught eleven years in elementary schools and experienced five years as a curriculum resource teacher, all of these experiences taking place in San Diego. This accumulation of understanding regarding the problems and issues in that school setting was seen as having had a positive effect in terms of the trainer/developer's knowledge of the system at both conceptual and strategy levels. The Vermont trainer/developer, although working in several school districts in a cooperative teacher education program which provided preservice students experience in public school programs, had as her primary workplace a university college of education. Thus, she was at least one step removed from the issues and problems faced daily by the teachers and others in the school systems with which she interacted. These differences in the trainer/developers, essentially institutional in nature, are believed to be related to the degree to which they were knowledgeable about and sensitive to the perceived reality of classroom teachers. There is some evidence to suggest that the California trainer/developer was more closely aligned with these perceived realities.

Although both trainer/developers demonstrated a repertoire of understandings related to teacher education, as evidenced in observed behavior and self-reports, the California trainer/developer appeared to have a more eclectic and less well-defined approach to training than his Vermont counterpart. The Vermont trainer/developer, by conviction based upon prior experience and training in special education, was more firmly disposed toward a single paradigm for training. This might be called a rational-empirical model dependent upon specification of outcomes prior to instruction, linearity of planning and execution, and accumulation of evidence related to the accomplishment of specified objectives. Although she appeared to become more flexible and accepting regarding other training models during the course of the IR&DT implementation period, there were repeated attempts on her part to recast the team's decisions regarding training into the rational-empirical framework.

Collaboration

As noted earlier, collaboration was hypothesized as being present in an IR&DT effort when there was parity among team members, equal responsibility in working through the r and d, working *with* as opposed to working *on* teachers, assumption of work by team members based upon their role expertise, assistance across roles as tasks were identified, and emergent or issue-specific leadership as opposed to designated or appointed leadership.

Findings demonstrated that, within the broad rubric of parity, i.e., equal ability to gain the attention of the team members, researcher members of both teams were likely to participate more extensively in team meetings than other *individual* team members because of their knowledge and skill related to research methodologies (the California researcher contributing 24.14 percent of the input across all team meetings and the Vermont researcher 26.15 percent). However, when teacher representation on the team was viewed as the product of all teachers representing one role function, the teacher input was higher than that of the researcher or trainer/developer (59.36 percent for the California team and 52.25 percent for the Vermont team). Regardless, the implementation of IR&DT demonstrates that the need for role expertise may be at odds with a simplistic notion of parity. For example, as suggested above, to deny team members the opportunity to learn from and react to the researcher during the research phase of their work, only to maintain some equality in terms of time and attention, would have been senseless. Parity had to be considered in concert with the needs of the team. The California and Vermont IR&DT teams attended systematically and sensitively to the issue of parity while at the same time acknowledging the need to provide for inclusion of certain "role" member skills when they were of potential utility.

Regarding responsibility for equal assumption of role-related functions in dealing with r and d problems, the two teams appeared to demonstrate different patterns of behavior. The California team was more participatory than the Vermont team in terms of r and d relevant interactions, whereas both teams were participatory in dealing with issues of collegiality and what might be termed personal support. Analysis of formal team meetings, interviews with participants, and analysis of correspondence indicated that the Vermont team depended to a considerably larger extent than the California team on the assumption that the responsibility for the r and d designs and final reports was that of the research and the trainer/developer. The California teachers actively participated in all phases of the r and d including report writing. Further, the California team engaged in more substantive and procedural discourse regarding r and d procedures and products (especially the formal, written ones) than the Vermont team.

The California team engaged in systematic discussion, formulation, review, critique, and revision cycles at almost every step of the IR&DT process, while the Vermont team only began to assume a systematic approach to their work when they entered the data collection step in their research.

What was seen, then, was collaboration at both sites but collaboration which included a more pronounced substantive focus in California. To illustrate, based on percent of total monitored talk segments for all IR&DT team members during the total IR&DT implementation period, the California team devoted 74 percent to research-related talk, 14 percent to development-related talk, and 12 percent to other talk. The Vermont team devoted 45 percent to research-related talk, 12 percent to development-related talk, and 42 percent to other talk.

Thus, while both teams achieved parity among team members, the California team demonstrated more equal assumption of r and d functions based on the individual team member's expertise, engaged in more systematic enactment of their respective roles, conducted an r and d effort that assumed a "work with" stance during more steps in the process, and worked with a leadership pattern vested in the researcher that was more substantively oriented than that of the Vermont team.

Problem Solving Focus

Relative to the problem focus for the r and d of the two teams, it is apparent that the California team's work as linked theoretically and practically to an issue which has a long history of attention from both research and conventional wisdom. On the other hand, the Vermont team's work had elements of historical attention (supportive instructional behavior) but conceptually depended upon a difficult-to-define human construct, mood. It might be concluded, therefore, that the California problem was a practice-related one with high visibility in local and national classroom settings whereas the Vermont problem was a person-related one which may or may not be found in subsequent inquiry to be central to the teaching-learning environment of the classroom.

Further, the California team made early and persistent attempts to determine, formally and informally, whether what they planned to study was as important to other teachers as it was to the teachers on the team. In contrast, the Vermont team presented a list of issues to teacher colleagues asking for a ranking of interest, but then engaged in more extensive systematic validation only as a consequence of Far West Laboratory technical assistance, which emphasized the need for validation.

Conducting Concurrent R and D

Both IR&DT teams exhibited enthusiasm for the possibility of temporary and conceptual linkage between the r and d they were expected to accomplish during the implementaion period. The inclusion of a trainer/developer on each team provided the groups with a persistent monitor of the entire implementaion process for potential development activities. Although in actuality development was given concerted attention only near the completion of the data collection stages of the research phase for both teams, there were repeated instances of attention to activities and procedures which might be used in the teams' training/development efforts from the beginning of the research effort, i.e., with the inception of question identification, particularly by the California team. As both teams began to consider systematically the training/development they would formulate, there was a consistent belief expressed that the procedures in which they, themselves, had engaged during the research phase would be powerful training opportunities for others. Consequently, as can be seen by examining the two teams' final training reports, both training programs included elements of the IR&DT process itself and the respective team's research procedures, as well as opportunities to examine and understand the team's research findings.

Thus, it can be concluded that the essential feature of concurrent attention to r and d was present in both teams. By this we mean that, in terms of team action, r and d overlapped conceptually such that a Venn diagram might illustrate properties which were in common from one phenomenon to another (research to development), but it also would illustrate properties of the same two phenomena which were separate. A more precise descriptor of what occurred might be "concurrent attention to and proximate implementation of r and d."

Maintaining the Integrity of the Classroom

Because much of conventional educational r and d was viewed as imposing artificial controls upon classrooms and persons in them, thereby transforming conventional aspects of a well-known social institution into those that were unrecognizable to practitioners, IR&DT has as an essential element the requirement that classrooms, teachers, and students be allowed to remain as natural as possible during the conduct of r and d.

Within the IR&DT strategy, it was believed that this element would be accomplished by ensuring that teacher sensitivity to classroom life was a major data source when decisions about r and d were made. This sensitivity was expected to result in greater than usual attention to the complexity of the classroom and reflection of that complexity in the data collection and intervention strategies formulated for the r and d.

This feature of IR&DT was realized at both sites. The two teams were resolute in their attention to maintenance of the classroom as a natural setting. Although observers were introduced into classrooms, a period of orientation and "getting acquainted" preceded data collection. Further, even the monitoring equipment (e.g., miniature lapel microphones for the California teacher subjects) was selected after a thorough search of available equipment with the principal criteria for use being the effectiveness of the equipment in terms of requirements of data collection and unobtrusiveness when in use.

IR&DT as an Intervention Strategy

One of the essential elements of IR&DT was recognition that participation in an IR&DT effort could serve as a change and/or professional development vehicle for the sites and the participants. Participation in IR&DT did appear to have consequences for individual participants and for cooperating institutional settings. It was shown that participants increased their awareness of educational options and possibilities partly as a consequence of the requirements of systematic inquiry into schooling. Although the evidence suggested that the Vermont team benefited more extensively on this dimension of the strategy, it should be remembered that the California team members, especially teachers, exhibited entry-level behaviors which might be termed more "professionally sophisticated" than those of the Vermont team members.

An intervention outcome that was sharply evident was the increased knowledge and skill regarding educational research and development exhibited by the participants. All members of both teams, through observation and self-reports, can be said to be more knowledgeable about, skillful in, and sensitive to research and development issues as a result of their participation in the implementation of IR&DT.

In addition, the historically persistent condition of teacher isolation was ameliorated for the participants. Teachers related one to another and to the researcher and trainer/developer in ways which were not typical. Systematic, focused, and interactive inquiry provided avenues of and for professional communication which had not been a usual pattern in their worklives. The institutional isolation, school from school and school from university, also was reduced to a degree. The concerns of the team and the actions upon those concerns "forced" the institutional relations which came about in the course of the implementation period.

Another intervention outcome was an increased belief that the work of other team members was of value and otherwise "prestigious" in their immediate workplaces and in the broader educational community. The combination of increased capacity to deal with r and d issues and the belief that the work which emerged out of that capacity was of positive value are seen as powerful antidotes to growing sentiments that teaching and teachers are of low status and low priority in terms of social action and reward systems at local and national levels of authority.

Although IR&DT did not have as an initial intention the significant alteration of professional practice by participants, such alteration did take place. Self-reports from participants indicated that teachers changed some of their instructional patterns, researchers learned and demonstrated new skills, trainer/developers revised and reordered certain beliefs and practices regarding teacher education, and so on. Some of these changes were a consequence of the *issue* under study in the teams' r and d efforts, some a result of the processes engaged in during such study, and some related to the requirements of *interaction* with other educators.

There also was an indication that participants began to rely less upon what might be called "conventional wisdom" and more upon prior research and/or expert testimony as their work proceeded. In both teams, although more markedly so for Vermont, initial discussions contained information more often from what individual participants had experienced than from findings of more systematic inquiries into the issues. Particularly true for teachers, less so for trainer/developers, and occasionally so for researchers, team members eventually came to question one another and others regarding the accuracy of statements, reports, formulations, and the like. It is believed that IR&DT contributed to this shift partly because of the requirements of conducting research and partly because of the technical assistance aspects of the implementation.

Judgment of IR&DT Teams' R and D Outcomes

A basic assumption which has persisted from the initial planning period through the implementation of IR&DT is that research and development conducted in this mode will provide useful knowledge and contribute to theory development. To judge the r and d outcomes of each team in respect to this assumption, two constructs provided appropriate guidance: "rigor," intended to convey strictly precise, *and* accurate adherence to scholarly inquiry in terms of methods and procedures; and "usefulness," meaning, to be of practical use in doing one's work.

Six juries were organized to judge the teams' r and d outcomes for rigor and usefulness. Each jury was comprised of three persons. Juries were organized to reflect particular biases from among the constituent users of educational r and d, each of whom was considered to be expert in his or her respective educational role: teachers, researchers, teacher educators, and staff developers. Juries included (1) a jury of three researchers that judged the rigor with which research had been conducted as reflected by the research reports; (2) a jury of three researchers that examined the degree to which research as reported contributed to new knowledge and/or theory development; (3) a jury of two teacher educators and a staff developer that judged the rigor of the training as reported; and (4) three juries (a teacher jury, a staff developer jury, and a teacher educator jury) that judged the r and d outcomes from each site—both research and training as reported—for usefulness to their constituents.

Each jury met separately for one day. All meetings were scheduled within a two-week period in February 1979. Jurors were asked (1) to develop criteria for either rigor or usefulness, whichever was the jury's focus; (2) to use these to make independent judgments of each team's r and/or d in comparison with what the juror knew to be typical of educational r and d; and (3) to bring criteria and judgments to the meeting. Meetings were audio-recorded and transcribed, and served as the basis for the reports of jury deliberations. In addition, each juror reviewed the report of the deliberations for his or her jury for purposes of accuracy.

Seven additional experts representing the same appropriate constituencies and six counterpart constituents from each team's site responded to items on a questionnaire in relation to the team's r and d reports.

As a result of the judging of the IR&DT teams' r and d outcomes by the juries and experts, conclusions can be drawn about the r and d outcomes resulting from use of the IR&DT strategy. In addition, because the juries were required to generate the criteria to be used in judging the teams' work, information also is available relative to the content and characteristics of these criteria. In turn, the judgmental criteria and the jury procedure provide an exemplary model for judging the outcomes of other educational r and d efforts.

What Was Learned About Implementing IR&DT

Six notable findings that have relevance for future applications of IR&DT emerged from the implementation study. These may be summarized as follows.

1. *The characteristics, skills, and previous experience of participants appear to affect the degree to which IR&DT is implemented, with high occurrence of/congruence with the essential features of the strategy. The presence of these features, in turn, is related to the rigor and usefulness of the r and d outcomes.*

Beginning with the orientation sessions and proceeding throughout the implementation period, the California IR&DT team dealt with r and d issues systematically, persistently, and methodically. The team's procedures also were characterized by high involvement of all team members at each stage of the process. This involvement took different forms—shared responsibility alternating with specific group-mandated assignments for certain tasks and with whole-group critique and revision—which, taken altogether, were linear and rational.

The Vermont team, again from the orientation period throughout the study, illustrated a more erratic, less rational pattern. Particularly during the early stages of the implementation period, the Vermont group's efforts were somewhat sporadic in terms of coming to grips with the essentials of the r and d process. The team's apparent preoccupation with the personal-social dimensions of its members' relationships may have influenced the degree to which it could effectively and efficiently accomplish its primary IR&DT missions: the formulation and conduct of r and d on teaching.

This raises the important question of why this difference was present. For the most part, this can be explained by looking at team member knowledge, skill, and performance.

As was noted earlier, the Vermont trainer/developer role was filled by two persons, one of whom replaced the original member three months into the implementation period. The first trainer/developer was characterized as being much more interested in human relations' processes than in educational research and development. He appeared to use the term "interactive" more in terms of team processes than for the interrelationship of r and d. In addition, he exhibited confusion as to which role functions were most appropriate to the IR&DT effort. The period of his membership on the Vermont team was significantly less task-oriented and IR&DT-specific than subsequent periods of the team's interaction. Because the period of his membership coincided with the critical research design formulation phase of IR&DT, upon which much, if not most, of the subsequent efforts were based, it is informally hypothesized that, had the second trainer/developer been a team member from the beginning of the effort, the consequences and processes of implementation would have been different.

Another phenomenon was the apparent reluctance of the researcher on the Vermont team to assume substantive leadership during the early research phase of the project. Although the researcher was acknowledged by the team members as the leader throughout the implementation period, the nature of his leadership was, for some time, more procedural and human-relations-oriented than it was research-oriented.

The relative differences between teacher members of the two teams, in terms of prior experience related to "special" innovative program activities, also are considered to be critical to the process and product of IR&DT. The California teachers had had experiences which were aligned with the assumed requirements of IR&DT—using teaching as a base for changing institutional behavior, responding to and engaging in externally-required information-gathering and report writing, working on school improvement projects, participating regularly in professional development activities, and the like. The idea that IR&DT was somehow "exotic" to the setting was expressed only minimally by the California teachers but was pronounced for the Vermont teachers. What might be concluded is that the IR&DT experience was better accomplished by persons, particularly teachers, who had had other similar experiences during the course of enacting their professional roles.

2. *Commitment to educational r and d and previous involvement in such efforts by the participating institutions also influences the conduct of IR&DT.*

There is believed to be a relation between institutional history and successful IR&DT based upon the data collected for the implementation study. The more successful team was located in an organizational context which was marked by decades-long attention to issues of professional development; curriculum revision; innovative program development, implementation, and evaluation; involvement in state and federal special programs; support of an organizational unit designed to support and encourage professional growth; and so forth. The Vermont team, however, was located in a setting which had a history of less attention to such issues. In California, then, there was a set of institutional norms, not present at all, in the Vermont context. For the Vermont team, it was necessary to *create* a new setting. In contrast, for California it was necessary to determine how best to *use* the accustomed setting.

3. *Orientation to IR&DT is important. It should be designed to fit the needs and context of the participating people and institutions. If the required participant skills do not exist, training in these skills should be included.*

The orientation sessions held prior to initiating IR&DT were found to be important. The differences between the two teams at the time of entry into IR&DT—these differences becoming more evident over time—suggest that the orientations which purposely were similar in content and process should have been conducted differently with different foci and different emphases. Although it was not conceived originally as such, IR&DT, like other school change efforts, appears to be situation specific. That is, knowledge of the context and of the participants should influence to a marked degree the nature and expected outcomes of IR&DT orientation. Most likely, such intervention should include the training of participants in the skills they lack, given what has been learned regarding the relation between appropriate participant characterisitcs and successful IR&DT.

4. *Technical assistance should be available throughout an IR&DT effort.*

Even the most exemplary schools and school systems often can be described correctly as "closed systems." Thus, introduction of external perspectives, input, and monitoring is desired in IR&DT regardless of the location of the effort and the surrounding support structures. From the beginning of the IR&DT experience, it was apparent that the technical assistance provided by the Far West Laboratory staff and a National Advisory Panel comprised of two researchers, a researcher/developer, and a teacher played an important role. The role played was what the term implies, assistance of a technical r and d nature. Occasionally, however, the role could be characterized as being more personal-professional. That is, in addition to offering r and d information and advice, it was beneficial to let the participants in the process know that "someone cared" about their efforts and to make public that caring. The importance of technical assistance of both types was seen during the implementation period in terms of the impact upon what was done, and how IR&DT members felt about what was done, and the rigor and usefulness of the outcomes.

5. *The typical time lag between research and development can be reduced with the IR&DT strategy.*

The implementation of IR&DT by the two teams demonstrated that IR&DT can reduce the typical time lag between production of research findings and development of training opportunities based on those findings. One reason for this reduction in time, it must be admitted, was the external imposition of contract requirements by Far West Laboratory which grew from its own contractual commitment with NIE. In addition to these externally imposed deadlines, dimensions of IR&DT also appear to have contributed to the reduced time lag. First, both teams believed that the research procedures and team interactions during the first phases of IR&DT were so beneficial to them that they included these aspects of the IR&DT effort in the training opportunities they developed. Therefore, the processes which were adopted for training were ones which were familiar, had been experienced, and were conceptualized as a consequence of that experience and familiarity. Second, since the trainer/developer was involved in the r and d process from the beginning, it was not necessary for a "naive" developer to engage in the difficult and arduous tasks of translating and transforming the research processes and findings for the purpose of formulating a development vehicle. This overlap of procedures and persons in the form of IR&DT membership and activities is seen as a powerful contribution to the much more efficient r and d cycle which was demonstrated during the implementation. However, all team members recommended that the time allotted to IR&DT be increased from 15 months to 24 months in future efforts. It is not known whether more time available would have enhanced the r and d outcomes but even a 24-month cycle would be significantly shorter than is typically the case.

Future Recommendations

Based on the overall findings and the information obtained in the IR&DT Study relative to the requirements of successful implementation/application of the IR&DT strategy, the following recommendations are advanced regarding the strategy.

Recommendation 1

> The IR&DT strategy should be used for conducting a portion of the educational r and d effort at the national, state, and local education levels. The more the r and d outcomes are intended to result in improvements in education that are to be used in classrooms by teachers, the more important the use of the strategy becomes.

The value and workability of the IR&DT strategy has been demonstrated in the implementations that were carried out for the purposes of the study reported herein. In particular, the California IR&DT team demonstrated the potential worth of the strategy to the field of education.

Given that an enactment of IR&DT at a high level as per the essential features of the strategy results in research outcomes that are considered to be the product of rigorous inquiry *and* are seen as *more* useful than most research outcomes by practitioners, IR&DT warrants use as an r and d process.

Further, regardless of the quality and worth of the products produced via IR&DT, the strategy has also been shown to be an effective mechanism for bringing about changes in people and institutions that previously have been difficult to effect. Such changes were particularly evident for the participants in the Vermont IR&DT implementation effort.

However, because of the limited length of the IR&DT Study and the use of only two implementation sites, questions remain regarding such factors as the permanence of the changes that occurred in institutions and in participants and the actual adaptation/use of the r and d outcomes.

Hence, there are limitations in the recommendation. We encourage the use of IR&DT to increase participation of teachers as equal partners in r and d, to increase the perceived usefulness of r and d, and to provide a powerful personal and institutional change strategy for school problem-solving. At the same time, we recognize that IR&DT should be considered as one of several viable r and d strategies. As indicated in the recommendation, a decision to use IR&DT should take into account the intended results of the r and d effort. For some knowledge and theory building purposes, IR&DT most likely is not the best r and d strategy to apply, but for others it most likely is. When making this decision, the goals of the proposed r and d effort should be taken into account. Regardless, teachers, researchers, trainer/developers (teacher educators and staff developers), and federal and state funding agencies are urged to consider IR&DT as an available and productive option for conducting educational r and d.

Recommendation 2

> Site and participant selection and/or training of participants prior to initiating IR&DT efforts are important antecedents to enactment of IR&DT in an "ideal" form. This is particularly important because ideal conduct of IR&DT is necessary for achievement of r and d outcomes that are more rigorous and more useful than "typical" educational r and d products.

The entry level skills and experiences of the California and Vermont IR&DT participants differed considerably. The California participants' r and d skills had been developed and applied on a regular basis in their respective positions in the school district. They had participated in the planning and implementation of several innovative classroom-based instructional programs and they were able to analyze and structure instructional programs in terms of various types of needs. The Vermont participants lacked most of these experiences and had had little recent training in research, development, or teaching skills.

Further, the institutional support system available in California was more extensive and facilitative than that in Vermont.

The differences both in the way the California and Vermont teams enacted the IR&DT strategy and in the outcomes of their r and d efforts also were marked, with the California team achieving a more "ideal" enactment of the strategy than the Vermont team, and the California research and training products receiving substantially higher rigor and usefulness ratings by other researchers, trainer/developers, and teachers.

However, in terms of professional growth and institutional change, the changes that occurred as a result of participation in the IR&DT effort were greater in Vermont than in California.

These data suggest that when r and d is being conducted for the purpose of contributing to the advancement of knowledge in the field of teaching (or in other areas of education), thereby necessitating high quality outcomes, the site(s) and participants should either possess the skills, knowledge, and support characteristics evidenced by the California team or, if such do not as yet exist prior to initiating IR&DT, training should be designed and conducted to build them.

If, on the other hand, the IR&DT strategy is being used for intervention purposes—that is, to bring about change in persons and institutions as a means for improving a local education program—one may intentionally elect to begin where persons and institutions are lacking in the "desired" skills. Even in this situation, orientation to IR&DT should be designed to provide experience in analyzing and restructuring programs and to acquaint the participants with what is to be done at each of the r and d steps to be carried out by the team. This is particularly important when the researcher on the team is lacking in r and d experience. Otherwise, the work of an IR&DT team could become of such low quality that the changes that did occur might not be desirable.

Recommendation 3

Some form of external review and assistance is recommended for all IR&DT efforts.

Three aspects of the IR&DT strategy make it essential to utilize external resources since each demands more expertise than one reasonably can expect to find on any given team. These aspects are: (1) the complexity of the problems teachers identify for study, (2) the use of multiple research strategies that most often are required by the problems that are selected, and (3) the ideological "shakeup" that is a "normal" occurrence in an IR&DT effort.

Both the California and Vermont IR&DT teams selected research issues that were challenging and complex. Arriving at operable, observable, measurable definitions/descriptions of variables such as distractions and coping strategies (in the California research) and mood and supportive instructional behaviors (in the Vermont research) was a difficult task. An important role in "tightening up" and improving the research design for both teams was provided by input from Far West Laboratory staff and the National Advisory Panel regarding identification of (a) research efforts in which similar variables had been studied, (b) strong and weak points in various definitions, (c) alternative ways to measure the variables, etc. Further, review and critique of the Vermont team's thinking regarding the variables to be studied and the procedures to be used to obtain information about them was considered essential to the quality of the r and d by the National Advisory Panel and Far West Laboratory staff and was seen as helpful by the Vermont team members, particulary the researcher.

As might be expected in a research study that is to take place in the "natural" classroom setting, the researcher on the California team found that he needed to utilize data collection and analysis methods with which he was unfamiliar. As a result, he asked Far West Laboratory staff to train him in ethnographic research methods. Such training was offered to the researcher and trainer/developer on both teams. It is expected that other IR&DT teams will need a similar capability to tap the skills of persons from a variety of research methodologies.

The professional growth that results from participation in an IR&DT effort already has been mentioned. As persons and institutions change, support, guidance, and reassurance are needed. Typically, such help is requested from and provided by people external to the immediate setting in which change is occurring. IR&DT teams need this help.

Recommendation 4

Changes in resource allocations (funding/budgetary policies) of federal, state, and local educational agencies will be necessary in order to utilize IR&DT extensively.

A major feature of IR&DT is that the question/problem that is the focus of the r and d effort is identified by the teachers on the team, usually in collaboration with other teachers in the school district(s). This requirement is imposed in order to increase the likelihood that the research issue will be of high interest and concern to teachers and to stress the problem-solving purposes of r and d.

However, including such a requirement in the IR&DT strategy places the strategy in confrontation with the funding procedures utilized by federal, state, and other funding agencies. Typically, a federal education agency, e.g., the National Institute of Education of United States Office of Education, or a state department of education issues a request for a proposal (RFP) to do work in a problem area that *already* has been stipulated. Further, in order to obtain funds to conduct r and d related to that problem, the applicant must indicate in advance what will be studied and how. These details of the r and d effort are even specified by the RFP.

Given these circumstances, it is inappropriate to utilize the IR&DT strategy. There is no guarantee that the specific problem identified by the federal or state agency will be of high priority (concern or interest) to teachers. Most often, prior to being funded, time and resources are not available to bring teachers, researchers, and trainer/developers together to "check out" the problem with other teachers, identify important variables (if such flexibility exists), or try out various data collection strategies to determine whether they interfere with the natural classroom setting.

To alleviate such hindrances to the use of IR&DT, we recommend that funding agencies increase the use of an already existing funding strategy—the planning grant—and, in addition, develop a new policy that allows at least a small portion of the educational r and d effort to be funded on the basis of the skills, experience, background, etc., of the persons and institutions that comprise a proposed IR&DT team.

In the first instance, the planning grant can be used to bring together an IR&DT team to identify a problem/question of high concern and interest to teachers and to design an r and d effort that responds to that problem. Just as the California and Vermont research designs were reviewed and critiqued by the NAP, the federal, state, or other funding agency could conduct reviews of an IR&DT team's design and determine whether to continue funding based on these reviews. The only difference between this use of a planning grant and its typical use might be in the lack of restrictions on the problem(s) to be studied. Otherwise, this approach uses a common funding tool.

In contrast, funding a team based on its composition—utilizing the site and participant criteria included in Recommendation 2 and the purposes for using IR&DT outlined in Recommendation 1—is a marked departure from typical procurement and funding procedures. Nonetheless, we encourage agencies to explore the possibility.

Another avenue for funding IR&DT efforts is redefinition of dollars and responsibilities attached to staff development, educational evaluation, and educational dissemination positions and practices in a local or intermediate educational agency. The intervention outcomes of IR&DT suggest that persons in these positions would bring about as much, and more likely more, improvement in education if they were assigned to carry out IR&DT efforts as part of their regular work in lieu of workshops, etc. Were this to occur, costs for teacher involvement would have to be considered. But, given that improvement/innovation is desired, reallocation of funds and personnel to support IR&DT teams warrants serious consideration.

Recommendation 5

IR&DT should be implemented and studied in settings with participants other than those involved in the original implementation.

IR&DT as an alternative mode for conducting education r and d had teaching as its substantive focus for this initial implementation of the strategy. Further, that focus was upon teaching in the early years of elementary school. The findings of the IR&DT Study suggest that IR&DT may be an appropriate mode for conducting r and d at other levels of schooling and with different foci. For example, problems of administration and leadership, curriculum revision, school organization, school-community relations, school system articulation, and the like could be the objects of IR&DT attention. In the event that such extensions of the strategy were put into place, the practitioner role members of IR&DT teams would change to include not only teachers but also administrators, central office staff, community members, and the like. It is considered desirable to determine the degree to which such alterations in membership and problem focus would support or modify the effects of IR&DT which are reported for the IR&DT Study.

Further, the implementation study did not discover as much about the impact upon institutions, particularly higher education institutions, as would be desirable. It is considered necessary to engage in both follow-up and newly-conceptualized studies to determine more precisely the immediate and long-term effects upon institutional settings. In regard to institutional participation in IR&DT it also is necessary to examine other organizational configurations. For example, what would be the consequences of using IR&DT as part of a school networking strategy? What IR&DT role functions could be provided by linkage agents between and among educational institutions? How would IR&DT impact upon institutional r and d if contained solely within an instituion of higher education (IHE) as opposed to IHE representatives working through IR&DT in a public elementary or secondary school? What would be the effect of IR&DT in secondary school settings?

A third issue related to future research is to provide more evidence regarding the findings reported herein. In a study with a larger set of IR&DT teams, some with teaching as focus and others not, would there be support for the elements and findings which were central to the initial implementation? Do the recommended site characteristics and participant role functions hold up as supportive components of IR&DT? These questions and others illustrate the need to obtain data in addition to those provided in this report.

It is believed that the process and product findings in this study support the need for continued investigation and demonstration of IR&DT. Also, it is believed that the study of such further efforts can rely upon many, if not all, of the procedures outlined in this study of IR&DT.

Chapter 16:

PROFESSIONAL DEVELOPMENT THROUGH INSERVICE THAT WORKS

Henrietta Barnes and Joyce Putnam

Like it or not, inservice education often has a bad name. And changing the name to professional development is not likely to make a difference. What might make a difference would be to change what is done in the name of inservice so that it can be the catalyst for improving teaching and learning in schools to meet the expectations of teachers, teacher educators, and public officials.

We contend that what teachers need is not simplistic answers to questions they have not asked, or solutions to problems they have not defined, but rather an enhancement, through inservice, of the capacity to think about teaching, to define their own problems, and to determine the validity of different instructional strategies for their own classroom practices. Teachers need not be technicians implementing someone else's ideas but thoughtful decision-makers who have multiple ways of reflecting on their own teaching practice.

In order for their decisions to be productive in terms of desirable pupil outcomes in affective, cognitive, and physical domains, the teacher must have broad conceptual schemes for action. These schemes need to embody both the theoretical knowledge of the researcher and theoretician and the teacher's own practical wisdom. In short, the teacher must be a student of teaching and learning, committed to continuous professional development. Concurrently, teacher educators must be committed to studying teaching and learning in ways that allow them to learn from and with teachers about classroom realities.

If one assumes that the primary goal of inservice education is to engage teachers and teacher educators in a process of mutual professional development, then one approaches that task in a collegial way. This mode must provide both teachers and teacher educators with opportunities to learn from one another, and to discover that learning together may encourage new ways of thinking about teaching and teacher education. It must also be intrinsically rewarding for both teachers and teacher educators if they are to value such collaboration as a viable inservice model for professional development.

Faculty at Michigan State University have developed such a *collegial* model for inservice education. It has as its goal professional development for all participants through an emphasis on reciprocity and reflection. This model is built on several assumptions. First, teachers should be involved in every phase of teaching, dissemination, and curriculum development. Second, both teachers and teacher educators have much to gain from the study of the impact of various theoretical conceptions of classroom teaching on practice. They can both learn from studying ideas together. Third, teachers and teacher educators both have specialized, but different, expertise which can illuminate the practical study and research of teaching and learning. Finally, teachers and teacher educators can learn more productively together than they can separately since their collective efforts create a synergistic effect.

Professional growth, then, is the goal, and inservice education the means through which continuing expertise in teaching is developed. This chapter describes the necessary criteria for the establishment of a collegial model and a released time system for accomplishing professional growth. The conceptual basis of the model is outlined. The remaining bulk of this chapter outlines the various phases of the model giving appropriate attention to the critical attributes of an inservice "delivery system," designed to improve teacher effectiveness and satisfaction.

Establishment of Collegial Relationship

A major premise of this model is that teachers and teacher educators must establish collegial relationships. This belief is based on a recognition that substantive change is rarely accomplished by an outsider telling a teacher what he/she ought to be doing. Teachers need to receive support for their daily struggles, and encouragement from someone they trust if they are to be expected to try new responses to teaching demands. We believe support and encouragement can be provided by teacher educators committed to establishing collegial relationships with teachers.

Historically, teachers and teacher educators have not enjoyed such collegial relationships. At least four factors contribute to this state of affairs. First, both groups tend to have negative stereotypes about each other, such as, the "ivory towered" professor and the "mindless" teacher. Second, neither group is seen as credible in the eyes of the other group. Third, there is a lack of reciprocity in relationships between the two groups. Teacher educators tend to be perceived as the helpers (givers, tellers) and teachers as the ones in need of help (takers, learners). Seldom are requests initiated in the opposite direction. The notion that teacher educators gain from the relationship has had little credibility with teachers or teacher educators. Finally, both groups hold assumptions about each other that do not facilitate the establishment of collegial relationships. Modifying non-facilitative assumptions and stereotypes through the establishment of mutual credibility and reciprocity is essential to productive working together. The strengthening of facilitative, or alteration of non-facilitative assumptions, is a continuing process affecting both strategies and outcomes.

Assumptions of both teachers and teacher educators must be carefully examined. The belief that both are capable professionals concerned about improving their teaching effectiveness should be encouraged. Other assumptions about teachers and teacher educators that should be fostered include: (1) individuals need to feel respected and appreciated as contributing members of a team, (2) individuals have diverse strengths to contribute to a joint enterprise, and (3) earned membership in a group project fosters intrinsic valuing of cooperative endeavors.

The development of mutual credibility is essential to this model. Credibility of teacher educators with teachers can be initially established through their willingness to "hang around" in classrooms, getting to know teachers' and students' behaviors and needs, and providing another pair of hands for any tasks that need doing. The presence of the teacher educator being there and working with teachers in their classrooms establishes a kind of credibility that is critical. Being able to offer and demonstrate alternative teaching actions is also important. Empathy for the teacher's daily demands probably cannot be built in a more productive manner. Teachers can establish their credibility with teacher educators as well through the sharing of their reflections of teaching situations, their concern for students' needs, and their desire to learn new ways of thinking and doing.

As both groups learn more about each other, negative stereotypes tend to disappear. The perception that teachers are technicians and teacher educators are "experts" is one sterotype, however, which may require continued dialogue. This stereotype is perpetuated by both groups. Teachers typically defer to teacher educators, and teacher educators, in turn, are often willing to be seen as "experts." In reality, both groups have expertise in differing but important areas of teaching.

Establishment of Released Time System

One of the most important organizational structures required for any inservice teacher education effort is related to the challenge of making inservice activities available at a time when teachers are fresh and relatively free from other distractions. Teachers and teacher educators alike lament the typical "after-school workshop" which reaches teachers when they are already at a point of overload. Both groups generally indicate that the fatigue and stress levels of teachers at that time of day are such that even the most motivating content presented by the most dynamic of teacher educators is less than effective.

Teachers are anxious to have "prime time" inservice teacher education; that is, inservice during teachers' regular work hours. On the other hand, many teachers will not participate in released time inservice unless there is some assurance that they will not return to a chaotic classroom created by "substitutes." Thus, teachers need to be not only physically released from their normal duties, but mentally released from the worry that their classrooms will not proceed productively without them. Finally, they need to know that they are not having to work twice as hard to get the released time. Most teachers will say that if they have to do all the planning, prepare all the materials, and have everything ready for someone else to use with their classes while they are gone, they would rather stay in their classrooms and do the teaching themselves. The extra work it takes to prepare for a substitute is usually not seen as worth the released time it produces. The primary challenge of any delivery system, therefore, is the development of an organizational system which makes qualitative released time a reality.

Michigan State University has utilized a unique procedure for providing for the mental as well as the physical released time teachers require for inservice teacher education. By combining a preservice elementary education program with the inservice teacher education program, the educational opportunities of both groups can be optimized. Some background may be useful at this point to clarify the MSU arrangement. A preservice elementary education program has been developed through a six-year cooperative effort involving Lansing teachers and administrators,

MSU undergraduate students in elementary education, and MSU faculty. This program, which is largely field-centered, features unified content-methods and practice, and foundational principles which are systematically integrated throughout the students' course work and field experience. Students are admitted into the program as sophomore pre-interns after participating in a detailed selection process. During their sophomore year, pre-interns spend two to three half-days per week in schools performing general instructional tasks and instructing small groups of students in content related to the campus content and methods courses. During their junior year, the pre-intern field experience increases in amount of time spent and complexity of tasks performed as well as responsibilities assumed. By the third term of their junior year, pre-interns are spending four half-days a week in school and have taught both small and large groups in all content areas under teacher or university supervision. By the fall term of their senior year, students who are now in their formal internship experience are ready to assume full responsibility for at least two half-days of complete instruction. When they begin a "normal" full day student teaching experience, normally during the second or third term of their senior year, interns are ready to assume complete instructional responsibility for planning and actual instruction for the entire day for the minimum ten week internship experience.

The high level of expertise exhibited by these undergraduate students is due in large part to the assignment of a field instructor to each student. This MSU supported staff member performs a number of valuable services for interns, teachers, and the program. Critical among the tasks performed is the supervison of planned instruction, classroom management, and personal interactions with immediate constructive feed-back and life-long learning skills. The field instructor provides necessary linkages between the university and the public schools and between theory and classroom practices. Because interns have demonstrated their ability to participate as full team members with their cooperating teachers, many of the problems usually associated with released time for inservice teacher education are eliminated. Because the undergraduate intern begins teaming with the cooperating teacher on the opening day of school, he or she is accepted by the children, parents, and other staff as a regular teacher. Inservice schedules are coordinated so that field instructors can be in the building and available in classrooms to assist their interns if problems should arise. Because inservice sessions are held *within* the school building, teachers are always available to return to their classrooms if serious problems come up.

While both teachers and interns benefit from this team teaching arrangement, others profit as well. The presence of the intern provides unique opportunities for *analysis and evaluation* of teaching practices (see Chapter 11 for further elaboration of a clinical supervison model). Through the negotiation of objectives and strategies, both teachers and interns are encouraged to examine their assumptions and procedures in terms of desired pupil outcomes. Children also benefit from this arrangement since there is another concerned individual to help provide educational experiences for them. Children are not only exposed to different and sometimes new ways of teaching and learning, but they are generally able to receive more individual assistance with particular learning problems. (A more complete description of this program—*Toward Excellence in Elementary Education*, is available through the College of Education at Michigan State University.)

Conceptual Basis of the Collegial Model Delivery System

Inasmuch as the vehicles one uses and the structures one creates depend largely on the outcomes one has in mind, it is important to describe those goals which motivated our development of this released time delivery system. First, we wanted both pre- and inservice teachers to be autonomous decision makers regarding their curricula. It is our firm belief that teachers are the best judges of what to teach and how to teach it to their particular set of learners. Second, we wanted teachers to become life-long learners who had a sense of professional competence and the feelings of pride that accrue from that knowledge. Third, we wanted an opportunity for teacher educators and beginning teachers to gain a reality base for their conceptions of professional teaching.

If one assumes that a professional teacher is a person who has special knowledge, then one must ask not only what that knowledge is but how one comes to know. What does it mean to "know" something? According to Piaget, one knows a thing when one can do something or act on the basis of information one has (Furth, 1970). Further, one comes to know and be able to do as a result of the experiences one has. The more concrete, relevant, and similar initial learning experiences are to the real world setting in which that knowledge can be used, the more likely it is that the knowledge will be useful to the learner. Knowledge which is useful for developing professional teaching competence, then, would be information accumulated from experiences designed to help teachers translate relevant concepts into internalized action schemes. Figure 1 illustrates critical phases involved in this process of development.

FIGURE 1

Phase One		Phase Two	Phase Three
"Learning About" in Real World Context	plus	Directed Practice and Reflection in Real World Setting	Integrated Decision Making and Action in the Real World Classroom

Our pursuit of the goals stated earlier has led to an elaboration of these phases into a professional development model for initial and continuing teacher education. The delivery systems utilized have emerged from the need to provide experiences designed to promote teacher development through these phases. The model encompasses professional development for preservice teachers, inservice teachers, and teacher educators. Figure 2 illustrates this professional development model for teacher education.

Explanation of Phases in the Model and Related Delivery Systems

Our goal of educating professionals to become more autonomous decision-makers who act in thoughtful and considerate ways as they plan for and enact their professional roles is achieved through a carefully sequenced set of educational experiences. For preservice teachers these experiences are designed on the assumption that abstract theoretical explanations can be transferred to the complex environment of most public school classrooms when they are presented initially in and related to a real world context through opportunities for practice. Such an instructional approach presents not only relevant content but also methods for teaching and opportunities for practice in a unified sequence. For example, teachers might study fractions (content), check to be sure they could work with them themselves, plan lessons to teach fractions to a group of children in their classrooms, teach the planned lesson, receive feedback from others, and reflect on the experience in a continuous learning model. This unified content/methods and practice sequence is quite the opposite of many college course sequences which typically teach all the content (usually done by a department or college outside of Education) with methods taught by yet another instructor at a later time, and practice waiting until the final term of student teaching (in the case of inservice or graduate work it is usually not provided at all) when all content must be simultaneously taught to an entire class.

We have found that an instructional sequence which gradually introduces a teacher to a content area, or sets of related content areas such as

FIGURE 2

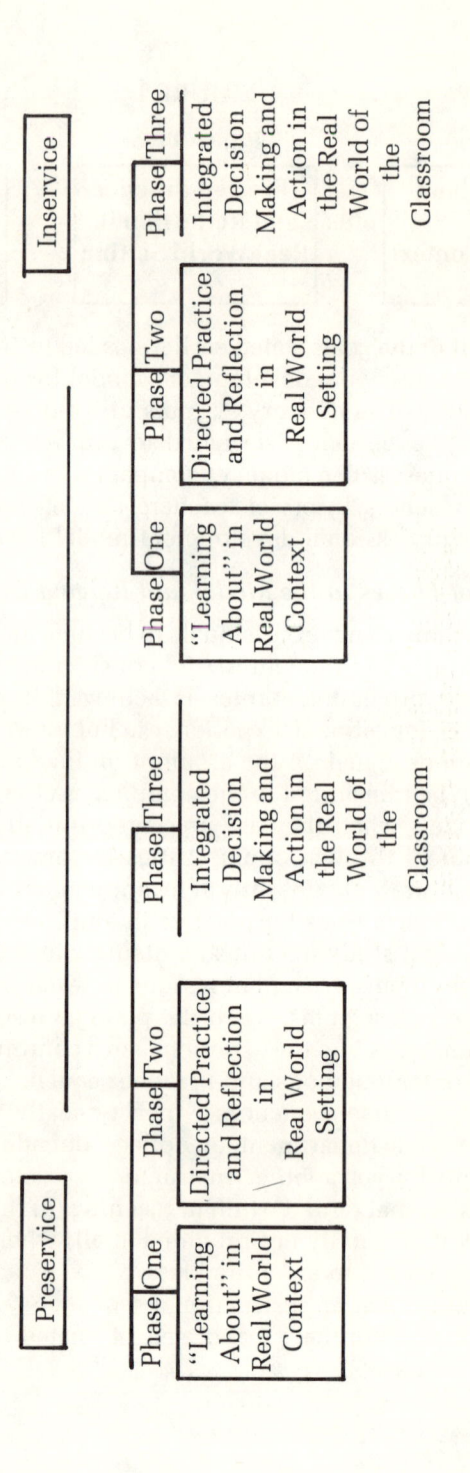

Preservice		
Phase One: "Learning About" in Real World Context	**Phase Two**: Directed Practice and Reflection in Real World Setting	**Phase Three**: Integrated Decision Making and Action in the Real World of the Classroom

Inservice		
Phase One: "Learning About" in Real World Context	**Phase Two**: Directed Practice and Reflection in Real World Setting	**Phase Three**: Integrated Decision Making and Action in the Real World of the Classroom

instructional design, mathematics, or classroom management, and allows for the sequential accommodation of that content through gradually intensified field experiences is effective for *both* pre- and inservice teachers. If we want teachers to adopt new ways of thinking and doing, we must facilitate initial learning about these ideas and provide ample opportunities for suitable practice and feedback.

The experiences are intended to be additive. Thus, it is the task of the teacher education program to sequence instruction and experiences so that each set of experiences can cumulatively enrich the teacher's professional abilities. Nothing is taught in isolation. Rather, teachers are expected to apply knowledge learned and internalize patterns of action. What begins as separate content gradually becomes autonomous behavior grounded in theory and a conscious rationale.

Phase One: "Learning About" in Real World Context

Regardless of the content being taught, certain conditions must be present if the "Learning About" step is to accomplish its purpose. These conditions are:

1. *Clear content definitions* (facts, concepts, principles, ideas, and skills) must be presented.
2. *Real world exemplars* and non-exemplars must be available. These should be as concrete as possible; however, films, pictures, and models can be used initially, if necessary.
3. *Discrimination practice* should be provided. Here the learner is choosing between exemplars and non-exemplars to demonstrate concept acquisition. Again, if real world examples are not accessible, role plays and simulations are useful in increasing the likelihood of transfer.
4. *Opportunities to socialize* about the new learning are essential for concept acquisition. Sharing perceptions and clarifying points of disagreement are important as teachers fit new content into existing conceptions of teaching.

In Figure 3, the various formats and activities involved in *phase one* ("learning about" the content and process of teaching in a real world context) are illustrated in a matrix scheme. The activities can occur in large groups, subsets of a large group, small groups, dyads, triads, or on an individual basis. Possible instructional activities include: discussions, readings, speakers, lectures, films, role playing, simulations, observation, writing, sharing, demonstrations, interviews, and teaching others. Since it is important that theoretical work be tied to classroom practice, both teacher educators and pre- and inservice teachers need opportunities for common classroom observation. Thus, some sessions must be held in schools where access to classrooms is available to teachers, teacher educators, and preservice teachers. Appropriate space for feedback on these classroom experiences must also be available.

FIGURE 3

Instructional Activities

Group Types	Discussion	Readings	Speakers	Lectures	Films	Role Plays	Simulation	Observation	Writing	Sharing	Demonstration	Interviews	Teach Others
Large Group	X		X	X	X		X				X	X	X	X
Subsets of Large Groups		X				X	X			X	X		X
Small	X	X	X	X	X	X	X	X	X	X	X	X	X
Dyads	X	X				X	X	X	X	X	X	X	X
Triads	X	X				X	X	X	X	X	X	X	X
Individuals		X			X			X	X			X	X

A variety of strategies are planned employing various combinations of group types and instructional activities which promote learning of theoretical constructs and their practical applications. For example, role playing done in small groups, triads, and dyads is helpful in learning procedures (e.g., steps for no-lose conflict resolution), gaining skill in practical application (e.g., responding constructively to participants' comments), and understanding the effects of a strategy as a participant. Classroom demonstrations observed by small groups, triads, or dyads, help teachers by providing concrete examples of theoretical constructs being studied. Abstract ideas such as Piaget's descriptions of how children think when they are at various developmental stages are much easier to comprehend when a teacher is able to actually question children who are at different stages. Having concrete experiences with different levels of thinking, the teachers are then better able to transfer Piaget's ideas to the selection of content and activities for children.

Phase Two: Directed Practice and Reflection

As new knowledge and skill are acquired, it is important that teachers have opportunities to apply this knowledge and skill in real world settings. It should be kept in mind, however, that the teachers tend to move back and forth between the "learning about" phase and the "directed practice and reflection" phase as they become more sophisticated about their practice.

The necessary conditions for the directed practice and reflection phase include initial practice and reflection.

1. Initial practice is directed and carefully planned for a "simplified" real world setting. That is, lessons are taught to small groups of students, and teachers are responsible for less of the total situation than would normally be their concern. As applications of the content become more familiar, the size and complexity of the teaching situation is gradually increased.
2. Through opportunities for reflection, teachers can consider alternative applications of the newly acquired knowledge and skill and weigh the potential outcomes that might be expected for each. Initial classroom trials are accompanied by opportunities for corrective feedback. Teachers need to know what they are doing well, and what they are doing not so well. Whether lessons are successful or not, reflection helps teachers see both intended and unintended consequences of instruction. Opportunities for feedback and reflection are essential to the development of the self-evaluation that is prerequisite to autonomous decision making.

The importance of directed practice and reflection to the ultimate goal of autonomous decision making and action must not be overlooked. Practice as used here means the implementation *in a school setting* of a particular concept, principle, theory, or skill which was the focus of instruction during phase one—"learning about." Implementation activities include: instructing students, role playing, demonstration, simulations, and on-site planning which allows for assessment and evaluation of curriculum, environment, materials, and discussion.

Instructing students as a practice activity is necessary for *teacher educators* as well as pre/inservice teachers. Instructing students allows teacher educators as well as pre/inservice teachers to have the opportunity to 1) increase skill levels and self confidence, 2) reality test theoretical ideas, 3) note *unintended* outcomes and/or necessary prerequisites, and 4) have a concrete experience as a basis for reflection.

In addition to the pupils and pre/inservice teachers who participate in these practice activities, teacher educators and one or two other pre/inservice teachers are frequently included. According to interview and questionnaire data, teacher educators, preservice and inservice teachers report that having another adult formally involved in team teaching or observing a practice lesson contributes significantly to an individual's growth.

The dyad and triad formats for directed practice activities are also beneficial to children. For example, when a field instructor, inservice teacher, and preservice teacher collaboratively plan, teach, and reflect on learning outcomes, all three participants grow professionally. In addition, the pupils benefit from participating in experiences which are the result of the collaborative work of professionals.

Reflection as used here means thinking about intended and unintended lesson outcomes of practice activities which are *directly related* to the content studied in phase one. While most teachers or teacher educators engage in reflection by themselves, (often in nonschool settings e.g., driving to school, doing the dishes, waiting to get a car repaired), such reflection frequently is not tied to specific theoretical constructs. Thus, improvement of teaching practice is less systematic than it might be. Reflection on one's practice is seen as an important contributor to the achievement of the goal of autonomous decision-making and action. Phase two activities are designed to provide opportunities for structured reflection. These reflection activities include discussions, stimulated recall, role play, writing, and sharing.

As can be seen in Figure 4, reflective activities usually occur in dyadic, triadic, or small group formats. It is in these settings that the teamed practice experience actually pays off. One member of the discussion group can act as the reflection stimulator for another member of the team. The reflection stimulator can ask clarifying questions, take part in a role play, share feelings and perceptions, and assist with tying the real world experience to theoretical constructs. Pre- and inservice teachers report that role plays done with a person who is knowledgeable about the content being studied and who was present during a practice session are helpful in learning alternative teacher behaviors, understanding a student's point of view, and increasing teacher skillfulness.

FIGURE 4

Instructional Activities

Group Types	Instructing Children	Discussion	Role Plays	Simulation	Writing	Sharing About Practice Experience	Demonstration	On Site Planning	Listening/Viewing Audio or Visual Tapes
Large Group						X			
Subsets of Large Group						X			
Small	X				X	X	X		X
Dyads	X	X	X	X	X	X	X	X	X
Triads		X	X	X	X	X	X	X	X
Individuals	X				X			X	X

Phase Three: Integration into Decision Making and Action

The goal of phases one and two is a teacher who has integrated relevant content into a body of professional knowledge which can be represented as integrated decision-making and action. Persons who have achieved this level are characterized as flexible and articulate about the lessons they teach. They have a body of knowledge at an *operative* level. They can make efficient and accurate decisions about *when* and under *what circumstances* various alternatives are most appropriate. They are intentional in their behavior and objective in their problem identification and solution. They can indicate their professional needs and use resources efficiently and well.

As content is integrated at this level, teacher education relationships assume a somewhat different character. Interactions function on a level of reciprocity not entirely possible before. Participants now have varying levels of expertise and can better provide mutual support and reinforcement for each other. Positive reinforcement of particular behaviors on an intermittent schedule may be suitable; however, personal satisfaction and spontaneous sharing will generally maintain desired behaviors.

Figure 5, Integrated Decision Making and Action in the Real World, is an illustration of the activities which need to occur to support the transition to and maintenance of this phase. These activities include: 1) self-evaluation, sometimes making use of another adult to help sort information; 2) problem identification and solutions; 3) sharing practical experiences; 4) initiating requests for feedback; 5) demonstrations of teaching for dissemination to other teachers and teacher educators; and 6) teaching others.

FIGURE 5

Delivery Systems for Integrated Decision Making and Action in Real World

Activities

Group Types	Self Evaluation	Problem Identification and Solutions	Development of Support Systems	Intermittent Reinforcement	Sharing About Practical Experience	Initiating Request for Feedback	Demonstration	Teach Others
Large Group			X					X
Subsets of Large Group			X			X	X	
Small		X	X		X	X	X	X
Dyads	X	X	X	X	X	X	X	X
Triads		X	X	X	X	X	X	X
Individuals	X	X	X	X		X		

Development of Professional Competence

Inasmuch as teaching others has proved to be especially effective as an instructional delivery system, it warrants further elaboration. As individuals integrate new knowledge into their existing conceptual schemas for teaching, we see the initial level of integrative decision-making in operation. Through their concrete experiences of "learning about" and "directed practice and reflection," teachers can apply the knowledge acquired to their classroom teaching situations. They tend, however, to limit their use of this new knowledge to lessons and uses practiced during the "directed practice" stage. They are limited in their ability to articulate a rationale that goes much beyond their initial insights as it relates directly to their own teaching situation. That is, they have not acquired a sense of professional competence that allows them to state with assurance the advantages, disadvantages, intended outcomes, and reasons for choosing to teach as they do. They tend to be tentative in their recommendations, limited in their ability to encourage others to try similar approaches, and uncertain about how various ideas would work for others. Bound by their past experience, their autonomy may be restricted to the areas of success they have personally achieved.

The process of teaching others has the potential of providing an expanded knowledge and sense of professional competence not otherwise possible. The demand to teach others what one knows requires the teacher to reconsider the knowledge she or he has and to organize it conceptually so that it can be translated for others. Having to fit knowledge into reasonable applications for new and different situations, different from one's own, forces a level of conceptual understanding not achieved through personal experiences alone. The flexibility one develops through such a process encourages a level of sophistication in knowledge and use that can only be characterized as professional. The teacher, thus, knows not only what works for him or her, but *how and under what circumstances it might work for a variety of others.*

Thus, one engages in a whole new process of "learning about" which leads to practice of a broader range of applications at a more sophisticated level. The level of autonomy in teaching decision making and action is similarly more flexible, integrated and rich in educational outcomes. Figure 6 illustrates the spiral process that is operational when teachers teach others an instructional delivery system.

In summary, we have presented a view of a professional development model for teacher education which is built on the assumption that the activities selected, the way in which teacher education plans are made and carried out, whether for pre- or inservice teachers or teacher educators, must reflect the outcomes one hopes to achieve. In the case described, that outcome is increased feelings of professional competence, belonging and worth for all participants, prospective and practicing teachers as well as prospective and practicing teacher educators. A collegial model which emphasized reciprocity and reflection has been designed to achieve this outcome.

FIGURE 6
Levels of Professional Competence

Level One: Initial Learning	Initial "Learning About" in real world context	Initial directed practice and reflection in real world setting	Integration with decision making and use in real world classroom
Level Two: Internalized Learning for Self	"Learning About" more elaborate conceptual schemes	Practice and reflection for self is more complex and sophisticated	Integration is more autonomous, activities are more complex, elaborate, and better integrated and reflection is self-initiated
Level Three: Ability to Teach Other	"Learning About" how to adapt knowledge to fit new and different teaching situations	Practice and reflection on teaching others forces expansions of possibilities and greater flexibility	Autonomous decision making reflects ability to use content in many different ways to meet needs of others

Teaching Others

REFERENCES

..Furth, H. G. *Piaget for teachers.* Englewood Cliffs, N.J.: Prentice-Hall, 1970.

Chapter 17:

Achieving the Goals of P.L. 94-142 Through School Focused Inservice Education: Implications for Leadership

Dean Corrigan

Introduction

The quest for equity and quality in education took a quantum leap foward with the passage of the *Education for All Handicapped Children Act*, Public Law 94-142 in November of 1975.

This chapter identifies key educational concepts in P.L. 94-142, describes some of the reforms needed in schools to implement these concepts, and draws implications for leadership in *school-focused* inservice education to bring about these reforms.

The Promise of P.L. 94-142

In my opinion, this is the most important piece of educational legislation passed in recent history. It has far-reaching implications for all levels of education and it could be the vehicle through which education emerges more truly as a profession—that is, if educators can develop the knowledge, skill, and courage to implement the concepts in it. It should be noted that the Education of All Children's Act, P.L. 94-142, passed the Congress with a 404-7 vote in the House and 87-7 vote in the Senate. Educators can undertake the goals of P.L. 94-142 knowing they have a clear mandate from Congress to do so.

Basically, this act must be considered a piece of Civil Rights legislation and cannot be fully understood except from this perspective. Review of the congressional testimony on P.L. 94-142 indicates that the basic rationale in support of providing access to educational opportunity for persons with handicaps is that they are human beings living in America and therefore have a right and access to educational opportunity, even if it costs more. The roots of this act are found in the Civil Rights movement of the 60's. The rhetoric of human rights is now being written into the legal and the legislative structures of this land; e.g., handicapped, racial integration, consumer advocacy, women's rights, deinstitutionalization of prisons and mental health centers, and senior citizens rights.

Perhaps the most significant aspect of P.L. 94-142 is that it reminds Americans that in a democracy the education of other people's children is as important as the education of their own. The act calls on educators to eliminate isolation of the handicapped, the prejudice and discrimination that isolation breeds, and the mockery that this isolation makes of the fundamental right of *access* to equal educational opportunity.

P.L. 94-142 will require social, political, and economical reforms as well as educational reforms. If we ever needed a specific example of the use of education as an instrument for social progress, this act is it.

The Paradox of P.L. 94-142

At this stage in the implementation of P.L. 94-142, it is vital that the public and the members of the education profession realize the paradox that exists. This act, which has been hailed as the Magna Carta for all handicapped Americans, has created an anomalous situation. A society which has kept its schools as relatively closed institutions, is now asking these same schools and the educators who staff them to become this country's primary instrument for social progress. When the current state of our educational system is examined in the light of the requirements of P.L. 94-142, it is realized that massive reforms will be needed not only in the kind of teachers who staff the schools, but in the nature of the school itself. Today's schools are not designed to achieve the objectives of P.L. 94-142 and today's teachers have never been prepared for the responsibilities it expects of them. Such complex educational functions require a high level of professional knowledge and skill, and the conditions which enhance professional practice.

To add a sense of urgency to the task, Reynolds (1978) reminds us that events and needs relating to P.L. 94-142 are already running far ahead of the necessary changes in training programs—literally hundreds of thousands of teachers and related professionals are being required, at this moment, to undertake duties for which they are unprepared. Unfortunately, the precious time being squeezed out of the educational system for inservice education to meet the educational imperatives of P.L. 94-142 has thus far focused primarily on how to "fill out the forms" for the

"IEP's" and set up the mechanisms of due process hearings. The lofty educational purposes for which P.L. 94-142 was created are in danger of getting lost in the paper shuffle.

A review of the key concepts in P.L. 94-142 dramatizes the need for comprehensive school reforms and inservice education for teachers to bring about these reforms.

Key Concepts in P.L. 94-142

P.L. 94-142 provides for identification of handicapped children, assessment, and placement in programs with individual treatment plans. There is also evaluation of progress with assurance that the program is in the least restrictive environment with procedural safeguards which allow parents to be consulted at each important step in program development.

The purpose of the act is to assure that all handicapped children have available to them, within the time periods specified, a free, appropriate public education which emphasizes special education and related services designed (1) to meet their needs, (2) to assure that the rights of handicapped children and their parents or guardians are protected, (3) to help states and localities provide for the education of all handicapped children, and (4) to assess and assure the effectiveness of efforts to educate handicapped children.

The Individualized Education Program (IEP) is defined in Section 602 of P.L. 94-142, as "a written statement for each handicapped child developed in any meeting by a representative of the local education agency or an intermediate educational unit who shall be qualified to provide, or supervise the provision of, specially designed instruction to meet the unique needs of handicapped children; the teacher; the parents or guardian of such child; and, whenever appropriate, such child (Federal Register, 1976, p. 4). Thus we see that the current law will require detailed record-keeping and systematic notification of parents along each of the steps necessary.

For years, we have talked about individually designed education, but P.L. 94-142 requires it. If such individualized education is not provided, due process procedures are described which offer parents legal alternatives to insure an individualized education for their children. It is critical to note that the legislation talks about individualized programs and individualized plans, not just individualized instruction.

Another goal we have discussed for years is parent-school interaction. This act requires a sign-off by the child's parent, guardian or surrogate on the individualized plan. These child-parent-teacher relationships which are developed starting with the "child find" will be critical in achieving the goals of this act and restoring the public's confidence in its schools.

The beneficiaries of this act are 12% of the human beings in the United States between the ages of three and twenty-one. At this point each state has been expected to complete a "child find" and provide services for the age group five to seventeen. By 1982, the age range receiving services should be extended to include persons ages three through twenty-one. Since many agencies work with these age groups, school personnel must now view themselves as part of a human service delivery system rather than as a school system.

The act uses the terminology "least restrictive environment" and if other settings are used, movement to such settings must be justified. The implications of using the regular classroom are enormous, not the least of which is that all educators—regular classroom teachers, counselors, administrators, and other support personnel—must now be educationally prepared to work with persons with a handicap. This will call for a change in roles of all education personnel and especially a change in role for special educators.

These concepts have far-reaching implications for the schools.

Reforms Needed in Schools

P.L. 94-142 calls for free, appropriate public education for all.

A number of fundamental changes must occur in the current school setting to make a reality of the concept of free *appropriate* public education.

(1) We must eliminate the labeling and classification of children, the social stigma that this labeling produces and the notion that schools ought to function as screening stations for other institutions.

Instead, we must develop schools based on the principle of "no rejects"—schools based on the firm assumption that every human being has a right to an education and the right to be treated as a person (as a subject not an object or a symbol on a chart or a category in a student grouping structure.)

(2) We must eliminate the marking system and the illegitimate comparisons it makes, the pressure it creates, and the failure it produces.

Instead, we must develop a continuous progress reporting system with diagnostic profiles describing each student's human variability, exceptionality, and intellectual-personal growth.

(3) We must eliminate the over-reliance on normative testing and the

misinterpretation and misuse of intelligence, achievement, and aptitude tests.

Instead, we must develop criterion or domain-referenced evaluation systems in which the concepts of expectancy and capacity are related more to access to competent teaching and adequate educational resources than inherent individual learner traits.

(4) We must eliminate overcrowding and the resulting class loads, easy anonymity and shallow teacher-pupil contacts, the objectivity model fostered by a mechanical approach to accountability which prevents meaningful relationships from developing among administrators, teachers, students, parents and the "right answer syndrome" which discourages values clarification and risk-taking activities.

Instead, we must develop the kind of personalized relationships between teachers and students in which students are free to say out loud what they do not know as well as what they do know; a relationship based on the realization that academic freedom for teachers and students is reciprocal. One cannot exist in an educational community without the other.

(5) We must eliminate curricular tracking, the caste system it fosters, and the grade level lock-step which ignores what we know about the ways in which unique selves develop and learn.

Instead, the educational setting should be organized so that students know what they can do to achieve a *success* experience. The methods used to differentiate instruction should be neither exclusively behavioristic nor cognitive, child-centered nor discipline-centered. They should be purposefully eclectic.

(6) We must eliminate the inflexible and non-variable time schedule and the conformity it demands.

Instead, the school must utilize the individual's own rhythm, own learning speed, and own style of learning.

(7) We must eliminate the paucity of curriculum options and the boredom it creates.

Instead, the school must be integrated into the community and be an integrator of the community.

(8) We must eliminate the failure to take responsibility for progress achieved by all students, the "push outs" as well as the merit scholars, while they are under our guidance.

Instead, no matter how bad home conditions are, students ought to know and feel more at 3:00 p.m. than they knew and felt at 8:00 a.m. They should know and feel more in June than they did in September and certainly more in 1981 than in 1971. We must stop blaming the victims.

(9) We must eliminate the stereotyped view of teachers as people who perform the same role fifty years after they started their careers as they did when they started.
Instead, differentiation of roles in schools and in a variety of human service settings should characterize teaching. Support systems should be established in which teachers share their specific knowledge and skills with other human service professionals.

(10) We must eliminate racial, religious, social-class, generational-isolation, the isolation of the handicapped, and the prejudice and discrimination that isolation breeds; the "defeatist" or "snobbish" self-concepts it nurtures; and the mockery that this isolation makes of the fundamental right of access to equal education opportunity.
Instead, we must reaffirm our belief that all human beings have a right to become all they are capable of becoming and that the education of other people's children *is* as important as the education of our own.

The most vivid truth that emerges from any analysis of the goals and concepts included in P.L. 94-142 and a review of educational practice as it exists in this country today is that we are not going to succeed if we continue with special education in a conceptual framework separate from regular education at any level of the educational spectrum. Furthermore, until we get rid of this dualism in our teacher education, our public schools will continue to be a mirror image of the conditions present in teacher education. Therefore, we must prepare all teachers to implement the concepts in P.L. 94-142. We must reform all aspects of teacher education.

It appears obvious that the preparation of any teacher for any subject and for any level, beginning immediately, must include knowledge and skills necessary to competently teach human beings with handicaps. The sharp boundaries between what we have called special education and regular education are down as far as P.L. 94-142 is concerned.

In the end, if the individualization plan, the zero reject principle, the due process requirement, the parent involvement directive, and the integration imperative of P.L. 94-142 are implemented for handicapped children, they will be extended to *all* children. Thus *special education* could become *general education*, and *general education, special.*

Whether or not this vision of education becomes a reality will depend upon the quality of teachers and the quality of teacher education that is provided in the future.

A New Strategy for School Improvement

The strategy for improving the schools has been to prepare new professionals with the most recent knowledge in their field, and send them out as crusaders to improve the schools. In a large part, this strategy has failed—the new recruits and their ideas were swallowed up by the system. The experienced professionals, those in the field who are 40 to 45 years old with 20 to 25 years of service left, are the "career" professionals. Unless we reeducate them right along with the new professionals, the schools will not improve significantly. In a world whose most constant characteristic is change, teachers more than any other professionals must keep up to date on the latest knowledge in their subject field as well as the most recent knowledge of "ways" to improve teaching and learning. The major educational challenge facing this country in the next five years is to reeducate two million experienced teachers and it cannot be done between 8:00 and 8:30 in the morning or between 4:00 and 5:00 in the afternoon.

The key to making the concepts in P.L. 94-142 come alive in the schools of this country is a new commitment to the reeducation of America's teachers.

Up to now, the public has blamed educators and held them accountable alone for the conditions in the schools. That kind of behavior has not produced results. Educators, just like every other professional group, must be provided access to the opportunity to *learn* new knowledge and skills before they can be expected to improve their performance. At the root of the problem is the lack of public understanding regarding the complexities of teaching and the need for financial support for the continuing education of career teachers.

The problem is not that we cannot prepare teachers but that we do not prepare them. We have been unwilling to provide the "life space" (time and money) necessary for true professional preparation. We have taken a shortsighted, cheap, approach to teacher education and we have gotten exactly what we have paid for.

Even though the knowledge base needed by educators has developed rapidly during the last decade, there is at present no significant effort to disseminate this knowledge meaningfully to the two million teachers in the schools and the thousands of educators who teach, administer and counsel in educational programs in community agencies beyond schools. Other professions, (e.g. medicine, law, industry, etc.) recognize the need, especially in times of rapid change, to provide for the reeducation of their practitioners. Eastman Kodak, for instance, reinvests at least ten percent of its gross profits in research and training to improve the knowledge and skill of its employees. IBM requires nearly eighty days a year for professional development activities related to the work of service personnel. The military invests a great deal in the improvement of the performance and capabilities of its personnel. Public Health, Internal Revenue Service and Cooperative Extension Services of Agriculture are continuously engaged in learning activities designed to increase knowledge and skill related to the work setting.

The American people face a crucial choice concerning school improvement. Either they reaffirm their faith in education through increased financial and psychological support or they will witness the demise of public education. In the future the public and the teaching profession must view the continuously learning teacher to be as important as the continuously learning child.

In the 1980's resources, both financial and personal, must be directed toward strategies that link schools seeking to change with teacher-education institutions seeking to break out of established patterns. The primary goal of teacher education should be the improvement of all aspects of the education of children and youth. Training should be developed as a by-product of a joint search for better ways to improve educational practice. From this cooperative school-college commitment to the larger end in view, serving children and youth, the training program will receive and sustain its relevance and its vitality.

School-focused inservice education as it is described in this book could provide one realistic means to achieve this new school-college teacher education partnership. However, a new brand of educational leadership will be needed to make it a reality.

Leadership for School Focused Inservice Education

Leadership will have to be redefined if it is to respond to the new complexities of school-focused inservice education.

In the process of redefining leadership, let us not confuse administrative ability with leadership qualities. Administrative ability many people and agencies have. It is merely facilitative and only instrumental; it gets acceptable or familiar things done. It is a stablizing force. There are custodial boards of trustees and individual administrative caretakers who are gifted with such abilities. They perform ceremonial functions but they do not *lead*.

Things don't just happen, they are caused. Leadership ability is creative and dynamic and influences people to do things they ought to do, even when they think they do not have the capacity to do them. Leadership ability points to a better way; it represents a constant process of releasing human potential.

Some of the other implications of school-focused inservice education for leadership are highlighted here.

Cooperative Decision-Making. In the past, there have been difficulties in offering effective inservice training programs, relative to objectives, methods, and content. It has been amply demonstrated that the personal and professional experience of the trainees, their motivations, their working milieu—in short, their condition as adults working in a given environment—were not sufficiently taken into consideration; The participation in decision-making by those who are most directly affected by such decisions was not sufficiently developed.

School focused inservice education believes that involvement of adults in the self-management of their training is a way to bring meaning to what is studied. If the role of teachers is to carry out orders—to be "executors" rather than persons who can make a difference—then teachers will not want further training. Motivation for inservice is directly connected with the potential opportunity to change practice. If teachers have an autocratic manager, there is a major difference in motivational factors for being a better teacher.

Teachers as Leaders. The hierarchical structure of schools must be changed. The current approach to administration and supervision is contradictory to professionalism and has too often inhibited what teachers were able to do with the education and experience they already possessed. Teachers have been trained to implement innovations conceived by supervisors or outsiders, but very rarely have they been trained to manage the system themselves. If teachers are to make a decision workable and effective they should be involved in making the decision. Individuals do not fully identify themselves with a situation until they are truly involved in decision-making. Teachers will not be truly involved unless what they think and what they say actually counts. After this is achieved, the only limiting factor is the combined potential of the people involved, and if each is constantly utilizing all available resources the total potential is ever-increasing quality as well as quantity.

Teachers function according to the various "representations" of their role (their own perceptions, the perceptions of the pupils, parents, administrators). Their view of themselves depends on the professional context in which they operate. Constructive peer relationships and cooperative learning and decision-making should pervade the schools' administrative structure as well as the classroom. Teachers will act like professionals when they are treated like professionals.

Shared Authority and Responsibility. In the future, the source of professional authority should be expertise, not title or position. The more leadership depends upon status, the less productive it will be toward creativity. An authoritarian approach automatically limits the accomplishments of the group to the capabilities of the one in command. When people behave because someone in authority is watching them, they are learning to beware of authority and therefore, they are not necessarily improving their own values. If the behavior of teachers is predominantly the result of instructions, then the product will be somewhat predetermined. In other words, an authoritarian approach by the administrator places a high premium on conformity—consequently, there is a danger that teachers and the situation in which they function may not rise above mediocrity. One of the best ways for educational leaders to exert leadership is simply by honest participation with others in solving mutual problems.

Decentralization of Authority. The point of decision-making should be as close to the source of the situation as possible. Administration should provide for decentralization of authority and responsibility to the greatest extent practicable. The unique purposes of education and the processes which it involves demand a high level of responsibility and participation in decision-making by those directly concerned with teaching of students. Centralizing administrative operations might seem to lead to greater efficiency. However, efficiency should not be seen as the most important criterion. Rather, the effect on individual effort, initiative, and growth should be considered. Developing a new method of rating students or a new curriculum guide might be more efficiently done by a well-qualified person, such as an expert in the central office. But, such new curricula or rating procedures would likely lack acceptance and fail because they were not developed by the individuals who are to make them workable.

Creating a Milieu—The Person and the Setting. The security of all personnel is essential for a creative atmosphere. Maximum results can be achieved only in a threat-free climate. The program should never become completely fixed, for it must provide for autonomy and individual differences. The ideal program is one that is neither too rigid nor too flexible. If one extreme or the other exists there is a danger that individuals will be placed in a position where they are pressured to stretch themselves beyond the probabilities of their potential, or on the other hand, may not be challenged to work to their capacity.

In this regard, leaders for school-focused inservice education must utilize knowledge of adult learning theory. Movement form one stage of personal and professional development to the next occurs through cycles of challenge and response, cognitive dissonance, cultural discontinuity, differentiation and integration. It occurs when a person confronts situations for which old ways are not adequate and which require new ways of thinking and acting. The experience may be upsetting and uncomfortable; coping with disequilibrium, learning new skills, assimilating new knowledge, resolving value conflicts, does not always happen simply and smoothly. The trick is to achieve that optimal distance between where the teacher is and what the new situations require so that the teacher is challenged but not bowled over, so change is possible without provoking trauma, entrenchment, or flight. This means that a very diverse array of resources, school based educators, field experiences, instructional materials and learning alternatives must be available if a diversity of adult learners are to be appropriately served in inservice teacher education programs. Professional growth, particularly when it involves the exchange of old habits for new, breeds considerable insecurity. We now know that if educational leaders fail to attend to teachers' emotions as well as to their minds, they will blunder. Professional development is obviously both an affective and cognitive process.

Inservice Education as a Personal Process. Teachers are more likely to identify a person than a course or program as a key influence on their intellectual-personal lives. Though such persons are sometimes called "advisors" for program planning purposes, they actually function as mentors. The mentor-student relationship is a unique one, exemplifying an acceptance and friendship well beyond narrow academic consultation. The mentor is a model not simply of a variety of teaching modes and subject fields, but of the humane professional. Mentors are needed in inservice as well as preservice education.

Because curriculum development, just like teaching and learning, is a very personal matter, leaders for inservice education should realize that an educational program cannot be transplanted successfully but must grow from where it is in its present surroundings. Building a new program is a continuous process. The administration doesn't build a program, it provides for it. Educational leaders must start with the teachers in the program and where these teachers are in relation to their experience, professional and personal maturity, and their capacity to grow. In the organization and development of a program, a change may be needed; but it must be made at the right time. *Persons, settings,* and *process* are all important elements in bringing about effective inservice education.

Conclusion

Key Concepts in School-Focused Inservice Education

Three major commonalities, or key concepts come through in the descriptions of the "real world" of inservice education described in this publication. These common elements are:

(1) An emphasis on the teacher as a developing *person*, and as one capable of designing and implementing personal-professional development. Teachers are viewed as active, often self-directed, adult learners. The direction of learning is from the teacher out. The adult learner's needs or demands are considered in the design of inservice, and the teacher is encouraged and expected to take responsibility for professional development. Mandated or forced change does not appear in the descriptions of effective inservice practices.

(2) A focus on the work setting as the most appropriate inservice *context*. This pattern generally stresses the importance of the educational "setting" as the source for deriving personal-professional goals and practices. *School-focused* inservice is viewed as the way to make knowledge useful and the training meaningful.

(3) A preference for experience-based inservice in which reflection upon practice is the key *process* characteristic. Teaching strategies proposed are those which utilize the concrete—the direct experience of the teacher or of others in the work site. Delineated this process is one in which teachers as adult professional practitioners respond to real situations (often problematic ones) by analysis, observation, solution design, application, and reflection.

The two key questions for teachers as they consider inservice education are: (1) Will it work (instrumentality)? *and* (2) Will it be worthwhile (educationally, personally)?

The major conclusion that emerges from the case studies and scenarios is that no significant changes will take place in teachers or the teaching profession until the situation in which teachers work is changed. Reforming the "setting" is a thread which runs through all of the chapters in this book. This is the primary reason that the term *school-focused* inservice education is so appropriate as a focus at this particular period in the history of American education.

School-focused does not imply that colleges or departments of education will be excluded from the process of inservice education. However, it does mean that educational change must move in both directions—to colleges as well as to schools. Indeed if colleges and departments of education are to be the training and development arm of the profession, they must become partners in reforming the schools so that the knowledge and skills learned in programs of continuing professional education can be *used* in the schools. If the content of teacher education cannot be used in the work place of the teachers, then colleges of education will be viewed as out of touch and obsolete.

Inservice teachers understand the realities of the workplace. They process formal experiences in teacher education in terms of these realities. They will not be interested in individualizing instruction if they believe that in the community in which they teach individualization is not possible, valued, encouraged, or even permitted. Nor will they plan continuing education or other professional activities after school if they must suffer large classes and heavy burdens every working day.

As President Lyman (1980) of Stanford University recently reminded his colleagues, "Our work with the schools will not be effective unless, to use a phrase beloved by the Quakers, it 'speaks to the condition' of the schools. To the actual condition, that is, and not to some idealized form that may exist in the minds of sheltered university faculty members, but is unattainable in the real world. One reason why the dividing line between schools and universities in this country so often seems more like a Grand Canyon than a grade crossing is because school teachers and university scholars have so little sense of being involved in a common enterprise."

Colleges and universities will serve the teaching profession and the schools best by helping to create conditions favorable to professional practice as well as professional study. The aim of teacher education in the 1980's must be to change the setting for teaching and learning as well as the teacher.

If our educational institutions are to become the kind of powerful instruments for social progress envisioned by P.L. 94-142, a new design for teacher education will be needed. Central to this new design is recognition of the fact that schools and colleges are interrelated and interacting components of *one* educational system. Currently schools and colleges are unnecessarily isolated from one another, to the detriment of both. The present disconnected approach must be replaced with a new partnership that provides an interlocking process of educational reform and training of "career" teachers in the kind of *school focused* inservice teacher education described in this book.

References

The Education for All Handicapped Children Act of 1975 (P.L. 94-142) Congress 5.6 *Federal Register*, December 30, 1976, p.4.

President Lyman and the state of the schools. *Stanford Educator*, edited by Shirly Stein, Stanford University School of Education Newsletter, No. 22, Spring 1980, p. 3.

Reynolds, M. Basic issues in restructuring teacher education. *Journal of Teacher Education*, 1978, p. 60.

A000016396159

DATE DUE

Demco, Inc. 38-293